The Dibble Family

Weymouth, Somerset, England

to

Dorchester, Massachusetts and Windsor, Connecticut

and

Charleston, South Carolina

E. Louise

Published by Phoenix Publishers Columbia, South Carolina

ISBN 979-8-9893861-0-9

Printed in the United States of America

In Commemoration of

Andrew Henry Dibble, Sr., Great-Grandfather

Harriet Catherine Dibble Taylor, Grandmother

John Benjamin Taylor, Jr., Father

To the Future Generations

and

Amanda, Elizabeth, Rebecca, and Gwendolyn

Dibble   Arms

Andrew Henry Dibble, Sr.
1825-1873

The Dibble Family

Contents

Introduction

_____

"Not to know what happened before we were born
is to remain perpetually a child. For what is the worth of
a human life unless it is woven into the life of our ancestors
by the records of history? The influence and achievements
of our ancestors we not escape."

Cicero

When my sister Catherine (Kate) and I started our family genealogy research more than fifty years ago, many persons questioned, *"Why?" "What do they hope to find?"* and *"What are they looking for?"* These were the questions of many persons we knew or encountered! Some family members, also wondered, *"Why?"*

Quite often, these questions arise many times when genealogists begin their search. Some persons research their family in order to become a part of such organizations as the *Daughters of the American Revolution*, or even the *Sons of the American Revolution*. Whereas, others start their research because they think they belong to a very prominent family, or may have prominent ancestors. When Kate and I began our Dibble Family genealogy and research in the 1960's, it was very rare. In fact, very few persons of color were even involved in genealogy at this time. Of course, today, nearly sixty years later, there are many more persons who are now interested in their family genealogy. Today, genealogy has become a hobby or past-time for many people and there are numerous genealogical societies and organization across the country, the most recognized is the National Genealogical Society, of which I have been a member for more than fifty years.

Our family research came about because of several different things. Our father, John B. Taylor, Jr., and his sister, my Aunt Catherine Springs Taylor were both big-talkers or story tellers. They constantly talked about the past and their growing up in South Carolina. They often spoke of their parents, grandparents, aunts, uncles, and cousins. These fascinating stories filled our Sunday afternoons, when we all sat around the table after dinner, and we as youngsters, would listen with intense interest, holding on to every word, phrase, and sentence. These stories, we grew up with, told of so many things of the family and how close they all were and their experiences while visiting their grandmother, and uncles in Camden, South Carolina. We heard of their love for the years of their youth. We heard of many things that sparked a keen interest in our wanting to know more about our father's family, especially since we were somewhat closer to my mother's family. As a youngster, we visited my father' first cousin, Charles Wendell Maxwell, a physician, living in Philadelphia, whom we called Cousin Wendell. During this visit, I was fascinated and excited to hear him speak of my paternal grandmother, who he grew up with and was his aunt, yet was near his age. Cousin Wendell's stories of the grandmother, I never knew, inspired me to want to know more about my father's family. Cousin Wendell's generosity and kindness, left an unforgettable impression, which resulted in my naming my eldest son for Cousin Wendell. This also contributed to my lifelong interest in family genealogy and research. As we grew older and had families of our own, this interest was still there, although time had prevented our doing much research while our children were very young.

During the years of my youth and young adult years there were numerous stories told to me in reference to my father's heritage. These stories were oftentimes portrayed to be on a grand scale and told of the way of life of these early ancestors. Among this family lore was the fact that my great- grandfather Andrew Henry Dibble, was the son of Andrew Comstock Dibble, of Connecticut and later Charleston, South Carolina, which had a long-standing, majestic, and portly heritage, which stemmed from both his maternal and paternal side. My father often spoke of his grandparents, and in particular, his grandmother, Ellie Naomi Naudin Dibble, who he knew well and spent a great amount of time with, while a youth and young adult. His grandfather, Andrew had died while his mother was still an infant. Yet, he had heard numerous stories of his grandfather and his heritage from both his mother and grandmother. These stories often told of the explorations of both of Andrew's parents. Andrew's mother who descended from the early Cleland/Cleveland Family of Scotland and England, who ventured into the West Coast of Africa before settling in Charleston in the 1760s; his father Andrew Comstock Dibble who descended from an early Dibble who ventured from England and settled in Dorchester, Massachusetts and Windsor, Connecticut during the 1600's. Numerous grandiose stories were told to him and his sister, as well as those he over-heard, while sitting on his grandmother Ellie's long rambling front porch, in Camden. During those hot summer evenings, as the adults were sitting in their rocking chairs telling of years gone by, youngsters gathered and sat listening. There were also fascinating stories of Ellie Naomi Naudin's paternal ancestors. Ellie's Grandfather, John Naudin, a Native of France settled in Camden, South Carolina in the late 19th century. Much of the oral history has been passed down for more than 160 or 170 years through seven generations of the Nandin-Dibble Family. This enduring legacy left by our early ancestors, continues into the twenty-first century. Thus, was the beginning of what we are known as today, the "Naudin-Dibble Family" of South Carolina.

In the mid-to-late-1960's, I decided to go to the National Archives in Washington, D.C., to see what I could find on my family. To my surprise, I was fascinated and excited to be able to fine my great-grandparents, Ellie Naudin Dibble and Andrew Henry Dibble, in the 1850 United States Census, living in Camden, South Carolina. When I found this first document, I was so excited. The excitement of your first find, can never be repeated. This was the beginning of many trips to the Archives, often dragging my daughter Felicia and my younger son William alone with me. This was also the beginning of their interest in our family research, as well. About this same time, my father's first cousin, Josephine Dibble Murphy, shared the "Andrew Dibble Freedom Papers" with a colleague, Dr. Horace Mann Bond, of Atlanta. In February 1967, *The Atlanta Inquirer* featured an extensive article that told of Andrew Dibble and his papers. This article also helped to spark further interest for both my sister and I. However, more than sixty years later, as I move forward through the years, I have discovered so much more information and so many more records. I continue to discover new things, which is continuing to document who I am.

With this being more of a genealogical collection tracing the paternal heritage of my Great-grandfather Andrew Henry Dibble (1825-1873), I did feel it was necessary to tell a little more about the descendants of my great-grandfather Andrew. Therefore, I have tried to include the information that I have on the older generations and information that has been obtained from public sources, on those who are still living. This was very important since I had already traced Andrew Henry Dibble's maternal heritage in the book, *Elizabeth Clevland Hardcastle, 1741-1808: A Lady of Color in the South Carolina Low Country,* which was published in 2001. Although this collection is mainly about my Great-grandfather Andrew Henry

Dibble, I have included a fair amount of information on the South Carolina Dibbles, who are the numerous descendants of both brothers, Andrew Comstock, and Philander Virgil Dibble, which I have collected in my Dibble Family Tree on Ancestry.

This is such an extraordinary American story. As we embrace our American history that documents several of our English ancestors who arrived here in the New England British Colony of Massachusetts so early in the United States History, we are very fortunate that this information was available and found. This story tells us of our early "Dibble (Deeble)" ancestry and what these many persons faced and endured during those early years. It also tells us that we are all connected by blood. I am sure many "Dibble" descendants of the majority population might question or are unwilling to accept this, but the true facts do not lie, they only substantiate what my family has always known. Although we have this from our family oral history, I have been able to confirm this by the Dibble Y-DNA markers and the Autosomal Dibble DNA markers that match descendants of numerous descendants of the Connecticut Dibble family through both Ancestry DNA and Family Tree DNA (FTDNA). In 2009, we had our Dibble Y-DNA tested with Ancestry.com and repeated it again in 2022, along with the autosomal-DNA with FTDNA. Both tests confirmed our relationship with the larger Dibble family.

A well-respected genealogist, Rachel Mills Lennon stated in her *"Report on the father of Andrew Henry Dibble,"* which provides enough evidence to support the fact that Andrew C. Dibble is the father of Andrew H. Dibble. She further states:

> *"Proving shrouded paternity in the early American South is a difficult task, particularly among racial minorities. The lack of any direct link between Mindah Cleveland and candidates for her son's father required exhaustive research, correlations, and analysis to put people into time and place, follow their movements, and define their person and environmental spheres…*
>
> *"…shows Mindah to have been an independent woman of comfortable financial means before her relationship with Andrew and the birth of her son. Indeed, her freedom to act independently at such a young age is above norms for the time and place. She clearly was on par—socially and economically— with the up-and-coming Andrew and not financially or socially subservient to him. Nor was she subservient to the Ravenals with whom she lived in Charleston. Her access to Andrew, then, is more conceivable on these terms."*

This publication also includes information on other ancestors of this same era, such as *"The Comstock Family," "The Trowbridge Family," "The Starr Family,"* and *"The Fyler Family."* This has been a tremendous task that has taken numerous years to compile and fully document, and I am deeply humbled and thankful.

All of us who descend from my great-grandfather, Andrew Henry Dibble, and his wife Ellie Naomi Naudin Dibble are *"Dibble Descendants,"* as well as, *"Naudin Descendants."* However, since the formation of the *"Naudin-Dibble Family Heritage Foundation,"* we are all *"Naudin-Dibbles."* While tracing this heritage, it became evident that all branches of this strong family tree were still tied to their South Carolina ancestors of more than two centuries before.

Andrew and Ellie became the parents of twelve children. Ten children grew to adulthood. Of the twelve children, three daughters married and had families and three sons (recently discovered the descendants of a fourth son) married and likewise had families. Andrew and Ellie's remaining three sons (John Moreau, William Smith, and Wyatt Naudin) did not marry and do not have known descendants.

In 2018, there were approximately 409 known descendants of **Andrew Henry DIBBLE** and **Ellie Naomi Naudin DIBBLE**.

    12 - Children, born between 1846 and 1873
    23 - Grandchildren born between 1871-1910
    53 - Great-grandchildren born between 1894 and 1942
    94 - Great-Great-grandchildren born between 1922-1979
  139 - GGG-grandchildren
    66 - GGGG-grandchildren
    23 - GGGGG-grandchildren

Included in these numbers are the known number of descendants of the three daughters and three sons of Andrew Henry and Ellie Naudin Dibble.

    67 - Martha Louisa Dibble and Senator Henry Johnson Maxwell, Sr.
    67 - Andrew Henry Dibble, Jr., and Elizabeth Levy
  105 - Representative Eugene Heriot Dibble, Sr., and Sarah "Sallie" Rebecca Lee
  108 - Ella Naudin Dibble and Theodore John Levy, Jr.
    15 - Rufus Dennis Dibble and Elizabeth "Bessie" Lee Greenlee
    47 - Harriet Catherine Dibble and Reverend Dr. John Benjamin Taylor, Sr.

It is interesting to note that Andrew and Ellie's children were born over a 27 year-span, yet, as time passed, the next several generations, the difference increased tremendously. This tells us that families were marrying much later than they had initially and therefore the many generations over-lapped as far as their ages. This was seen early in our history where my grandmother Harriet Catherine was the youngest of the original twelve Dibble children, being born in 1873, whereas, her eldest sister Martha Louisa was born in 1846. Harriet had nieces, Cassandra J. Maxwell, Ella Louise Maxwell, and Catherine Cleveland Dibble, being born in 1871, 1873, and 1872, respectively. Therefore, Harriet palled around and attended school along with her three nieces, who were all her age.

As subsequent generations came the span increased: of the 23 grandchildren, the years increased to 39 years; of the 53 Great-grandchildren the years increased to 48 years; of the 94 Great-Grandchildren, the years increased to 59 years. With Harriet Catherine Dibble being the youngest child of Andrew and Ellie, her descendants were always a generation or more younger than the generations of her older siblings.

Most of the information and documents compiled in this collection regarding Andrew Henry Dibble's paternal heritage was initiated more than fifty years ago, about the same that I was researching and documenting his mother's heritage. Although I started my Dibble genealogy years ago, I recently felt it was necessary to put it into some form for the future generations to have, and hoping my years of Dibble research would be preserved. Most of the information included in this collection, is in the public domain.

PART I

The Dibble Name

A generation may bind itself as long as its majority
continues in life; when that has disappeared

another majority is in its place, holds all the rights and
powers their predecessors once held, and may change their laws

and institutions to suit themselves. Nothing then is
unchangeable but the inherent and unalienable right of man.

Thomas Jefferson, 1824

The "Dibble" name in this country and England goes back several centuries. In this country, the name "Dibble" has many variations, including Dibblee, Dibbell, Dible, Daboll, Diabol, Diable, Deble, Debill, Deeble, and others. Robert "Dible" (sometimes seen as "Deeble") with his wife and son and daughter, Thomas and Frances were among the earliest settlers in the New England colonies of America that possessed the name of "Deeble or Dibble." They embarked from 'Portus, Weymouth (Weymouth, in Dorset) on 'ye 20th March, 1635,' Thomas Dibble. Certainly, the name as a surname, in all its various spellings, seems to have become popular from the 12th century in Britain. The word "dibble" is a word of English origins and is a sharp stick or pole used for planting seeds. It is very likely that there were people who found employment in the planting of crops and that, when surnames came into general usage, some assumed the name of their primary occupational tool. I have heard a contemporary English person use the word "dibbling" as a synonym for gardening. Clearly there is a long-term, historical connection between agriculture/gardening and the family name. Some seem to think that this unusual surname is of French derivation, but that has not really been proved. It was introduced by the Normans after the 1066 invasion, but in fact, the true origin is much older, and maybe pre-Christian. It has two possible derivations, the first from the Roman (Latin) 'debil-is', which seems to have been a metonymic for a doctor or healer, one who dealt with the sick. The first recorded spelling of the family name is shown to be that of "William Debel," which was dated 1197, in the pipe rolls of Yorkshire, during the reign of King Richard 1st, known as 'The Lionheart', from 1189-1199. Surnames became necessary when governments introduced personal taxation. In England this was known as Poll Tax. Throughout the centuries, surnames in every country have continued to "develop" often leading to astonishing variants of the original spelling. The spelling as "Dibble" is known to go back as far as 1584, when an Andrew Dibble lived in West Bagborough, England. The present family spelling of "Dibble" in this country began with Ruben Dibble who was born about 1763. Spelling was not very important in the

English language before the 19th century, thus resulting in the many variations of the spelling. Many people with these names are part of one huge interrelated family. There is a coat of arms associated with the name, and it prominently features the gardening implement known as a *"dibble" or "bean-setter." The arms are recorded in the Visitation of Cornwall, by Vivian in 1887. The Deeble shield is purple, with three dibbles or beanseters of silver. Crest a gold dibble. The Dibble name also appears on the tombstone of Reverend Samuel Dibble who died in 1750 and was buried in Charles Church Yard, Plymouth, England.* There were hundreds of Dibble Wills preserved in the Bishop of Exeter's files before World War II, which I believe would have given more of our ancestry in England, but they were all destroyed in the "Blitz."

The Dibbles of Massachusetts and Connecticut

Van Buren Lamb, Jr., (1898-1980) of Old Lyme, Connecticut, with the help of his mother Ida Lewis Tanner, who was the granddaughter of Sally Dibble of Saybrook, Middlesex, Connecticut and Atwater, Ohio, was a tireless Dibble family researcher. He compiled the best-known and most extensive genealogy of the Dibble family/families in North America. He was considered the most detailed and best-known researcher on the Dibble Family, spending more than 60 years travelling to Dibble Family sites, corresponding, researching and collecting nearly 5,000 pages of notes placed in a notebook, along with numerous church records, documents, letters, etc. In the 1940s, he published his work in the magazine "Your Ancestors" which included Dibbles who descend from Robert Dibble of Dorchester, Massachusetts through eight or nine generations. His work remains a heroic and invaluable effort. Most of his research concerned the vast extended network of descendants of Robert Deeble (Dibble). Among Mr. Lamb's many sources in collecting information and documentation on the Dibble Family, he was able to gain much information on the birth and death of individual persons with the Dibble name from the Bethel Connecticut Library. In the Bethel Connecticut Library there is a document, part of a larger collection, which contains information from the grave stones of Bethel's cemeteries. The material was compiled in November 1934 under the auspices of the Federal Emergency Relief Administration (FERA), later the Works Progress Administration (WPA). The project was sponsored by the Connecticut State Library and is often referred to as the Hale Collection for Charles R. Hale, State Military Necrologist who directed the project. For example, my ancestral, 3rd great-grandfather, Samuel Dibble, died October 14, 1860, age 90 years, 10 months. Samuel is the father of my Great-grandfather, Andrew Comstock Dibble who settled in Charleston in 1821

After the death of Mr. Lamb, this large compilation of information on the Dibble Family, including all the records, were passed to a relative named Reverend Stephen Dibble and later passed to Mr. George Arthur Dibble, III, of Sacramento, California, who has maintained them and put them on a disk for any descendant of these early Deeble (Dibble) members to use for their research.

ROBERT DIBBLE

ROBERT DEEBLE (DIBBLE) (c. 1586 to 1590) was a Puritan who immigrated to America on the ship *Recovery* and settled in Dorchester, Massachusetts, founded by the Massachusetts Bay Company. Robert and his wife evidently became members of the Dorchester Congregation, prior to 6 May 1635, which was formed in 1629 in Plymouth, England, under the leadership of the Reverend John Warham of Exeter. Some of the members of this congregation sailed from Plymouth for America. On March 31, 1633/34, a Robert Dibble and his wife appeared on the list of the 26 passengers on the *Recovery of London*, who were preparing to depart for New England from Weymouth. Not all the passengers arrived in Massachusetts Bay; some may have decided not to sail. Although the ship was sailing from Weymouth, England, records state that Robert Dibble was a native of Somersetshire, England. No authentic record of his wife's name has been found, but a "Goody" Deeble is named in the Dorchester church records. These Puritans, sometimes known as "decenters," were a group of English Protestants in the 16th and 17th centuries who were dissatisfied with the limited extent of the English Reformation. This great migration of the 1630s, came about because of the anger and resentment of many at the behavior of King Charles I, which resulted in the English Civil War of 1642-1651. They identified with various religious groups advocating greater purity of worship and doctrine, along with personal piety. The modern usage of the word "puritan" is often used to describe someone who adheres to strict moral or religious principles. The Puritans of New England brought together their own regional customs and beliefs. The Congregationalist tradition is one such Protestant denomination that claims descent from the Puritan traditions.

ROBERT DEEBLE (Dibble) probably arrived in Massachusetts in 1632/33. About two years later, Robert's son and daughter, Thomas Dible, *"husbandman" (farmer), age 22, and Frances Dible, "soro" (sister), age 24, appeared on the passenger list of the ship Marygould preparing to depart for New England from Weymouth, Somerset, England. His son Thomas Dible (Dibble), who was born in 1613 in Somersetshire, along with his daughter Frances left Weymouth bound for New England on 20 March 1635, with 106 passengers.* Their ages given at this time was Frances, age 24 and Thomas, age 22. Robert Deeble's estimated birth is about 1586 to 1590, based on the ages of his children. Although Thomas and Frances names were spelled as "Dible," and their father's name was spelled "Deeble," tells us spelling was not as uniformed as it today. The below information on Robert and Thomas obtaining land in December 1635, also confirms the fact that Thomas is the son of Robert with both spelling their names as "Deeble."

There are several documents that have survived to document Robert Dibble's involvement in the duties of the community in which he lived during the years following his arrival in the British Colony. Robert Dibble, early settler of the Massachusetts Bay Commonwealth, became a freeman at the General Court on May 6, 1635. He would have had to be admitted to the Dorchester Church before he could become a freeman. Robert is said to have been the fourth of the five Dorchester men to become a "freeman." The term "freeman" was used by these early settlers, letting others know he had an advantage in dividing the lands and were members of the general court, until the representative court system was established. Robert received a grant of land in Dorchester, Massachusetts on January 4, 1635.

According to *The Great Migration*, on December 17, 1535, the town of Dorchester, Massachusetts (today, part of Boston) *"ordered Robert Deeble shall have enlargement of two goad (a goad was 9 linear feet) in length from his house upward, and that his son Thomas Deeble shall have six goad next to his to go with a right line up from the pale before his house on condition for Thomas Deeble to build a house within one year or else to lose that goad granted him." "Robert Deeble and his son, to have thirty aces in the great lots at the bounds betwixt Roxbury and Dorchester at the great hill."* In the March 18, 1637 division of land, "Robert Deeble" received two acres and three-quarters and twenty-two rods in the neck and two acres and three-quarters and twenty rods in the cow's pasture.

On March 18, 1637, *"Robert Deeble is chosen bailiff (tax collector) for half year or till another be chosen and it is ordered that he shall levy all fines, rates and amercements for the plantation.... It is ordered that Robert Deeble is to continued bailiff for a year following with the same power according to the order of the former year, 31 October 1638."* He served in this capacity until 1641. The job of bailiff required integrity and ability to deal with money and handle all fines. This position tells us that he was a Freeman of the town, which meant that he could vote in the general meetings, and was one of the "select men" who ran the town between the general meetings.

The records of the Dorchester Congregational Church in February 1642, list Robert and his wife as original members. His signature appears on the flyleaf of the History of Dorchester, Massachusetts, setting up maintenance for a new free school in Dorchester. The majority of those who immigrated to the colonial colonies were mainly of an intelligent, better class and could afford the passage, unless they came as indentured servants. His death date is unknown, but probably died after the 1646 account of constables. Savage claimed that Robert Dibble *"was living in Dorchester in 1652,"* but no evidence for this has been found. Some others believe that Robert may have moved to Windsor along with his son Thomas. Still others suggest that he returned to England. At this time there was much dissension in the Dorchester Church. Many of the members returned to England and many went to Windsor, Connecticut.

The below signature of Robert Deeble, lets us know that he was one of the upper-class immigrants, for many of those migrating to the New England Colonies during these early years, were unable to write.

Signature of Robert Deeble on the document about setting up maintenance for a new free school in Dorchester.

It is believed that **ROBERT DIBBLE** had about seven children:

> Robert Dibble (c.1607-08) (came to New England as a servant to Joseph Hull)
> Oliver Dibble (c.1610), of England
> Frances Dibble (c.1611), Arrived in New England with her brother, (but no other
>   information is found)
> **THOMAS DIBBLE (c.1613, died 17 Oct 1700, in Windsor, Connecticut)**
> John Dibble (c.1615, died 7 Oct 1646 in Springfield, Massachusetts)
> Abraham Dibble (c.1616, d.31 Dec. 1690, in Suffield, Connecticut (was Hampshire
>   County, Massachusetts until 1803)
> Miriam Dibble (c.1619)

Thomas, John, and Abraham founded the impressive **Dibble Family** line which was prominent in Connecticut, Massachusetts, and eventually spread out to the upstate of New York, the Carolinas, Michigan, Minnesota, California, and other places. No further information has been found on his daughter Frances. Many of the early records are using the "Deeble" spelling for their name, but later the spelling becomes "Dibble." Robert's son John who died in 1646 had several children; his son Abraham died in 1690, married Lydia Teffe and had numerous children. All records point to a close relationship between Robert's three sons: Thomas, John, and Abraham.

THOMAS DIBBLE

THOMAS DEEBLE (DIBBLE) (c.1613-1700) *(Robert)* Born in England in 1613, he sailed from London, England on the ship *Marygould,* and arrived in the Massachusetts Bay Colony in May 1635, one year after his father, **Robert Dibble's** arrival on the ship *Recovery.* Thomas died 17 October 1700 in Windsor, Connecticut, at 87 years. While in Massachusetts, Thomas Deeble was *"ordered"* to build a house on the land grant, but probably never did. He appears to have moved from Dorchester, Massachusetts to Dorchester {later, Windsor}, Connecticut between May and October 1635. Thomas was among the first settlers of Windsor, Hartford, Connecticut. In 1640, Thomas was granted land of the Plantation on which he built a house which he sold to Robert Watson. In 1670, he purchased the William Hubbard house on the Palisado between Matthew Grant and a Mr. Phillips.

Thomas Dibble, the son of Robert, married Mary or Miriam Grant (1614-1681), who died 14 May 1681 in Windsor, Connecticut. He then married Elizabeth Browne (who was the widow of John Hawke (1625-1662) and Robert Hinsdale (1617-1675)]. Elizabeth Browne (1621-1689), daughter of William Browne and Lydia Ward, was born in England and died 25 September 1689 in Windsor, Connecticut.

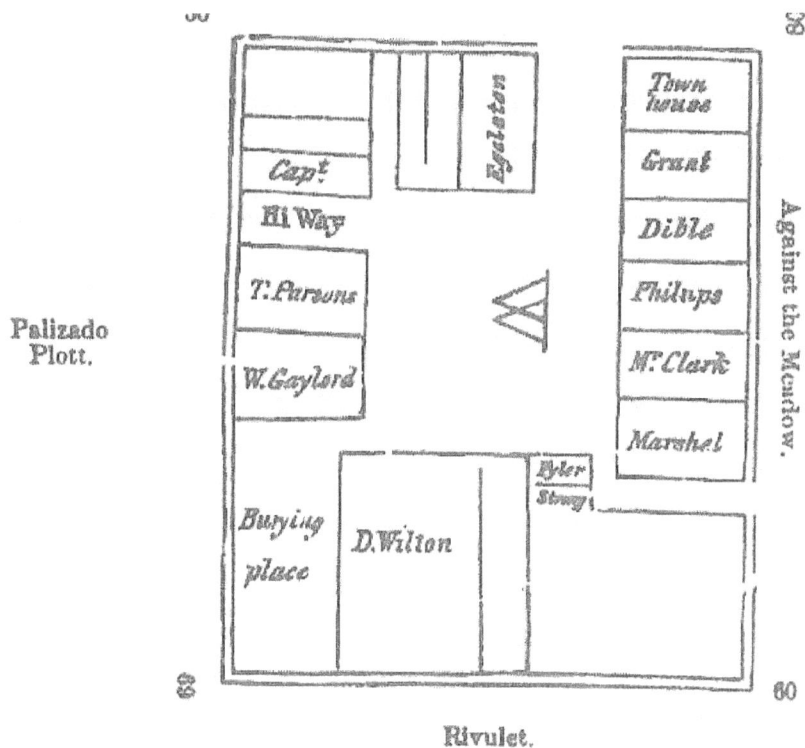

Plan of the Ancient Palisado Plot in Windsor, 1654.

This plan of the plot of the Palisado shows where Thomas Dibble had his property, in Windsor. Plot taken from Henry R. Stiles *"History of Ancient Windsor, (1859) (2018).*

The Will of Thomas Dibble is dated 17 February 1699/1700 and stated he was of Windsor. The inventory was taken on November 1, 1700, and it was proved on November 13, 1700. He did not mention a wife in this Will, therefore she was probably already deceased. In the Will, he did mention his sons, Samuel and Thomas and their wives, as well as daughters, Miriam and Hepzibah's husband, Samuel Gibbs (Hepzibah, already deceased), and numerous grandchildren.

> *"I, Thomas Dibble, Sr., of Windsor, doe make this my Last Will and Testament: To my son Samuel and his wife, I give the north half of my orchard whereon he liveth, ... To my son Thomas Dibble and his wife, I give the other half of my orchard during his life, and the remainder to his son Abram...I give to my daughter Miriam Gillett that two acres of meadow she now possesseth....*

> *Thomas Dibble, Sr.*

Thomas and Robert Dibble's names are among the 137 names included on the large granite monument, called the *"Founders Monument of Windsor,"* in Windsor, Connecticut. It is located on the Palisado Green, which was dedicated on May 1, 1930, celebrating the 300th Anniversary of the First Church of Windsor. However, recent historians are not sure Robert migrated to Windsor with his son Thomas, who is among the founders of Windsor. This is a beautiful monument, seen later in this collection. Thomas owned two pieces of property in Windsor. One parcel of land was located south of the Bissell Ferry Road, in the area where Robert Winchell had his land. Later he owned land in the City Plan of Palisado, where William Hubbard's name is seen on a Windsor map. Thomas bought Hubbard's lot. Thomas also contributed to King Philip's War by making pouches for the men.

Thomas Dibble, like his father was literate, he could write his name, whereas many of these early Puritans could not. He like most of these early Puritan's were farmers, as well. His signature is seen below.

THOMAS DIBBLE and MIRIAM GRANT (1624-1681) became the parents of:

Israel Dibble (29 Aug. 1637; d. 12 Dec 1697, in Windsor), mar. Elizabeth Hull Samuel Dibble (31 May 1640; died 31 May 1640, in Windsor, Connecticut)
EBENEZER DIBBLE (26 Sept. 1641), mar. MARY WAKEFIELD
Hepzibah Dibble (bpt. 25 Dec. 1642; d. 22 Feb 1697/98), mar. Samuel Gibbs
Samuel DIBBLE (9 Feb. 1643- d. 5 Mar 1708/09), mar. (1) Abigail Graves (1645-1666).
    Their daughter Abigail DIBBLE (1666-1725) mar. George HAYES (1655-1725). (See below.).m. (2) Hepzibah Bartlitt, (3) Frances Cranston
Miriam Dibble (15 Feb. 1645; d. 18 Apr 1687), mar. Jonathan Gillette
Thomas Dibble, Jr. (1 Feb. 1647; d. before 1719), mar. Mary Tucker
Joanna Dibble (bpt. 1 Feb. 1650; died, 1651 in Windsor, Connecticut).

MAP OF CONNECTICUT AND NEW HAVEN COLONY

Windsor, Connecticut (Near the Massachusetts Border).

PLAN OF ANCIENT WINDSOR

This Plan of Ancient Windsor (1640-1654), includes the names of many of the early settlers in Windsor during this time. It was developed by The Descendants of The Founders of Ancient Windsor.

EBENEZER DIBBLE

EBENEZER DIBBLE (1641-1675) *(Thomas, Robert),* was baptized on 26 September 1641, in Windsor, Hartford, Connecticut, and died on 19 December 1675 in a Swamp fight. He married **MARY WAKEFIELD (1645-1703)**, on 27 Oct 1663 in Windsor, Connecticut, the daughter of JOHN WAKEFIELD (1615-1667) and ANN LITTLEFIELD (1625-1703). Mary was baptized 21 August 1645, in New Haven, Connecticut and died 24 September 1703. Mary endured the early death of her husband, Ebenezer Dibble (1641-1675) who was killed in the Great Swamp fight in King Phillips War, at age 34, leaving seven young children, and great debts. The inventory was taken 11 February 1676. Mary later married James Hiller. Ebenezer's father Thomas Dibble (1613-1700) was also involved with the war, making pouches for the soldiers during the King Philip War.

EBENEZER DIBBLE's brother **Samuel DIBBLE (1643-1709)** and his wife, Abigail Graves are the parents of Abigail DIBBLE (1666-1725). Abigail DIBBLE was born 19 January 1666, the second wife of George Hayes (1655-1725) who was born in Scotland and migrated to Windsor, Connecticut. George Hayes and Abigail DIBBLE are the 3rd great-grandparents of our 19th President of the United States, Rutherford B. Hayes (1822-1895), of Ohio. Abigail and George Hayes had about fourteen children, in which our President descends from their son Daniel Hayes, who was born in Windsor on 26 April 1686 and died in Simsbury, Connecticut, on 23 September 1756.

EBENEZER DIBBLE and MARY WAKFIELD are the parents of:

> Mary Dibble, (24 Dec. 1664) probably in Simsbury, Hartford, Connecticut; died
> Unknown and married John Eno.
> **WAKEFIELD DIBBLE (15 SEPT. 1667)**, in New Haven, died 1734 in Stratford,
> Fairfield, Conn; mar. (1) Mary Loomis, **(2) JANE FYLER**
> Martha Dibble (10 Mar. 1668, died 30 June 1670), in Windsor, Connecticut
> Ebenezer Dibble, Sgt. (18 Aug.1671, in Windsor Hartford, Connecticut),
> mar. 3 times: (1) Mary Loomis, (2) Ann Horton, (3) Mary Lewis died in
> Colchester, New London, Connecticut, 24 June 1758.
> John Dibble (9 Feb. 1673) in Windsor. Mar. Mary in Windsor, Hartford, Connecticut;
> died about 1710, in Colchester, New London, Connecticut.

KING PHILIP'S WAR

In 1620, Plymouth, Massachusetts was established with the help of Squanto and Massasoit, chief of the Wampanoag Indian Tribe. Many thousands of Colonists settled in New England during the Great Migration to the New World during the years that followed. As the Colonists numbers increased, the New Englanders expanded their settlements along the regions coastal plain and up the Connecticut River valley. By 1675 they had established a few small towns in the interior between Boston and the Connecticut River settlements. The Wampanoag Tribe had entered into an agreement with the Plymouth Colony and believed that they could rely on the colony for protection. However, in the decades preceding the War, the Wampanoag realized that the Treaty did not protect them from the English expansion, and tensions began to rise, as the English colonists continued pressuring the Indians to sell land and their continued encroachment.

The colonists' growing desire for more land, coupled with mutual cultural misunderstandings by both the colonists and the Indians, set the stage for numerous wars of varying degrees of ferocity and length. One such war was King Philip's War in 1676. King Philip's father was one of the first Indians to befriend the Pilgrims who arrived in America on the "*Mayflower*" in 1629. Philip maintained good relations with the colonists until the unauthorized acts (which were apparently in violation of treaty agreements) of some of the young men of his tribe forced Philip into a war with the colonists. Based on questionable evidence and fear, the commissioners of the United Colonies became convinced that the Narragansett Indians were deeply involved with King Philip and his tribe' conceived "plans" against the colonists. The colonists decided to attack the Narragansett at their headquarters in a preemptive strike. Despite the bitter New England winter, the colonists decided to attack the Narragansett before they dispersed from their winter quarters and scattered to different parts of the country until the spring.

King Philip's War of 1675-1676, was fought between the colonist in Massachusetts and Connecticut and the Wampanoag, Nipmuck and Narragansett Indians led by "Metacomet/Metasom" (c.1638-1676). Metasom was the son of the Wampanoag chief Massasoit, who had peacefully assisted the Pilgrims during their first winter in this New World. Metasom was called "King Philip" by the colonists. Most men who served in King Philips War were between the ages of 16 and 60. The fighting lasted fourteen months and destroyed twelve frontier towns, killing 600 Puritans and approximately 3,000 Native Americans lost their lives. This was the last major effort by the Native Americans of southern New England to drive out the English settlers, who had become greedy and continued to take over their lands. There are numerous accounts of this deadly war with many details. It was considered one of the bloodiest wars in American History. One such account mentions my ancestor, Ebenezer Dibble.

> "*Ebenezer Dibble was killed in the Great Swamp Fight by the Narragansett Indians during King Philip's War, dying 19 Dec 1675, 34 years old. The battle in which Ebenezer was killed was especially Bloody. Forces from Plymouth and Massachusetts were present with the Connecticut Volunteers. Ebenezer died insolvent, with debts exceeding his estate…. it mentions widow Mary, and gives the names and ages of their seven children. The inventory was taken 11 Feb. 1676. The following letter from a Mr. Jones to Governor Lute is indicative of the plight of Ebenezer's widow: ' Sir, I pray be pleased what you can to favor and further the bearer, the Widow Dibble, that her husband's estate may be settled. He was killed at the Swamp Fight, died in debt more than his estate. 'T' were a work of mercy to consider the poor widow and fatherless children'*"

20-foot Granite Monument, surrounded by four squat blocks. South Kingstown, R. I.

Monument to the Great Swamp Fight

According to the, *History of Ancient Windsor,* written by the distinguished historian, Ezra Stiles (1727-1795), who in 1746 graduated from Yale and later became President of Yale College, gives an account of the "Swamp Fight" in which Ebenezer Dibble died.

"King Phillip was named by the colonists. His name was Metacomet. He was Massasoit's son. Massasoit and Squanto were the Indians who met the pilgrims at Plymouth. Phillip led a confederation of Native American nations: Wampanoags, Narragansetts, Nipmucks, Pequots, and Mohegans. The settlers had tried and hung 3 Natives in Plymouth. 1675, Phillip led the war. The Great Swamp fight, the Indians had taken refuge in a dense swamp. Guided by Indian scouts more and 1000 militia men were led through the swamp and marshes and came upon a great walled fort where there were 3000 Native Americans waiting. The battle was one of the most-bitter fights that ever took place on American soil. There were very heavy casualties on both sides. Many settlers and many Native women and children were killed also. The Great Swamp fight did not end the war, Phillip was eventually hunted down and killed.

The year 1675 is memorable for the breaking-out of King Philip's War, during which the united colonies lost as many as 600 men, and had as many as 600 dwelling-houses reduced to ashes. Philip, an able warrior, whose Indian name was Metacomet, ruled the Wampanoags, and resided at Mount Hope, near Bristol, In., Rhode Island. Observing the encroachments of the English on the hunting-grounds, and instigated by the execution of three of his tribe for the murder of John Sassamon, he artfully secured the aid of other tribes, and commenced hostilities by an attack, June 24, on the people of Swansey while returning from church, during which eight or nine of them were slain. In September, seventy young men, the flower of Essex County, were massacred and buried in one grave at Bloody Brook, in Deerfield and Northfield and Hadley were attacked. In an encounter with the Narragansetts in a swamp in Kingston, R.I., in December, Gov. Winslow with an army of 1,800 troops, killed and wounded about 1,000 Indians, burned 600 wigwams and thus seriously weakened Philip's power, who nevertheless continued during the winter his savage work, burning the towns of Lancaster, Medfield, Marlborough, Groton, Sudbury, and murdering or caring many of the people merciless captivity. But tribe after tribe deserting Philip, he returned to Mount Hope; and, his wife and son being soon after captured, he said, "Now my heart breaks: I am ready to die." On the 12th day of August, 1676, Captain Benjamin Church with a small body of men came upon him. An Indian of the party shot him through the heart; and thus fellthe last king of the Wampanoags and with him the power of the Indians of New England."

**Bethel Cemetery, Elmwood Section, Fairfield, Connecticut
where Wakefield Dibble is buried**

WAKEFIELD DIBBLE

WAKEFIELD DIBBLE (1667-1734) *(Ebenezer, Thomas, Robert)* was born in New Haven, Connecticut on 15 September 1667 and died in Stratford, Fairfield, Connecticut in 1734. This Wakefield DIBBLE is the son of EBENEZER DIBBLE (1641-1675), who lost his life in the Great War with the Narragansett Indians mentioned above. Wakefield first married Sarah Loomis, who was born on 1 February 1667 and died in 1693. She was the daughter of Thomas Loomis (1624-1689), a native of England. Wakefield married secondly, on 20 September 1694, to **JANE FYLER (1671-1760),** daughter of Zerubbabel (1644-1714) and Experience (Strong) Fyler (1650-1714). JANE was born on 1 June 1671 and died in 1760. Wakefield had about ten children by his second wife Jane born between 1695 and 1715. Wakefield moved to Danbury about 1703. Wakefield lived in Windsor, Danbury and Stratford, Connecticut. In Stratford, he related to his brother John Dibble in Church affairs. Wakefield's Will, dated 31 January 1733/34 in Starfield, probated on 2 May 1734. It mentions his wife Jane and children Ebenezer, Elizabeth Starr, Sarah Hudd, Abigail Starr, Experience Dibble, Ezra (who is identified as the oldest son), Nehemiah (who is described as very lame), John, "who has property at Pocono, between Danbury and Newton," and Mary Hicock (deceased). Three of Wakefield Dibble's children married three of the children of Josiah Starr. Executers were sons Ezra, John and Nehemiah. Wakefield is buried in Bethel Cemetery in Connecticut, Elmwood Section.

Wakefield's second wife Jane Fyler is the Granddaughter of Lieutenant Walter Fyler (1613-1683), who came to Massachusetts from England in 1630 and served in the King Philip War. He is one of early Puritans who settled in Danbury, Connecticut. His son Zerubbabel married Experience Strong, the daughter of Elder John Strong (1605-1699) and his wife Abigail Ford (1619-1688), who also arrived in the Massachusetts Bay Colony in 1630. The names of Walter Fyler and Thomas Ford are also included on the Founder's Monument in Windsor.

WAKEFIELD DIBBLE and JANE FYLER are the parents of:

> Ezra Dibble (12 June 1695 and died 20 June 1695)
> Ezra Dibble (7 October 1697), mar. (1) Hannah Star (2) Elizabeth Purr
> Mary Dibble, (1698-)
> Sarah Dibble (9 Feb 1701), mar. Jonathan Hurd
> Abigail Dibble (1 Oct 1703), mar. (1) Samuel Starr (2) Joseph Walker
> Nehemiah Dibble (1706),
> mar. Rebecca
> **JOHN DIBBLE (1708-1790), LT., mar. SARAH LEWIS, 27 August 1727**
> Experience Dibble (1710-),
> Elizabeth Dibble (1712-), mar. Thomas Starr
> Ebenezer Dibble (18 July 1715- 1799), mar. Joanna Bates

LT. JOHN DIBBLE

JOHN DIBBLE, (Lieutenant) (1708-1790) *(Wakefield, Ebenezer, Thomas, Robert)* was born in 1708 in Danbury, Fairfield, Connecticut and died 11 March 1790 in Danbury, the son of Wakefield Dibble and his second wife, **Jane Fyler (1676-1760)**. He married **SARAH LEWIS** on 27 August 1727. She was born in 1706, in Danbury, Fairfield, Connecticut and died 27 Feb 1787 in Bethel, Connecticut. They are buried in the Congregational Church yard at Bethel, Connecticut and the inscription on their stone says, *"They lived together 58 years, 6 months and 2 days."* He was commissioned as a Lieutenant on 4 May 1754, as he served in the French and Indian Wars. Thus, my 5th great-grandfather Lieutenant John Dibble (1708-1790) served with the 2nd Connecticut Regiment under Colonel Thompson.

Lieutenant John Dibble also served in the 2nd Connecticut Regiment under Colonel Thompson during the Revolutionary War. In his father's Will of 31 January 1733-34, mentions son, John Dibble, "who has property at Pocono, between Danbury and Newton." This same land was land held by the Indians until the white settlers arrived in 1684, in Danbury. The bridge over the Still River just north of Brookfield Junction was long called the "Pocono Bridge" and that immediate spot may have been an Indian Camp. A gentleman named, Ezra Beach Dibble, mentions in a 1903 DAR document that, *"Lieutenant John Dibble, father of Captain Ezra Dibble, was an Ardent Revolutionist."* This Ezra Beach Dibble is the great-great-grandson of Lieutenant John Dibble (which is my 5th Great-grandfather, 1708- 1790) and great-grandson of the Revolutionary Patriot Captain Ezra Dibble, who is the son of this same Lieutenant John Dibble, who is also my ancestor.

Lt. John Dibble (1708-1790), wife Sarah (1705-1787). Congregational Cemetery, Bethel, CT.

Here Lies the Body of Lieut John Dibble who departed this Life March 11th 1790 aged 82 Years

I personally visited the gravesite & photographed the marker, 31 May 2009, Gary Boughton.

Here lies the Body of Mrs Sarah Dibble the Wife of Mr John Dibble who departed this Life February 27th D 1787 in the 82d Year of her Age they lived together 58 Years 6 Months & 2 Days

THE FRENCH AND INDIAN WAR OF 1754-1763

Lieutenant John Dibble served in the Connecticut Militia during this war. This significant war, sometimes referred to as the "Seven Year War" in the colonies, was fought between Great Britain and her two enemies, the French, and the Indians of North America. In the early eighteenth century, the Appalachian region of North America remained the same as it had for some centuries. Frenchmen from Canada and Englishmen from the British Colonies, travelled through its woods and rivers, but the principal occupants of the region were the Native Americans who were being displaced from their lands. As the British Colonies became more populated and prosperous, their citizens began to look toward the rich lands across the Appalachian Mountains as providing new opportunities for settlement and economic growth. The French, who claimed the entire watersheds of the Mississippi and Saint Lawrence Rivers, which include the Great Lakes and the Ohio Valley, became concerned about the British encroachments into this region and so began to set up a series of forts on the Ohio, Mississippi and Missouri Rivers.

In 1752, the governor-general of New France was given instructions to take possession of the Ohio Valley, removing all British presence from the area. Sometime later, the Lieutenant Governor of Virginia was granting land in the Ohio Valley to citizens of his colony. These events led to the French and Indian War. The French setup new forts in the upper Allegheny River and the British decided to also build a fort there, named Fort Prince George, which was later taken over by the French and renamed it Fort Duquesne (present-day, Pittsburgh, Pennsylvania). There was much military activity during 1755, 1756 and 1757, in the frontier areas of Pennsylvania and New York, however it was not until 1756 that the British officially declared war on the French and the Indians who were their allies. The British was also driving the Native Americans off their land to make way for new settlers from England. Most of the fighting between France and Britain in North American ended in 1760. The official war in North America ended with the signing of the Treaty of Paris on 10 February 1763, thus ending the Seven Year War between France and Great Britain, resulting in France giving up its holdings in North America.

LT. JOHN DIBBLE and his wife SARAH LEWIS (1708-1787) are the parents of:

> John Dibble, II (1730-1779)
> Mary Dibble (1732-1790)
> Eleazer Dibble (1734, in Danbury; d. before 1780 in Bethel) (French and Indian War)
> Nathan Dibble (11 Aug 1736, in Danbury; d.1784, in Danbury) (Revolutionary War)
> > married Abigail Stevens (1738-1810)
> Sarah Dibble (1738-)
> Jane Dibble (1739-1820) married Matthew Barnum (1736-1806)
> Ezra DIBBLE, (Capt.) (Revolutionary Patriot) (1739-1809),
> > married Lydia Benedict (1741-1804). They lived in the southern part of Brookfield (then Danbury) and are interred in the old private ground below Brookfield Junction west of William Blackman's residence. Ezra Beach Dibble, (DAR Application dated 30 April 1903, approved 30 September 1903), indicates that both of his ancestors, "LT. John Dibble, father of Capt. Ezra Dibble, was an Ardent Revolutionist."
> **SAMUEL DIBBLE, Sr. (1742-1821),**
> > **mar. SARAH TROWBRIDGE (1743-1861)**
> Hannah Dibble (1745-1825), married Lemuel Beebe (1743-1813) (Revolutionary War.

SAMUEL DIBBLE, SR

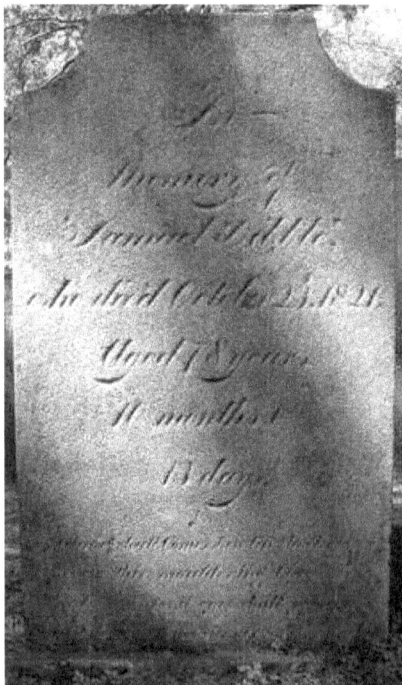

Samuel Dibble Sr. (1742-1821)
Son of Lt. John Dibble & Sarah Lewis

Sarah Trowbridge (1743-1772)
Daughter of Samuel Trowbridge, Jr. & Sarah Seeley

SAMUEL DIBBLE, SR. (1742-1821) *(John, Wakefield, Ebenezer, Thomas, Robert)* was born on 8 December 1742 in Danbury, Connecticut and died on 23 October 1821, in Danbury, the son of Lt. John Dibble and his wife Sarah Lewis Dibble. Samuel married **SARAH TROWBRIDGE (1743- 1772),** the daughter of **SAMUEL TROWBRIDGE (1700-1782)** and his wife **SARAH SEELEY**. Sarah Trowbridge was born on 27 April 1743 in Worcester, Massachusetts and died 15 July 1772 in Danbury, Fairfield, Connecticut. Samuel and Sarah are buried in Stony Hill Cemetery in Bethel, Fairfield County, Connecticut. His marker states: *"Died at age 78 years, 10 months, and 17 days."*

SAMUEL DIBBLE, SR.'s wife SARAH TROWBRIDGE was born on 27 April 1743 and died 15 July 1772, probably in childbirth of her last child, Sarah. Sarah Trowbridge was the first wife of Samuel Dibble, Sr., (1742-1821) of Danbury, Connecticut. **Sarah** had five children, with only one son, Samuel.

Samuel Dibble, Sr.'s second wife was Phoebe Benedict (1750-1828), who he married on August 4, 1774, had seven children. Samuel's third wife was Ruth Benedict. *(See Appendix I: "The TROWBRIDGE Family"*

Samuel DIBBLE, Sr. and his first wife **Sarah TROWBRIDGE** are the parents of:

> Mabel Dibble (1763-1861)
> Rodah Dibble (1765-)
> Sallome Dibble (1767-1807)
> **SAMUEL DIBBLE, JR., (1769-1860)**
> > mar. (1) Rue Marie Benedict (1768-1796);
> > **mar. (2) MARY "POLLY" COMSTOCK (1778-1866)**
> Sarah Dibble (1772-1772)

Samuel DIBBLE, Sr. and his second wife **Phoebe BENEDICT** are the parents of:

> Mary "Molly" Dibble (1776-)
> Rene Dibble (1778-)
> Adah Benedict Dibble (1779-1844) Amelia Dibble (1781-)
> John Dibble (1784-1878)
> Phebe Dibble (1788-1879)
> Lucy Dibble (1790-1882), married Andrew Benedict

SAMUEL DIBBLE, JR.

Samuel Dibble Jr. (1769-1860)

Mary "Polly" Comstock Dibble (1778-1866)
Died: *"87 Yrs., 9 Mos. & 25 Days"* (1769-1860)

SAMUEL DIBBLE, JR. (1769-1860) *(Samuel, Lt. John, Wakefield, Ebenezer, Thomas, Robert).* He was born on 6 November 1769 in Danbury, Connecticut and died on 14 October 1860. Samuel married first to Rue Maria Benedict (1768-1796) on 20 September 1791 and had one daughter Sarah (1793-1816).

He married second, **MARY "POLLY" COMSTOCK (1778-1866),** the daughter of **ANDREW COMSTOCK ((1752-1789)** and **Mercy Hickok STARR (1750-1841**), and had seven children. Mary "Polly" was born on 19 June 1778 and died 14 April 1866, in Danbury, Connecticut. Both Samuel and Polly outlived their son, Andrew Comstock Dibble, who died in September 1846. They are buried in the Stony Hill Cemetery, in Bethel, Fairfield County, Connecticut. *(See Appendix II: The COMSTOCK Family)*

Samuel Dibble and his second wife Mary "Polly" Comstock are the parents of the following:

> Polly Mariette DIBBLE (1798-1876)
> > married Frederick Seeley
> **ANDREW COMSTOCK DIBBLE (1800-1846),** migrated to Charleston, South Carolina
> > on 10 December 1821.
> > **(rel.) MARTHA "Minda" SMITH (1800-1849), of Charleston, SC**
> > Henrietta M. Wagner (1812-1882), (mar. 9 April 1828) of Charleston, SC
> Horace Benedict DIBBLE (1803-1819)
> Rue Maria DIBBLE (1806-1807), died as infant

Philander Virgil DIBBLE (1808-1883),

> **married Frances Anna Evans**
>
> **(1815-1891); migrated to Charleston, South Carolina 16 August 1827.**

Samuel Lorenzo DIBBLE (1812-1896),

> married Sarah Smith (1816-1929) in Danbury, Connecticut and had about twelve children. Delevan (1824-1886), in Danbury, Connecticut and had about seven children, with one son named Andrew Comstock Dibble (1845-1936), who was born in Danbury and died in Nevada.

Cornelius Augustus DIBBLE (1815-1900),

> married Nancy Jane Polly Mariette

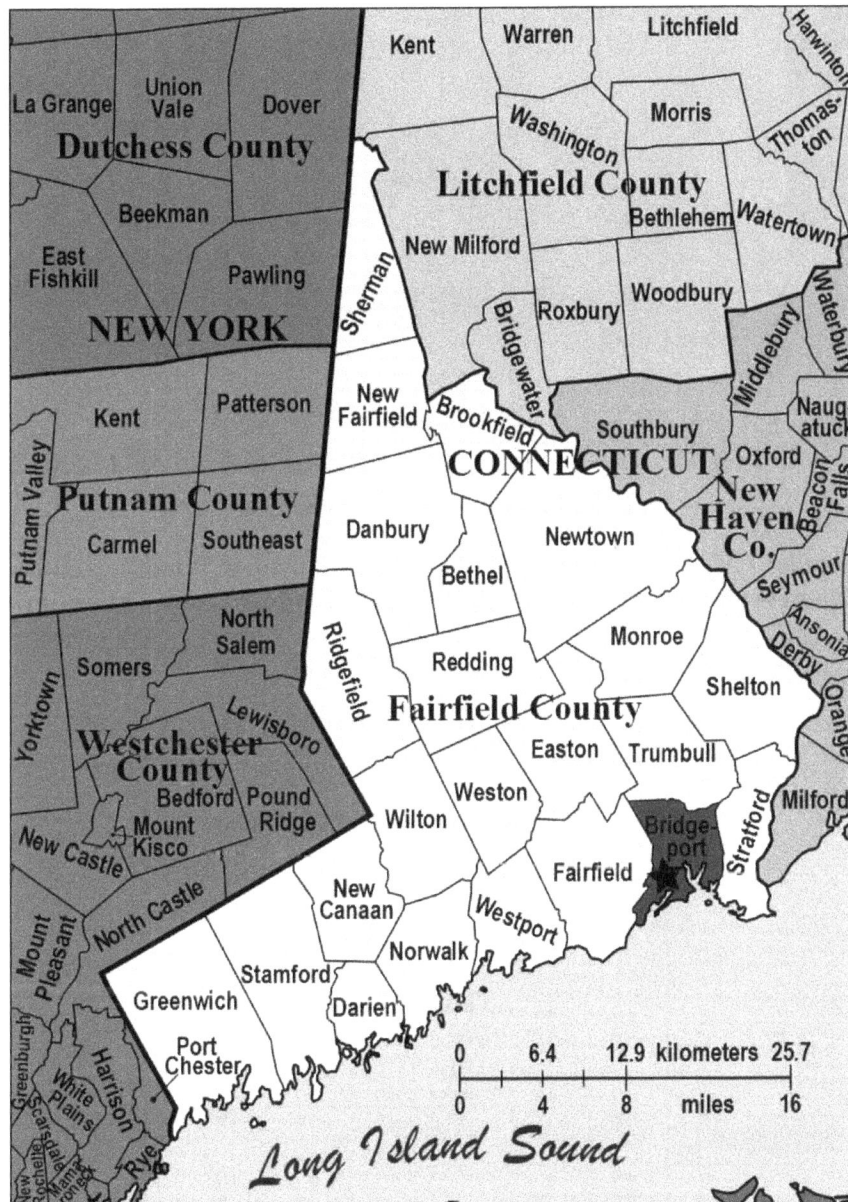

Fairfield County, Connecticut Danbury, Home of the Dibble Family

FOUNDER'S MONUMENT, WINDSOR CONNECTICUT

Founder's Monument, Windsor, Connecticut

Founder's Monument, this large granite monument, in Windsor, Connecticut
has the names of about 140 persons who founded Windsor and lived there prior to 1641.

**Ancestors of ANDREW HENRY DIBBLE, SR. (1825-1873)
whose names are included on the Founder's Monument**

Thomas and Robert Dibble

Lt. Walter Fyler

Simon Hoyt

Thomas Ford

PART II

The Dibble Family of South Carolina

Many a man and woman in the South
Have lived in wedlock as holy as Adam and Eve,
and brought forth their brown and golden children. . .

W. E. B. DeBois (1868-1963)

SAMUEL DIBBLE, JR. (1769-1860) *(Samuel, John, Wakefield, Ebenezer, Thomas, Robert).* Samuel of Danbury, Connecticut, and his wife Mary "Polly" Comstock (1778-1866), were the parents of seven children. Two of their sons ventured to Charleston, South Carolina, in the 1820s, to establish their hat business. The eldest son, Andrew Comstock Dibble (A.C.) (1800-1846), born in Danbury, Connecticut, came to Charleston on 10 December 1821, as a twenty-one years old young man. Their third son and fifth child, Philander Virgil Dibble (P.V.) (1808-1883), was also born in Danbury, Connecticut on 30 November 1808. He arrived in Charleston as an 18-year-old young man, in August 1827. These two brothers, A.C. Dibble and P.V. Dibble and their descendants are the only "Dibbles" in South Carolina from the early 1820s through the early 1900s.

ANDREW COMSTOCK DIBBLE (1800-1846) *(Samuel, Samuel, John, Wakefield, Ebenezer, Thomas, Robert)* was born in Danbury, Connecticut on 5 May 1800 in Danbury, Connecticut and died on 22 September 1846 in New York, New York, while on a visit.

The earliest document found in reference to A.C. Dibble, is in the (*City Gazette Newspaper*, Charleston, S.C.) when he is arriving as a passenger on the ship, *Allen* from New York arriving in the Port of Charleston on December 10, 1821. A classified advertisement of his Hat business is seen in the *City Gazette Newspaper* (Charleston, SC), June 10, 1822. From 1823 through 1846, there are 371 notices seen in the Charleston, South Carolina Newspapers (mostly in the *City Gazette* and *Charleston Courier*) of either A.C. Dibble arriving or his merchandize being received by him in the Port of Charleston, by ship from New York. During the twenty-five years he lived here, he had to establish a place to open his hat shop and then purchase the stock, and supplies to operate it. As we see these many notices, we see that those persons who lived in the Charleston community were dependent on their necessary goods to be shipped by boat from New York. It appears he travelled to New York quite often during these years to acquire supplies and merchandise for his hat shop, which appears to have been very successful. During this time in our history, businesses in Charleston had to import all their items and stock from New York.

This information obtained from these many newspapers, which tells me that Andrew Comstock Dibble was living in Charleston from 10 December 1821 until his death in September 1846.

It appears that Andrew Comstock Dibble came to Charleston to work in the Waldman Hat Shop, which was established by Zalmon Wildmon, with the intention of eventually opening his own hat shop. I have been very fortunate to have located a letter written by Andrew Comstock Dibble on "8 Nov. 1824" (envelope dated, 8 Nov. 1822) to a Mr. Zalmon Wildman, who was the Post Master in Danbury, Connecticut, at this time. A. C. Dibble discusses his plans to soon open his Hat Shop, in Charleston. In this letter he also discusses the Yellow Fever and the risks associated with Yellow Fever that was prevalent in Charleston at that time.

Mr. Zalmon Wildman (1775-1835) was a U.S. Representative from Connecticut, serving in 24th United States Congress, and was appointed Postmaster of Danbury from 1805-1835. Occupationally, Wildman was a hatter and he established the first hat stores in Charleston, South Carolina, and Savannah, Georgia, in 1802. This, also further documents the fact that Andrew Comstock Dibble was living in Charleston in 1822/1824, when he wrote this letter to this family friend and relative in Danbury, Connecticut. A. C. Dibble also mentions his parents, who both survived him. Mr. Wildman was married to Mary B. Dibble (1776-1856), a native of Danbury, Connecticut who was the granddaughter of Nehemiah Dibble (1706-1820), who was the brother of Lieutenant John Dibble (1708-1790), who was great-grandfather Andrew Comstock DIBBLE, thus, making them cousins. It is evident that Mr. Waldman was instrumental and encouraging Andrew Comstock Dibble to venture to Charleston to open his hat shop.

Letter from Andrew Comstock Dibble who was living in Charleston, South Carolina to Zalmon Wildman, who was the Postmaster of Danbury, Connecticut:

November 8th 1824
Z. Wildman, Esq.

Sir,
I arrived here on the 1st of November after a pleasant passage of 78 Hours from New York in the Ship LaFayette. The weather was then cool but moderated on the 3d & 4th and was quite warm until yesterday when the wind shifted Northerly & became cool again.

There has been several cases of [Yellow] Fever since I arrived but were confined to those who have remained here through the summer — the seeds of the disease having been sown in the system for some time. It is generally thought that there is no danger attending strangers coming in here now although some differ in opinion. Yet I do not know of any strangers having taken the Fever & there are many who have been here for 3 weeks past.

I have not opened my store yet but shall in about 3 days. Neither have I been down town but once but the weather is so cool I shall go down today. But what is my loss is your gain, for since I have been here. I have sold not less than 20 of my old Broad St. customer Hats. On Saturday, had I been opened, I have not the least doubt but I would have sold 150 or 200 dollars. Last week sale here was very good and the countrymen begin to come in fast.

The [ship] President arrived yesterday but none of our Northern hatters have yet arrived. She was full of passengers. The Lafayette Stamp goes very well and we have to iron most of the brims flat. The retail is small brims, I.E., for the city, but the country trade require as usual larger brims.

Respectfully yours, — A. C. Dibble

P. S. If my father enquires, please tell him there is no danger from Fever — at least I think there is none.

During the period of several years, Andrew Comstock Dibble's Hat Shop was located at several locations in the same block on Broad Street, where he was probably renting the store. He is seen at 27, 31, 35 and 37 Broad Street, at different times. Since Martha also lived in this same block at 64/68 Broad at the Ravenel's home, he apparently had an opportunity to form a close relationship with Martha Smith, who was living a short distance away. According to the family *Bible*, their son Andrew Henry Dibble, was born on 1 January 1825, in Charleston.

Andrew Comstock Dibble (1800-1846) later married Henrietta M. H. Wagner on 9 April 1828, who was the daughter of Samuel J. Wagner, Esq., and his wife Margaret Wood Wagner, of Charleston. Andrew Comstock and Henrietta had about ten children born to this union. Andrew is seen in the *1830 U. S. Census*, with his wife and one daughter, under age 5, (Margaret Ann, b. 1829) and one male *free person of color* (likely his son, Andrew Henry Dibble), living in Charleston, SC. (The 1830 United States Federal Census only includes the name of the head of household.) In the *1840 U. S. Census,* there are two U.S. Census reports; (1) has A.C. Dibble with his wife and 1 male, age 5-9; 2 females under 5 years; 2 females 5-9 years; and 11 enslaved persons. He and his family are living on State Street, in the business section of Charleston, not far from his Broad Street Hat Shop. The other 1840 Census (2) has Andrew C. Dibble, owning a plantation in Saint Andrew Parish, Charleston County, SC, includes A.C. Dibble, (white male) with 6 enslaved persons, which appears to be in the southwestern part of Charleston where he had a large plantation in a rural section of Charleston. (The *1850 United States Census Reports* was the first census that included the names of all persons within a household.)

It appears that A. C. (Andrew Comstock) Dibble owned several pieces of real estate, during the twenty-five years he lived in Charleston. He owned property at 37 Broad Street where he had his Hat Shop. The first document seen (15 Oct. 1835) in reference to this property, mentions it as a 3-story brick building, with "out-buildings" and is located on the south side of Broad Street. There are other documents associated with this Broad Street property, as well. He also owned a large plantation on Wappoo Creek of 198 acres, in Saint Andrew's Parish, Charleston County, which he purchased on 22 March 1838 from Edward B. Lining. Mr. Edward B. Lining had purchased this plantation from Benjamin Stiles in 1822. The 1840 Census of St. Andrew's Parish, Charleston County, shows A.C. Dibble. (At this time in the history of the Charleston community, many of the wealthy residents owned plantations across the Ashley River (only a few miles from downtown Charleston), in the Saint Andrews Parish of Charleston County. This tells one that there was no set standard of how these plantation owners and their enslaved persons were accounted for, especially since most of them had a residence in Charleston City. According to the Charleston County RMC Office, many persons are picked up on their plantations, as well as in the city for the same Census.)

Andrew Comstock Dibble's "*Last Will and Testament*" is dated February 27, 1839, about seven years prior to his death. He died on the 22 September 1846, and his Will was proved on 28 September 1846, six days later. It appears Andrew Comstock's father-in-law, wasted no time in filing these papers. Andrew Comstock stated in his will: "*... being weak of body but of sound and disposing mind memory and understanding ....*" This tells us that Andrew Comstock had been sick or his body had become weak with some illness approximately seven (7) years prior to his death, dying at age 46 years, six months. This also tells us that A. C. knew he had some medical condition when only 39 years old. His Last Will mentions "*beloved wife, Henrietta M. Dibble and the support and maintenance of my four children...*", but does not include the names of any of his children. However, he had eight living children by his wife, at the time of his death. The executors of his Will were Samuel J. Wagner and Edward Sebring. Samuel J. Wagner, was his father-in-law, and Edward Sebring (1799-1880), was a native of New York who had also migrated to Charleston about the same time as Andrew, to open a tailoring business. In 1822, Sebring is listed as a "Merchant Tailor," located at 30 Broad Street. He is later seen at 32 Broad, during the 1830s and 1840s. He later becomes a wealthy businessman and president of the State Bank. It is interesting that he was one of the executors of A.C.'s will, and evidently a close friend, and operated his tailoring shop very close to Andrew's hat shop on Broad, makes one suspect that this may be where Andrew Henry worked as an apprentice to become a Tailor.

Andrew Comstock died on 22 September 1846, at 46 years and 6 months, while on a business trip to New York City, probably to purchase supplies and merchandise for his hat shop. The New York City Newspaper (Barber Collection) death notices states: "Tuesday, Sept. 22, at residence of brother-in-law, Frederick Seeley, A. C. Dibble, of Charleston, S.C. Remains, Danbury, Connecticut." Andrew Comstock's elder sister, Polly M. Dibble (1798-1875) married Frederick Seeley on 20 January 1819, in Danbury, Connecticut. They are seen living in New York, Ward 2 in the 1850 U.S. Census.

After his death, his wife, Henrietta ran a rooming house, she purchased in 1851 on Queen Street, in Charleston City, not too far from the Broad Street hat store, in order to have an income to help with the maintenance of these many young children. At the time of Andrew Comstock Dibble's death, his son Andrew Henry Dibble was 21 years old and his other children's ages are as follows, about 18, with others to follow close afterward, with ages approximately 16, 12, 11, 9, and the four youngest, 6, 3, 1, and 0. The 1850 United States Census the youngest son, Marion Wakefield Dibble, is seen living with his grandparents, Samuel J. Wagner, and his wife Margaret Wood Wagner, in Charleston. Marion is said to be 4 years old in this Census. You will also see from the list of children below that Andrew Comstock lost 4 of his children while still babies or very young children. Henrietta's "Last Will and Testament," dated 9 August 1864, mentions her property on Queen Street (Southside), opposite Smith Street and this is where she had her rooming house.

Andrew Comstock Dibble
1800-1846

ANDREW COMSTOCK DIBBLE (1800-1846) (*Samuel, Samuel, John, Wakefield, Ebenezer, Thomas, Robert*) was born on 05 Mar 1800, the son of Samuel Dibble, Jr. (1769-1860) and his wife Mary "Polly" Comstock (1778-1866), in Danbury, Fairfield, Connecticut, USA. He died on 22 Sep 1846 in New York, New York, USA (Age at Death: 46; He was on a visit to his sister's home in NY.). He married **HENRIETTA MARY H. WAGNER** (daughter of Samuel Jasper Wagner Esq. (Customs Inspector) and Margaret Wood). She was born in 1811 in Charleston, South Carolina, USA. She died on 02 Nov 1864 in Columbia, Richland, South Carolina,

Obituary.

Departed this life, in the city of New-York, on Tuesday morning last, after a distressing illness of several day's continuance, Mr. ANDREW C. DIBBLE, of this city, aged 46 years. By the decease of Mr. D. our community has lost one who was highly esteemed for the noble qualities of his heart. Just in all his dealings, kind and conciliating to all with whom he associated, it may perhaps be said of him with more truth than almost any other man, that HE LEFT NOT AN ENEMY BEHIND. His death has created a void in a large circle of friends, and his afflicted widow and a numerous family of children, are left to mourn over the departure of the most affectionate of husbands, and kindest of fathers. He who "tempers the wind to the shorn lamb," will administer consolation to the afflicted ones. The remains of Mr. D. were taken to Danbury, (Conn) for interment.

Andrew Comstock Dibble and his wife Henrietta M. Wagner became the parents of five sons and five daughters. Two of his sons died early (six months, and four years and three months). Three sons grew to adulthood, serving in the Confederate Army during the Civil War, with one dying in the war. Of the five daughters, three married and one never married, and one died as an infant. It is very interesting to see that Andrew and Henrietta lost three of their ten children, while very young. The three daughters who married have descendants, and one son, William Jasper Dibble.

Andrew Comstock and his wife Henrietta May Wagner (1812-1864) Dibble became the parents of ten children:

> Margaret Anna Dibble (1829-1911)
> > m. Clarence A. Graeser (1806-1863)
> Mary Elizabeth Dibble (1830-1923)
> > m. William M. Patton, Sr. (1829-1884)
> Julia Henrietta Dibble (1831-1832), (died as an infant.)
> Samuel Wagner Dibble (1834-1865) (Sgt. Major, Civil War Confederate); died in war.
> Julia Henrietta Dibble (1835-1903)
> > m. William W. Smith (1827-1887)
> Horace Benedict Dibble (March 1838- Sept.1838, at six months old)
> Rosa Frances Dibble (1841-1922)
> William Jasper Dibble (1842-1918) (Civil War Confederate)
> > m. Eva Cooper (1848-1879)
> Andrew Comstock Dibble, Jr. (1842-1847) (Died 4 years, 3 months)
> Marion Wakefield Dibble (1845-1882) (Civil War Confederate)
> > m. Eliza. E. Ottolenghi (1852-1895)

CHILDREN

ANDREW COMSTOCK DIBBLE and Henrietta Mary H. Wagner had the following children:

1. **MARGARET ANNA (MAGGIE) DIBBLE** (daughter of ANDREW COMSTOCK DIBBLE and Henrietta Mary H. Wagner) was born on 10 Dec 1829 in Charleston, Charleston County, South Carolina, United States of America. She died on 06 Nov 1911 in Charleston, Charleston County, South Carolina, United States of America. She married CLARENCE AUGUSTUS GRAESER SR. He was born in 1806 in Columbia, Richland County, South Carolina, USA. He died on 18 Aug 1893 in Charleston, Charleston County, South Carolina, United States of America.

2. **MARY ELIZABETH DIBBLE** (daughter of ANDREW COMSTOCK DIBBLE and of Henrietta Mary H. Wagner) was born in 1830 in Charleston City, Charles, South Carolina, USA. She died on 05 Sep 1923 in Montgomery Alabama, USA. She married WILLIAM MOORE PATTON Sr. He was born on 26 Jan 1829 in Stanstead, Estrie Region, Quebec, Canada. He died in 1884 in Jackson, Hinds County, Mississippi, United States of America.

3. **JULIA HENRIETTA DIBBLE** (d. Infant) (daughter of ANDREW COMSTOCK DIBBLE and Henrietta Mary H. Wagner) was born in 20 July 1831 in Charleston, Berkeley, South Carolina, USA. She died in 7 September 1832 in Charleston, Berkeley, South Carolina, USA.

4. **SAMUEL WAGNER DIBBLE** (SGT. Major, Civil War) (son of ANDREW COMSTOCK DIBBLE and Henrietta Mary H. Wagner) was born about 1834 in Charleston, Berkeley County, South Carolina. He died on 15 Jan 1865 in Fort Fisher, North Carolina.

5. **JULIA HENRIETTA DIBBLE** (daughter of ANDREW COMSTOCK DIBBLE and Henrietta Mary H. Wagner) was born on 21 Feb 1835 in Charleston, Charleston County, South Carolina, USA. She died on 15 Apr 1903 in Charleston County, South Carolina, USA (Age at Death: 68, Magnolia Cemetery, Charleston). She married William Walton SMITH Sr. (son of Whiteford SMITH and Margaret Mary SHAND) on 08 Apr 1851. He was born on 07 Apr 1827 in Charleston County, South Carolina, USA. He died on 05 Jan 1887 in Charleston, South Carolina, USA.

6. **HORACE BENEDICT DIBBLE** (d. 6 months) (son of ANDREW COMSTOCK DIBBLE and Henrietta Mary H. Wagner) was born in Mar 1838 in Charleston, Berkeley, South Carolina, USA. He died on 8 Sept 1838 Died at 6 months old in Charleston, Berkeley, South Carolina, USA.

7. **ROSA FRANCES DIBBLE** (daughter of ANDREW COMSTOCK DIBBLE and Henrietta Mary H. Wagner) was born on 30 Mar 1841 in Charleston, Berkeley County, South Carolina. She died on 05 Oct 1922 in Atlanta, Fulton, Georgia, United States of America.

8. **WILLIAM JASPER DIBBLE** (Civil War, Confederate) (son of ANDREW COMSTOCK DIBBLE and Henrietta Mary H. Wagner) was born on 12 Dec 1842 in Charleston, Berkeley County, South Carolina. He died on 25 Mar 1918 in Atlanta, Fulton, Georgia, USA. He married EVA COOPER (daughter of George Franklin Cooper) on 02 Jul 1868 in Sumter, Georgia, USA. She was born in 1848 in Americus, Sumter, Georgia, USA. She died in Nov 1879 in Americus, Sumter, Georgia, United States.

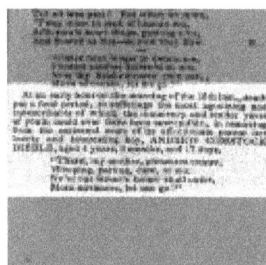

9. **ANDREW COMSTOCK DIBBLE JR**. d: 4 YRS 3 MO. (son of ANDREW COMSTOCK DIBBLE and Henrietta Mary H. Wagner) was born in Aug 1843 in Charleston City, Charleston, South Carolina. He died on 15 Nov 1847 in Charleston city, Charleston, South Carolina.

10. **MARION WAKEFIELD DIBBLE** (Corporal, Civil War Confederate) (son of ANDREW COMSTOCK DIBBLE and Henrietta Mary H. Wagner) was born on 31 Oct 1845 in Charleston County, South Carolina, USA. He died on 08 Nov 1882 in Magnolia Cemetery, Charleston. SC (Age: born 1845 (at 37 years)). He married ELIZA EMMA OTTOLENGIN (daughter of Jacob Ottolenghi and Eliza Emma JACOBS). She was born on 16 Dec 1852 in Charleston, South Carolina. She died on 24 Mar 1895 in buried in Charleston Jewish Cemetery.

GRANDCHILDREN

1. **MARGARET ANNA (MAGGIE) DIBBLE** (ANDREW COMSTOCK) was born on 10 Dec 1829 in Charleston, Charleston County, South Carolina, United States of America. She died on 06 Nov 1911 in Charleston, Charleston County, South Carolina, United States of America. She married CLARENCE AUGUSTUS GRAESER SR. He was born in 1806 in Columbia, Richland County, South Carolina, USA. He died on 18 Aug 1893 in Charleston, Charleston County, South Carolina, United States of America.

   Clarence Augustus GRAESER Sr. and Margaret Anna (Maggie) DIBBLE had the following child:

   i. **CLARENCE AUGUSTUS GRAESER JR. MAJ**. (Professor of French and German at the Citadel Military College, Charleston. (son of Clarence Augustus GRAESER Sr. and Margaret Anna (Maggie) DIBBLE) was born on 26 Aug 1869 in Charleston, Charleston County, South Carolina, United States of America. He died on 03 Feb 1953 in Charleston, Charleston County, South Carolina, United States of America (Age: 83 Magnolia Cemetery, Charleston, SC). He married (1) JEANNE ALICE PIQUET (daughter of Albert and Alice Piquet). She was born in Jun 1874 in Switzerland. She died on 26 Dec 1961 in Columbia, Richland, South Carolina, USA. He married an unknown spouse in 1896.

2. **MARY ELIZABETH DIBBLE** (ANDREW COMSTOCK) was born in 1830 in Charleston City, Charles, South Carolina, USA. She died on 05 Sep 1923 in Montgomery Alabama, USA. She married WILLIAM MOORE PATTON SR. He was born on 26 Jan 1829 in Stanstead, Estrie Region, Quebec, Canada. He died in 1884 in Jackson, Hinds County, Mississippi, United States of America.

William Moore Patton Sr. and Mary Elizabeth DIBBLE had the following children:

    i.   **HARRIS McWILLIE PATTON** (son of William Moore Patton Sr. and Mary Elizabeth DIBBLE) was born on 28 Apr 1859 in Jackson, Hinds County, Mississippi, United States of America. He died on 14 Nov 1864 in Greenville, Greenville County, South Carolina, United States of America.

    ii.   **WILLIAM MOORE PATTON JR** (child of William Moore Patton Sr. and Mary Elizabeth DIBBLE) was born on 02 Aug 1865 in Greenville, Greenville County, South Carolina, United States of America. William Moore died on 01 Mar 1875 in Jackson, Hinds County, Mississippi, United States of America.

    iii.   **MARY BERTHA PATTON** (daughter of William Moore Patton Sr. and Mary Elizabeth DIBBLE) was born in 1866. She died on 04 Jul 1897, of typhoid fever, in Jackson, Hinds County, Mississippi, United States of America.

    iv.   **STUART WAGNER PATTON** (child of William Moore Patton Sr. and Mary Elizabeth DIBBLE) was born in 1869. Stuart Wagner died in 1941. He married Kate Cawthon (1870-1960), in 1896.

    v.   **HENRIETTA C PATTON** (daughter of William Moore Patton Sr. and Mary Elizabeth DIBBLE) was born in 1881. She died on 30 Dec 1899, of typhoid fever, in Jackson, Hinds County, Mississippi, United States of America.

5. **JULIA HENRIETTA DIBBLE** (ANDREW COMSTOCK) was born on 21 Feb 1835 in Charleston, Charleston County, South Carolina, USA. She died on 15 Apr 1903 in Charleston County, South Carolina, USA (Age at Death: 68, Magnolia Cemetery, Charleston). She married William Walton SMITH Sr. (son of Whiteford SMITH and Margaret Mary SHAND) on 08 Apr 1851. He was born on 07 Apr 1827 in Charleston County, South Carolina, USA. He died on 05 Jan 1887 in Charleston, South Carolina, USA.

William Walton SMITH Sr. and Julia Henrietta DIBBLE had the following eight children:

i. **ANDREW DIBBLE SMITH** (son of William Walton SMITH Sr. and Julia Henrietta DIBBLE) was born on 13 Oct 1852 in Charleston, Charleston County, South Carolina, United States of America. He died on 15 Jul 1887 in Georgia, USA. He married Molly in 1875. She was born in 1855 in Charleston, South Carolina, USA.

ii. **JULIA GERTRUDE SMITH** (daughter of William Walton SMITH Sr. and Julia Henrietta DIBBLE) was born on 28 Apr 1854 in Charleston County, South Carolina, USA. She died on 11 Mar 1909 in Buried at Magnolia Cemetery, Charleston, South Carolina. She married Daniel Gabriel WAYNE Jr. (son of Daniel Gabriel WAYNE Sr. and Mary Elizabeth Kingman) in 1875. He was born on 30 Aug 1849 in Charleston County, South Carolina, USA. He died on 23 Sep 1905 in Magnolia Cemetery, Charleston, South Carolina.

iii. **SARAH "SALLIE" LOUISE GRONIN SMITH** (daughter of William Walton SMITH Sr. and Julia Henrietta DIBBLE) was born on 01 Aug 1856 in Charleston County, South Carolina, USA. She died on 27 Jun 1937. She married Robert Motte SMITH (son of Robert Shand Smith and Susan Mary Muncreeff Dart) in 1877. He was born on 16 May 1849 in Greenville, South Carolina, USA. He died on 02 Mar 1923 in Washington, County, Georgia, USA.

iv. **WILLIAM WALTON SMITH JR**. (son of William Walton SMITH Sr. and Julia Henrietta DIBBLE) was born in 1858 in Charleston County, South Carolina, USA. He died in 1932.

v. **SHAND SMITH** (son of William Walton SMITH Sr. and Julia Henrietta DIBBLE) was born on 04 Sep 1858 in Charleston County, South Carolina, USA. He died on 29 Jan 1955. He married Gay Edna "Gay" Trout Smith on 19 Apr 1892 in Salt Lake City, Utah, USA. She was born in Jul 1874 in Missouri. She died on 03 Dec 1962 in Alameda, Alameda, California, USA.

vi. **MARY "MAMIE" ELIZABETH PATTON SMITH** (daughter of William Walton SMITH Sr. and Julia Henrietta DIBBLE) was born on 24 Oct 1863 in Charleston County, South Carolina, USA. She died on 12 Feb 1937 in Columbia, Richland, South Carolina, United States (Buried at Sunnyside Cemetery, Orangeburg, SC at age 73). She married Edward Courtenay DIBBLE (son of Philander Virgil DIBBLE and Frances Ann EVANS, who was a cousin) on 08 Apr 1884 in Charleston, South Carolina. He was born on 22 Jul 1855 in Charleston, South Carolina, USA. He died on 13 Mar 1899 in South Carolina (Buried in Sunnyside Cemetery, Orangeburg, SC).

vii. **J. LAWRENCE SMITH** (son of William Walton SMITH Sr. and Julia Henrietta DIBBLE) was born in 1866 in Charleston Berkeley, Carolina, USA. He died in 1965.

viii. **FRANCIS "FRANK" MARION SMITH SR.** (son of William Walton SMITH Sr. and Julia Henrietta DIBBLE) was born on 20 Nov 1871 in Charleston Berkeley, Carolina, USA. He died on 21 Mar 1946 in Charleston, Berkeley, South Carolina, USA. He married (2) Maria "RIA" Stewart Harvey (2ND WIFE) (daughter of Wilson Godfrey HARVEY and Cornelia Julia ELBRIDGE). She was born on 12 Nov 1877 in Charleston Berkeley, Carolina, USA. She died on 06 Aug 1948 in Charleston, South Carolina. He married (1) May Louise MUCKENFUSS (1ST WIFE) (daughter of Allen Wesley MUCKENFUSS and Emily Laura WHEELER) in 1897. She was born on 11 Jun 1877 in Charleston, Berkeley County, South Carolina. She died on 02 May 1906 in Charleston, Berkeley, South Carolina, USA.

8. **WILLIAM JASPER DIBBLE** (Civil War Confederate) (son of Andrew Comstock Dibble) was born on 12 Dec 1842 in Charleston, Berkeley County, South Carolina. He died on 25 Mar 1918 in Atlanta, Fulton, Georgia, USA. He married (1) EVA COOPER (daughter of George Franklin Cooper) on 02 Jul 1868 in Sumter, Georgia, USA. She was born in 1848 in Americus, Sumter, Georgia, USA. She died in Nov 1879 in Americus, Sumter, Georgia, United States.

William Jasper DIBBLE and Eva COOPER had the following children

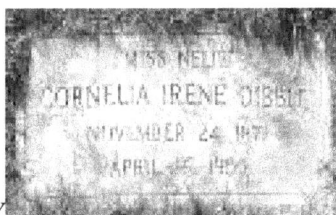

i. **CORNELIA IRENE DIBBLE** (daughter of William Jasper DIBBLE and Eva COOPER) was born on 24 Nov 1871 in Americus, Sumter, Georgia, United States. She died on 16 Apr 1955 in Fulton, Georgia (Age: 83 Years).

ii. **ROSA FRANCES DIBBLE** (daughter of William Jasper DIBBLE and Eva COOPER) was born on 24 Sep 1874 in Americus, Sumter, Georgia, USA. She died on 07 May 1948 in Fulton County, Georgia, USA. She married Walter Hunt GRANT (son of William GRANT and Mattie) on 25 Jul 1906 in Fulton, Georgia, USA. He was born in 1870 in Atlanta, Fulton, Georgia, USA. He died on 30 Jan 1942 in Atlanta City, Fulton, Georgia.

iii. **MARY LOUISA DIBBLE** (daughter of William Jasper DIBBLE and Eva COOPER) was born on 24 May 1876 in Americus, Sumter, Georgia, USA. She died on 05 Jun 1936 in Atlanta, Fulton, Georgia, USA. She married Henry Madison PEARSON on 07 Apr 1909 in Fulton, Georgia, USA. He was born on 16 Feb 1860 in Atlanta, Fulton, Georgia, USA. He died on 04 Jul 1942.

iv. **SAMUEL WAGNER DIBBLE II** (son of William Jasper DIBBLE and Eva COOPER) was born on 22 Feb 1878 in Americus, Sumter, Georgia, USA. He died on 19 Apr 1915 in Atlanta, Fulton, Georgia, USA (Age: 37). He married Gertrude WAYNE (daughter of Daniel Gabriel WAYNE Jr. and Julia Gertrude SMITH) on 16 Aug 1913 in Henderson, North Carolina, USA. She was born on 07 Jan 1882 in 30 Vanderhorst St. City, Charleston, South Carolina, USA. She died on 07 Jul 1920 in Polk, North Carolina.

GREAT-GRANDCHILDREN

6. **CLARENCE AUGUSTUS GRAESER JR. MAJ. (Professor of French and German at the Citadel Military College, Charleston).** (son of Margaret Anna (Maggie) DIBBLE) was born on 26 Aug 1869 in Charleston, Charleston County, South Carolina, United States of America. He died on 03 Feb 1953 in Charleston, Charleston County, South Carolina, United States of America (Age: 83 Magnolia Cemetery, Charleston, SC). He married (1) JEANNE ALICE PIQUET (daughter of Albert and Alice Piquet). She was born in Jun 1874 in Switzerland. She died on 26 Dec 1961 in Columbia, Richland, South Carolina, USA. He married an unknown spouse in 1896.

    Clarence Augustus GRAESER Jr. MAJ. and Jeanne Alice Piquet had the following child:

    i.   **ALBERT CLARENCE GRAESER** (son of Clarence GREASER, Jr. and Jeanne Alice Piquet) was born on 21 Apr 1898 in Darlington County, South Carolina, USA. He died in Dec 1965 in Woodstock, Ulster, New York, USA. He married Emily P. Parks. She was born on 01 Oct 1903 in New York. She died in Nov 1977.

7. **JULIA GERTRUDE SMITH** (Julia Henrietta DIBBLE, ANDREW COMSTOCK[1] DIBBLE 2nd GG) was born on 28 Apr 1854 in Charleston County, South Carolina, USA. She died on 11 Mar 1909 in Buried at Magnolia Cemetery, Charleston, South Carolina. She married Daniel Gabriel WAYNE Jr. (son of Daniel Gabriel WAYNE Sr. and Mary Elizabeth Kingman) in 1875. He was born on 30 Aug 1849 in Charleston County, South Carolina, USA. He died on 23 Sep 1905 in Magnolia Cemetery, Charleston, South Carolina. Daniel Gabriel WAYNE

Jr. and Julia Gertrude SMITH had the following children:

i. **JULIA WALTON WAYNE** (daughter of Daniel Gabriel WAYNE, Jr and Julia Gertrude SMITH) was born on 01 Jan 1877 in Charleston, South Carolina, USA. She married William Gayer Locke. Was born on 05 Sep 1871. He died on 08 Jun 1957 in South Carolina.

ii. **DANIEL GABRIEL WAYNE III** (son of Daniel Gabriel WAYNE Jr. and Julia Gertrude SMITH) was born on01 Feb 1878 in 133 Quinn St Charleston, South Carolina. He died on 18 Feb 1938 in Asheville, Buncombe, North Carolina. He married ELIZABETH "BETTIE" JAMES QUIN.

iii. **MARY LOUISE WAYNE** (daughter of Daniel Gabriel WAYNE Jr. and Julia Gertrude SMITH) was born in 15 Jan 1880 in Charleston, Berkeley County, SC., married Edwin Henry SCHIRMER. Jr. (1875-1948).

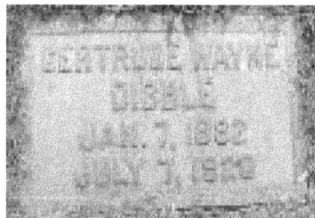

iv. **GERTRUDE WAYNE** (daughter of Daniel Gabriel WAYNE Jr. and Julia Gertrude SMITH) was born on 07 Jan 1882 in 30 Vanderhorst St City, Charleston, South Carolina, USA. She died on 07 Jul 1920 in Polk, North Carolina (Age: 38). She married Samuel Wagner DIBBLE II (son of Wm Jasper) (son of William Jasper DIBBLE (Civil War Confederate) and Eva COOPER) on 16 Aug 1913 in Henderson, North Carolina, USA. He was born on 22 Feb 1878 in Americus, Sumter, Georgia, USA. He died on 19 Apr 1915 in Atlanta, Fulton, Georgia, USA (Age: 37).

v. **WILLIAM WALTON WAYNE III** (son of Daniel Gabriel WAYNE Jr. and Julia Gertrude SMITH) was born on 11 Aug 1883 in Charleston, Berkeley, South Carolina, USA. He died on 20 Sep 1953 in Charleston, Berkeley, South Carolina, USA. He married Eleanor "Ellie" GREGG (1887-1952). She was born in Florence, South Carolina.

vi. **GEORGE FREDERICK WAYNE** (son of Daniel Gabriel WAYNE Jr. and Julia Gertrude SMITH) was born on 18 Sep 1885 in 32 Rubidge St. He died on 26 Feb 1957 in Richland, South Carolina, USA.

vii. **ROSA WAYNE** (daughter of Daniel Gabriel WAYNE Jr. and Julia Gertrude SMITH) was born in 1890 in Charleston, Berkeley, South Carolina, USA.

viii. **EMILY WAYNE** (daughter of Daniel Gabriel WAYNE Jr. and Julia Gertrude SMITH) was born 6 Oct 1889. In Charleston, Berkeley, South Carolia. She died 28 July 1966, Florence, South Carolina.

8. **SARAH "SALLIE" LOUISE GRONIN SMITH** (daughter of Julia Henrietta DIBBLE) was born on 01 August 1856, in Charleston, South Carolina, USA. She died on 27 Jun 1937. She married Robert Motte SMITH (son of Robert Shand Smith and Susan Mary Muncreeff Dart) in 1877. He was born on 16 May 1849 in Greenville, South Carolina, USA. He died on 02 Mar 1923 in Washington, Witts County, Georgia, USA.

Robert Motte SMITH and Sarah "Sallie" Louise Gronin SMITH had the following children:

i. **ANNA SMITH** (daughter of Robert Motte SMITH and Sarah "Sallie" Louise Gronin SMITH) was born in 1877.

ii. **ROBERT SHAND SMITH** (son of Robert Motte SMITH and Sarah "Sallie" Louise Gronin SMITH) was born about 1878 in Wilks County, Georgia, USA. He died on 15 Feb 1948 in Wilks County, Georgia, USA. He married ADONA S SMITH. She was born about 1878 in Alabama.

iii. **JULIA HENRIETTA SMITH** (daughter of Robert Motte SMITH and Sarah "Sallie" Louise Gronin SMITH) was born in 1879. She died in 1880.

iv. **SUSAN MARY SMITH** (daughter of Robert Motte SMITH and Sarah "Sallie" Louise Gronin SMITH) was born in Mar 1881 in Georgia. She died in 1967.

v. **WILLIAM "WILLIE" SMITH** (son of Robert Motte SMITH and Sarah "Sallie" Louise Gronin SMITH) was born in 1883. He died in 1883.

vi. **JULIA GERTRUDE SMITH** (daughter of Robert Motte SMITH and Sarah "Sallie" Louise Gronin SMITH) was born in 1885.

vii. **LAWSON MOTTE SMITH** (son of Robert Motte SMITH and Sarah "Sallie" Louise Gronin SMITH) was born in 1886. He died in 1887.

viii. **CHARLES IRVIN SMITH** (son of Robert Motte SMITH and Sarah "Sallie" Louise Gronin SMITH), born in Jan 1888 in GA. He died in 1951.

ix. **SARAH "SALLIE" LOUISE SMITH** (daughter of Robert Motte SMITH and Sarah "Sallie" Louise Gronin SMITH) born in 1891 and died in 1936.

x. **MARION VANCE SMITH** (son of Robert Motte SMITH and Sarah "Sallie" Louise Gronin SMITH) was born in 14 Jan 1892. He died in 2 Sep 1943, Wilkes, Georgia. He married Frances Ida Wolfe.

xi. **JULIETTE LEITHE "LILLIAN" SMITH** (daughter of Robert Motte SMITH and Sarah "Sallie" Louise Gronin SMITH), born in 1894 in GA.

xii. **ROBERT MOTTE SMITH JR.** (son of Robert Motte SMITH and Sarah "Sallie" Louise Gronin SMITH), born in Jan 1896 in GA. He died in 1949.

xiii. **WILIAM WALTON SMITH** (son of Robert Motte SMITH and Sarah "Sallie" Louise Gronin SMITH), born in 1898 in Georgia. He died in 1953.

9. **SHAND SMITH** (son Julia Henrietta DIBBLE,) was born on 04 Sep 1858 in Charleston County, South Carolina, USA. He died on 29 Jan 1955. He married Gay Edna "Gay" Trout Smith on 19 Apr 1892 in Salt Lake City, Utah, USA. She was born in Jul 1874 in Missouri. She died on 03 Dec 1962 in Alameda, Alameda, California, USA.

Shand SMITH and Gay Edna "Gay" Trout Smith had the following children:

i. **WILLARD WALTON SMITH** (son of Shand SMITH and Gay Edna "Gay" Trout Smith) was born on 27 Jul 1893 in Salt Lake City. He married Effie Jensen on 11 Aug 1923 in Salt Lake City, Salt Lake, Utah. She was born on 26 Dec 1899 in Salt Lake City.

ii. **NEIL F. SMITH** (son of Shand SMITH and Gay Edna "Gay" Trout Smith) was born on 07 Jun 1899 in Salt Lake City, Utah.

10. **MARY "MAMIE" ELIZABETH PATTON SMITH** (daughter of Julia Henrietta DIBBLE) was born on 24 Oct 1863 in Charleston County, South Carolina, USA. She died on 12 Feb 1937 in Columbia, Richland, South Carolina, United States (Buried at Sunnyside Cemetery, Orangeburg, SC at age 73). She married Edward Courtenay DIBBLE (son of Philander Virgil DIBBLE (Hat Store Charleston) and Frances Ann EVANS) on 08 Apr 1884 in Charleston, South Carolina. He was born on 22 Jul 1855 in Charleston, South Carolina, USA. He died on 13 Mar 1899 in South Carolina (Buried in Sunnyside Cemetery, Orangeburg, SC).

Edward Courtenay DIBBLE and Mary "Mamie" Elizabeth Patton SMITH had the following children:

i. **COURTENAY DIBBLE** (son of Edward Courtenay and DIBBLE and Mary "Mamie" Elizabeth Patton SMITH) was born on 06 Nov 1887 in Orangeburg County, South Carolina, USA. He died on 13 May 1888 in Orangeburg, South Carolina, United States.

ii. **JULIA GERTRUDE DIBBLE** (daughter of Edward Courtenay DIBBLE and Mary "Mamie" Elizabeth Patton SMITH) was born on 30 Nov 1888 in Orangeburg, Orangeburg, South Carolina, United States. She died on 04 Feb 1956 in Columbia Ward 1, Richland, South Carolina.

iii. **WILLIAM VIRGIL DIBBLE** (Methodist Minister) (son of Edward Courtenay DIBBLE and Mary "Mamie" Elizabeth Patton SMITH) was born on 25 May 1890 in Orangeburg city (north part), Orangeburg, South Carolina. He died on 10 Apr 1970 in Chatham, Georgia. He married AUGUSTUS "GUSSIE" MUCKENFUSS (daughter of Charles Henry Muckenfuss and Augusta E. Hicklin). She was born on 30 Jul 1887 in Charleston Berkeley, South Carolina, USA. She died on 14 Jan 1976.

iv. **FRANCES DIBBLE** (daughter of Edward Courtenay DIBBLE and Mary "Mamie" Elizabeth Patton SMITH) was born on 11 Nov 1891 in Orangeburg, Orangeburg, South Carolina, United States. She died on 22 May 1892 in Orangeburg, Orangeburg County, South Carolina, USA.

v. **MARY COURTENAY DIBBLE** (daughter of Edward Courtenay DIBBLE and Mary "Mamie" Elizabeth Patton SMITH) was born on 01 Jul 1893 in Orangeburg, Orangeburg County, South Carolina, USA. She died on 10 Nov 1998 in Orangeburg, Orangeburg County, South Carolina, USA.

vi. **BESSIE DIBBLE** (daughter of Edward Courtenay DIBBLE and Mary "Mamie" Elizabeth Patton SMITH) was born on 09 May 1896 in

Orangeburg, Orangeburg County, South Carolina, USA. She died on 22 May 1896 in Orangeburg, Orangeburg County, South Carolina, USA.

11. **FRANCIS "FRANK" MARION³ SMITH SR.** (son of Julia Henrietta DIBBLE) was born on 20 Nov 1871 in Charleston Berkeley, Carolina, USA. He died on 21 Mar 1946 in Charleston, Berkeley, South Carolina, USA. He married (2) MARIA "RIA" STEWART HARVEY (2ND WIFE) (daughter of Wilson Godfrey HARVEY and Cornelia Julia ELBRIDGE). She was born on 12 Nov 1877 in Charleston Berkeley, Carolina, USA. She died on 06 Aug 1948 in Charleston, South Carolina. He married (1) MAY LOUISE MUCKENFUSS (1ST WIFE), in 1897, (daughter of Allen Wesley MUCKENFUSS and Emily Laura WHEELER) in 1897. She was born on 11 Jun 1877 in Charleston, Berkeley County, South Carolina. She died on 02 May 1906 in Charleston, Berkeley, South Carolina, USA.

Francis "Frank" Marion SMITH SR. and May Louise MUCKENFUSS (1st wife) had the following:

i. **FRANCIS "Frank" MARION SMITH, JR.** (1897-1965), who married Irene M. Smith (1897).

Francis "Frank" Marion SMITH SR. and Maria "Ria" Stewart HARVEY (2nd wife) had the following children

ii. **WILSON HARVEY SMITH** (son of Francis "Frank" Marion SMITH SR. and Maria "Ria" Stewart HARVEY (2nd wife)) was born on 24 Jan 1909 in Charleston, Berkeley County, SC. He died 12 Jan 1991, in Charleston.

iii. **WILLIAM WALTON SMITH** (son of Francis "Frank" Marion SMITH SR. and Maria "Ria" Stewart HARVEY (2nd wife)) was born on 03 Mar 1911 in Charleston Berkeley, Carolina, USA. He died on 08 Aug 1994 in Charleston, Charleston, South Carolina, United States of America (Age: 83).

iv. **FRANCIS "FRANK" MARION SMITH JR.** (son of Francis "Frank" Marion SMITH SR. and May Louise MUCKENFUSS (1st wife)) was born on 12 Oct 1897 in Charleston, Berkeley County, South Carolina. He died in

1965. He married IRENE M SMITH. She was born about 1897 in South Carolina.

12. ROSA FRANCES DIBBLE (daughter of William Jasper Dibble (Civil War Confederate) was born on 24 Sep 1874 in Americus, Sumter, Georgia, USA. She died on 07 May 1948 in Fulton County, Georgia, USA. She married Walter Hunt GRANT (son of William GRANT and Mattie) on 25 Jul 1906 in Fulton, Georgia, USA. He was born in 1870 in Atlanta, Fulton, Georgia, USA. He died on 30 Jan 1942 in Atlanta City, Fulton, Georgia.

Walter Hunt GRANT and Rosa Frances DIBBLE had the following children:

ii.   **LOUISE GRANT** (daughter of Walter Hunt GRANT and Rosa Frances DIBBLE) was born on 15 Sep 1913 in Florida, USA. She died on 26 Apr 1933 in Randolph, Georgia. She married FRANK HEAD DAVENPORT (son of Frank Beall Davenport and Emogene Davenport). He was born on 16 Aug 1908. He died on 08 Dec 1963 in Georgia.

iii.   .**BABY GRANT** (daughter of Walter Hunt GRANT and Rosa Frances DIBBLE) was born in 1915.

13. **MARY LOUISA DIBBLE** (daughter of William Jasper) was born on 24 May 1876 in Americus, Sumter, Georgia, USA. She died on 05 Jun 1936 in Atlanta, Fulton, Georgia, USA. She married Henry Madison PEARSON on 07 Apr 1909 in Fulton, Georgia, USA. He was born on 16 Feb 1860 in Atlanta, Fulton, Georgia, USA. He died on 04 Jul 1942.

Henry Madison PEARSON and Mary Louisa DIBBLE had the following children:

    i.   **CLAUDIA PEARSON** (daughter of Henry Madison PEARSON and Mary Louisa DIBBLE) was born about 1902 in Georgia.

    ii.   **WILLIE PEARSON** (son of Henry Madison PEARSON and Mary Louisa DIBBLE) was born about 1906 in Georgia.

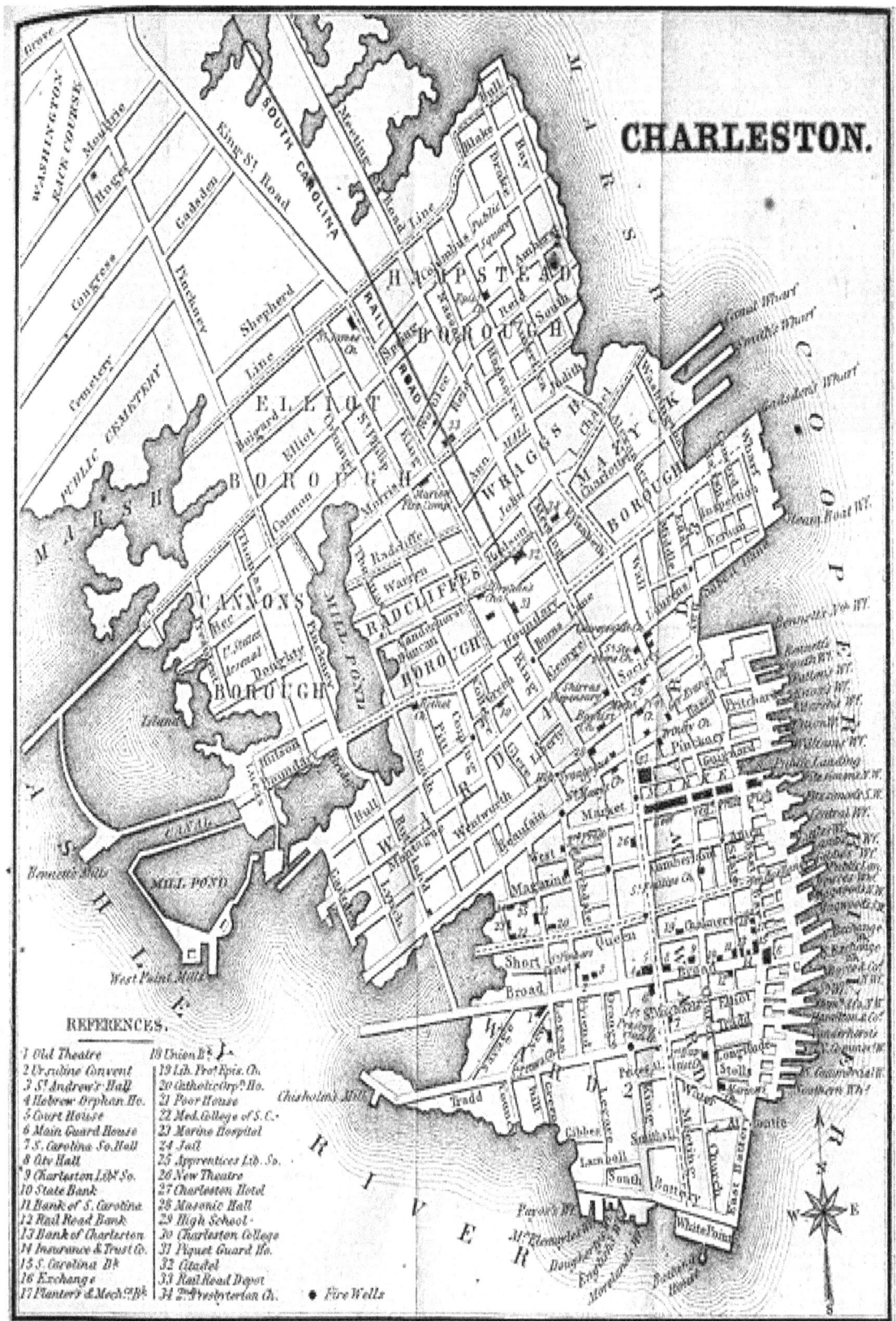

Broad Street: A.C Dibble Hat Shop and where Martha Smith Lived.

ANDREW COMSTOCK DIBBLE AND MARTHA "MINDA" SMITH

To connect Andrew Comstock Dibble with Martha/Minda Smith, I will look at where they both lived during these early days of the 1820s. The Charleston, *Free Negro Capitation Tax List* is an important document because it gives the residence of all free people of color, who lived in the city for a specific year. It appears that during Martha's early years she used the name of "*Minda Cleveland.*" In "*Andrew Henry Dibble Freedom Papers*" of 24 August 1860, it states: "*Mindah, known as Martha Smith….*" Martha is registered under "*The Free Negro Capitation Tax List,*" for Charleston, from 1821 through 1823 and 1826-1827 (the 1824 and 1825 lists are missing), as living at the home of Mrs. Catherine Ravenel, the widow of Daniel Ravenel, at 64 Broad Street. This Daniel James Ravenel (1762-1807), Secretary of State, is the same person who signed the document of 1807, stating that Catherine Cleveland arrived in South Carolina, in 1764, as a free person.

Catherine Clevland is Andrew H. Dibble's Great-Grandmother, who arrived in South Carolina along with her aunt Elizabeth Clevland, who later married a British medical doctor, William Hardcastle, will be discussed in more detail in the section on Andrew Heny Dibble.

The Ravenel home on Broad Street is a short distance from Andrew Comstock Dibble's hat shop on Broad. The Ravenels were among Charleston's wealthy and elite families, who had numerous servants, therefore Martha living there was not one of servitude but probably because of the long-standing relationships between Martha's grandmother, Catherine Cleveland, and great-aunt, Elizabeth Clevland Hardcastle (1741-1898) and the affluent Ravenel Family, which expanded several generations.

This Mrs. Catherine Ravenel (1769-1849), *"remembers her mother speaking of seeing Elizabeth Clevland (1741-1808), at Keithfield Plantation, which was the home of her Uncle William Keith."* as seen in the book*, Elizabeth Clevland Hardcastle, 1741-1808: A Lady of Color in the South Carolina Low Country.* It appears Elizabeth Clevland, as a youngster, stayed at Keithfield Plantation, while on a visit to South Carolina, some years before. Catherine Ravenel knew Elizabeth Clevland Hardcastle, who was Martha's Great-aunt, and both Elizabeth Clevland Hardcastle and Catherine Ravenel owned plantations in Saint John Parish, adjacent to each other, in the late 1700s.

A. C. Dibble Locations & Martha/Minda at the Ravenel Home on Broad Street.

49

The Ravenel Home, like other very large brick homes of this period usually had separate buildings in the rear where some of the servants and others lived. Oftentimes the plantation kitchen was a separate building, as well as the stables and carriage house. Martha's son, Andrew Henry Dibble (1825-1873), was evidently born while Martha was living at this location. We do not know what Martha's role was while living here, but evidently, she was a welcome part of this household.

Mrs. Daniel (Catherine) Ravenel Home
68 Broad Street, Charleston

The Ravenel Home Out-Houses

Martha moved from the Ravenel's Broad Street residence about the same time as Andrew Comstock's marriage to Henrietta Wagner in 1828. Possibly, she felt the need to move to a location which would put some distance between her and Andrew Comstock. According to the "Capitations Tax List," by 1832, Martha is living at the corner of Bull and Smith Streets, where she continues to live and pay her taxes through 1846. In 1843, we see Andrew Henry Dibble, Martha's son, also living at this address and paying his capitation tax, having reached the age of maturity, at age 18 years. At this address, Martha is last seen paying her capitation tax. *The 1840-41 Charleston City Directory*, Martha gives her address as "18 Bull Street," which is the same location she has been living for fourteen years, and presumably her son, Andrew has been living here as well.

This address was the home of William Blacklock (1733-1816), a native of Scotland, who was a wealthy merchant in the import-export business. He purchased Lots 16 and 18 on Bull Street in 1794, and built this large brick two-story home about 1800, which had a large brick basement. It was considered one of the largest residences in the city with Gothic windows overlooking a rear garden and two out-buildings. It is quite possible that William Blacklock probably knew Elizabeth Clevland Hardcastle, Martha's Great-aunt, since he was a native of Scotland as was Elizabeth's early Clevland ancestors.

The 1840 U.S. Census states that Martha is a free female of color, between 36 and 54, with two females under 10 years and one female between 10 and 23 years. The female between 10 and 23 is Andrew Henry Dibble's sister Catherine B. Smith (1828-1895) who married Richard Springs (1819-1871), a Charleston merchant. (The two females under ten years, must have died early, since I have not been able to locate them.) Catherine Smith Springs tells us in her Last Will and Testament, that Andrew is her brother. Also in this household are four enslaved persons: male 24-35, female, 24-35, with a boy and girl both under 10 years. I must assume that Martha was sharing this living arrangement with this other family who were part of the Blacklock's establishment, since she was living here. This is where Martha lived and probably Andrew, as well, for many years, most probably in one of the out-buildings, since it is unclear as to what

Martha's role was in relation to the Blacklock family. She might possibly have been considered a companion to the lady of the house or to one of the female daughters, or even a seamstress, this we will probably never know, just as we do not know Martha's role when she lived with the Ravenel family, those years before. We do know she was not a servant, because both families had numerous servants. However, I find this most fascinating and remarkable, to know that I have been able to document where my Great-great-grandmother, Martha Smith lived most of her adult life, in downtown Charleston. To be able to know this is unbelievable, since these two large, brick, and historic homes were not her homes, but where she lived, and possibly worked, with these two well-known families whose history and homes have been preserved for more than two hundred years. I find this most incredible, and extraordinary, to be able to document this.

The William Blacklock Home
18 Bull Street
Charleston, South Carolina

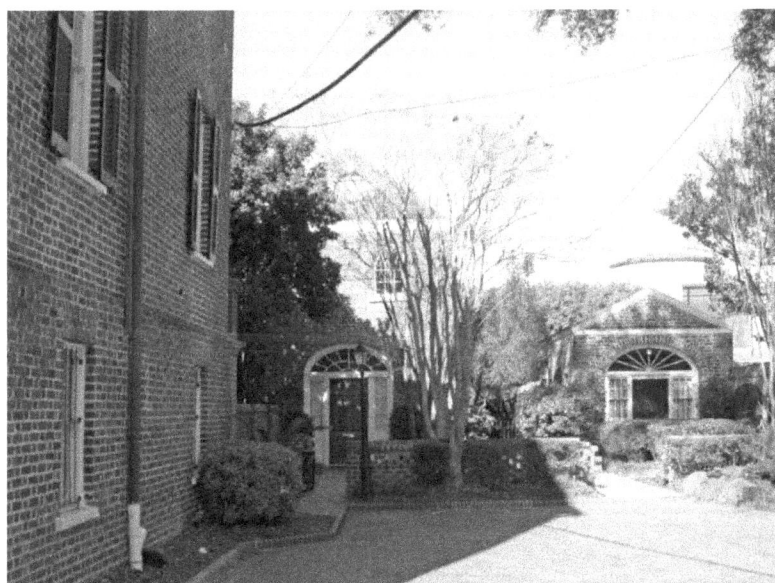

William Blacklock Home Out-Houses
18 Bull Street
Charleston, South Carolina

WILL OF ANDREW COMSTOCK DIBBLE

WILL OF

ANDREW C. DIBBLE

Box 36 } STATE OF SOUTH CAROLINA. In the name of God, Amen.
o
N. 7 } I Andrew C. Dibble of the City of Charleston and
State aforesaid being weak of body but of sound and disposing
mind memory and understanding blefsed be God for the same,
do make and declare this my last will and Testament in manner
and form following that is to say. First. It is my will and
desire that all my real and personal Estate together with all
my stock in Trade and all my household and kitchen furniture
should be sold at the discretion of my Executrix and my Executors hereafter to be named, and also that all my outstanding
accounts be collected and that the nett proceeds after the
payment of my legal and just debts be invested with the amount
received from the sale of my real and personal Estate. Secondly.
It is my will and desire that the above property be disposed
of as follows for the sole use and benefit of my beloved wife
Henrietta M. Dibble and the support and maintenance of my four
children under the immediate direction and attention of my
Executors. LASTLY. It is my will and desire that this Instru-
ment of writing which I hereby declare to be my last will
and Testament may be executed by my beloved wife Henrietta M.

<u>WILL OF ANDREW C. DIBBLE PAGE 2</u>

1

Dibble and my two friends Sam. J. Wagner and Edward Sebring whom I hereby nominate constitute and appoint for that purpose hereby revoking and making void all former wills and Testaments at any time heretofore by me made In Witness whereof I have hereunto subscribed my name and affixed my seal this twenty seventh day of February in the year of our Lord one thousand Eight hundred and thirty nine.

A.C.Dibble (Seal)

Signed sealed declared and published by the within named Andrew C. Dibble as and for his last will and Testament in the presence of us who at his request and in his presence have subscribed our names as witnesses thereto.

E.W Edgerton (LS)   A.C.Goodsell (LS) Richard Smith (LS)

Proved before Thomas Lehre Esq. O.C.T.D. 28th September 1846. At the same time qualified Samuel J. Wagner and Edward Sebring Executors.   Mrs. Dibble's renunciation as Executrix annexed to the Original Will.

Recorded in Will Book K 1845-51 Page 55

ANDREW COMSTOCK DIBBLE ESTATE PAPERS AND INVENTORY

Box 66, No. 7
(Pages 235 & 236)

Inventory and Appraisements of the goods and chattels of the Estate of A. C. Dibble. Shown to us by the Executors…...September 1846

Dep'd   *9*
Oct 1846.

South Chamber:

> One wardrobe, $25
> Two Drawers, $15
> Two Bason Stands, $5
> One child's crib, $1.50|
> Fender and Firedogs, $3
> Lot of Matting, .50 cents
> Nurse's chair, .50 cents

East Front Room:

> One Bedstead, $2
> Two mattresses, $2
> One Book case. $6 One set of Drawers, $4
> One Pine Press, $2
> I Fender for Fire dogs, $2

West Front Room:

> One Bedstead, One mattress, $2
> One dozen chairs, $1

Front Parlour:

> One sofa, $15
> Lot of milling on floor, $2
> One Center Table, $8
> Two Card Tables, $6
> Poker Shovel Tongs & Stand & Grate, $8
> 1 Dozen mahogany Chairs, $18
> 1 Rocking Chair, $10
> Two Ottomans, $2
> Four flower vases, $8
> One Lamp, $8
> 7 Prints, $2

Back Parlour:

One Side broad, $8

One Lamp, $1.50

One Sofa, $3

One dozen chairs, $4

4 Candlesticks, Snuffers and Tray, $1

1 Set of Dinning Tables, $10

One Center Table, $5

Milling on Floor, .50 cents

One Rocking Chair, $1

One Pair Foot Stools, .50 cents

One Large Brussels Carpet, $15

Two Kidderminster do $10

One State? Carpet, $4

One Looking Glass, $5 &

3 Window Blinds, $3

1 Grate & Fire Utensils, $10

Lot Glassware, Cake Basket, Cordial Stand…Water Pitchers on Side Board &
contents of live closets, $20

1 Ice House, $1

1 Lamp hanging, $2

Kitchen Utensils, Pots, Crockery & …, $3 ….

Silver Spoons by Weight, 22 ½ Oz @ $1, $22.50.

Servants:

Rosannah & Her Five Children: William, 16 yrs., Washington, 15 yrs.,
George, 11 yrs., Joseph, 10 yrs., Rose, 6 yrs., $350 = $2100…..

Clarissa and two Children, Edward, 5 yrs., Celia, 2 yrs., -- $700…

Dick and Sarah his wife, $325 = $650.

Contents of Store: 37 Broad Street:

5 -- BB Coney Hats, $3.75

5 -- Muskrat, $6.25….

11 -- Russed, $11.33….$28.87 ½

25 -- Old Stock, $18.75

19 -- $14.25

46 -- R & SC Pearl, $40.25

12 -- Fine Nutria, $42 …12 .. $42

9 -- $31.50

3 -- Angola, $6

1 --   Fine Drab Bea, $5

12 -- Fine Nutred, $42 12 -- $42, 12 .. 12..$42

9 -- $27

10 -- Common .. $750

12--   Fine Silk, $36, .. 12 .. $36, 11 .. $33.13 .. $15.25, 14 .. $28

12 -- Drab Bea, $42, 4 .. $14,

6 -- Plain & Russia, $12

11 -- Silk, $24.25

8 -- $18…

12 -- B B Drab Russia, $16.50

15 -- $28.12 ½

10 -- $28.75

7 -- Black Nutria, $9.62 ½

9 -- Black Caps, $10.12 ½

11 -- Pearl, $13.75

9 -- $6.75

12 -- $9

8 -- M B, $6

9 -- Black Russia, $11.25 12 -- $10.50

12 -- M B, $9

12 -- $10.50

12 -- $9

3 --.2.62 ½

12 -- Caps, $16.50

8 -- $76

10 -- Fash Blk Caps Hats, $6.25

12 -- M B Nutria, $16.50

11 -- Silk, $16.50

16 -- Fash, $16

Be -- Nutria $11.37 ½

38 --- Silk, $46.50

38 --- Angola, $13.25

30 -- Boys. $15

2 7/12 #3 Glazed Caps, $5.81 ¼

2 ½ - TM, $10

2----- Silk, $15

1-11/12 -- Com Cap Covers, $4.31

1/4 2 7/12 -----M, $9.03

1–11/12 ---- Silk, $11.50

8 ½---- Cloth Caps, $68

3 ½---------- elvet, $9.25

7 5/12   Cloth, $44.50

7-8/12 -- $57.50

1-9/12-- $14.75

6-11/12 -- $70

2-5/12 -- $10

87 ½ .. 11/12 -- $4.81 ¼

10/12   Sea Fishing, $10

30 Boys R C Hats, $18.75

15 Leghorn $11.25

8   Men's $6

5   Men's Panama, $15

1-8/12 Men's P H --- $3.28

4   Fine Otter Caps --- $26

2   Seal -- $5

8   Caps -- $5.25

Fine Castor, --- $46

50 – 7/12 R C Wool Hats----- $3.15

1 Glass Case, ---- $3

18- 3/12 doz. Band boxes, -- $17.37 ½

70 Boxes for Hats, ---- $52.50

25 Empty boxes, 9.37 ½

Counter Table & 2 Glasses, ----- $20

Looking Glass, ----- $3

Camphane Lamps, ---- $6

Contents of Draw No.3, ---- $7

1 Mahogany Desk, -- $2.21

Band Blocks, --- $5.25

Work Bench & Tools, -- $15

Oil Cans, --50 cents

1 Gun, - $10

3 Saws -- $2

4 Military Hats, -- $3

9 Hats, -- $3.37 ½

Paper, $3.25

15 Old Hats, --- $2

Lot of Caps, . -- 50 cents

3 doz. Of Hats, --- $54

8-9/12 Wool Hats, -- $30.61

10-4/12 Hats, --- $21.44

11-2/12 Hair Seal Caps, ---$27.90

19   Hair Seal hats, -- $2.37 ½

Cold Shuttle and Pipes, --- $3

6   Glased Hats, -- .50 cents

9   Sealette Caps, -- .56 ¼ cents

32   Boys Angola, --- $16

5   Doz. Russia's, -- $55

112   Band Boxes, -- $11.20

Orna Mental Sign, -- $5

Glass Cases, -- $50

E. M. Carey, John G. Milnor, P. V. Dibble

REAL PROPERTY OWNED IN CHARLESTON, SC

Andrew Comstock Dibble purchased several pieces of property in Charleston City and Charleston County, South Carolina during the twenty-five years he lived there, from December 1821 to the time of his death on 22 September1846. Properties are:

(1) 15 Oct 1835: three (3) story brick building, with "out-buildings," located on south side of Broad Street. (22 Aug 1836: Grantor Mordechai Cohen, Book P10, pg. 256) in downtown Charleston on Broad Street where he operated his Hat Store.

(2) Property (30 May 1837: Grantor, J. D. Yates, Book Q10, pg. 470) located on Elliott Street.

(3) Property (22 March 1838: Grantor Edward B. Lining, Book T10, pg. 400) in Saint Andrews Parish, Charleston County. This was a large plantation consisting of 198 acres. *Old Saint Andrew's Parish* was a rural section of Charleston County, which was located a short distance across the Ashley River, from downtown Charleston. Andrew C. Dibble purchased the 198-acre plantation from Edward B. Lining on March 22, 1838. Edward B. Lining had purchased this plantation from Benjamin Stiles in 1822. It was situated on the *Wappoo Creek* which winds between the Stone River and the West Ashley River. Many of the wealthy planters of Charleston also owned rice and indigo plantations in Old Saint Andrews Parish. Andrew C. Dibble is seen maintaining a plantation in Saint Andrew's Parish in the 1840 United States Census.

(4) Residence on Burnes Street, purchased in 1840.

PART III

Andrew Henry Dibble, Sr., and Ellie Naomi Naudin

Generations come and go but it makes no difference.
The sun rises and sets and hurries around to rise again
The wind blows south and north,
here and there, twisting back and forth, getting nowhere.
The rivers run into the sea but the sea is never full,
and the water returns again to the rivers, and flows again to the sea...
History merely repeats itself.
Nothing is truly new; it has all been done or said before.
What can you point to that is new?
How do you know it didn't exist long ago?
We don't remember what happened in those former times,
And in the future generations no one will remember
What we have done back here.

Ecclesiastes

ANDREW COMSTOCK DIBBLE and MARTHA SMITH are the parents of:
ANDREW HENRY DIBBLE (1825-1873), married
ELLIE NAOMI NAUDIN (1828-1920), of Camden, SC

ANDREW HENRY DIBBLE (1825-1873) *(Andrew C., Samuel, Samuel, John, Wakefield, Ebenezer, Thomas, Robert)* was born on 1 January 1825 in Charleston, South Carolina, the son of Andrew Comstock Dibble (1800-1846), and Martha Smith (c.1800-1849), of Charleston. Andrew Henry DIBBLE died on 29 September 1873, in Camden, South Carolina. Andrew Henry's mother, Martha Smith was the daughter of Rebecca Cleveland (1773-1849), and granddaughter of Catherine Cleveland (c.1759-1859), who migrated to the South Carolina British Colony in 1764, as a youngster of about four or five years old, with her Aunt Elizabeth Clevland; Elizabeth later married Dr. William Hardcastle, who was a surgeon with the British Army and a native of England, dying in 1771. Andrew's Great-Grandmother Catherine Cleveland is the Granddaughter of Captain William Clevland, RN (1720-1758), and Great-Granddaughter of Captain William Clevland, RN (1665-1735), of Devonshire, England.

Andrew Henry Dibble's father, Andrew Comstock Dibble was the eldest son of Samuel Dibble, Jr. (1769-1860) of Danbury, Connecticut and his wife, Mary "Polly" Comstock Dibble (1778-1866), of Danbury. Andrew Comstock Dibble was the grandson of Andrew Comstock (1752-1789) and Mercy Starr (1750-1841), the parents of his mother. Andrew Comstock Dibble migrated to Charleston on 10 December 1821, to start his business as a

Hatter, as a 21-year-old. We do know that Andrew and Martha Smith both living in downtown Charleston, had a personal relationship. According to the Family *Bible,* Andrew Henry Dibble was born in Charleston on 1 January 1825. At this time, there was no other Dibble man living in the State of Sout Carolina.

Andrew Henry Dibble grew up in Charleston and was apprenticed as a Tailor, as many of the free persons of color were given a trade where they could make a gainful and profitably living. The 1830 United States Census shows Andrew Comstock Dibble, having a male free person of color, living with him and his wife and two young daughters. Andrew Henry Dibble is seen in 1843 living with his mother Martha, at the Bull Street address, where both are paying their capitation tax which was required of free persons of color, over age 18.

In the early 1840s, Andrew Henry Dibble met Ellie Naomi Naudin, a free person of color and a native of Camden, who had migrated to Charleston to attend a Quaker school for free persons. Ellie was the daughter of Moreau Naudin (c.1801-1856), a Clerk of the Court in Camden and Harriet Conway (1797-1854), a free person of color. Moreau Naudin is the son of John (Jean) Naudin, a native of France, whose "Naturalization Papers" are dated November 9, 1803. Harriet Conway was the daughter of Bonds Conway (c.1763-1843), (also free) a native of Virginia who had migrated to the Camden community some years earlier. Andrew Henry Dibble and Ellie Naomi Naudin were married on 8 May 1845 in Charleston. After the birth of their first child, Martha Louisa Dibble (1846-1923), Andrew and Ellie migrated to Camden, which was Ellie's home. Family lore tells us that they came up the Wateree River from Charleston by boat, settling in Camden where they lived the remainder of their lives.

With the onset of the Civil War during the late 1850s, South Carolina Legislator became fearful of the many free persons of color. There were discussions on enslaving free persons of color that was debated in the South Carolina House of Representatives in December 1859. In the early months of 1860, Charleston's large community of free persons of color became frantic and fearful of being sold in bondage. The white Charlestonians were committed to enforce the laws of 1820 and 1822. Johnson and Roark in *Black Masters* States*:*

> *"A Free Family of Color in the Old South stated: . . .in August . . . Charleston authorities began to go door to door through the free colored community demanding unassailable proof of free status and proceeding to enslave those without it. These free people of color throughout the state were concerned about their survival as free persons. Many left South Carolina to settle in the north and Canada." Johnson and Roark also stated: "Between the August enslavement crisis and the firing on Fort Sumter the following April, hundreds of free people of color left Charleston."*

The country was in great turmoil at this time. President Abraham Lincoln was elected to the Presidency in November 1860 and took office in March 1861. South Carolina's secession from the Union took palace on 20 December 1860, and on 12 April 1861 the Confederate forces around Charleston Harbor fired on the Union forces at Fort Sumter, thus was the beginning of the Civil War. Numerous persons left Charleston to relocate in other places and many of the free people of color left the state to live in places such as Philadelphia and Ohio as several members of the Cardozo Family.

Thus, in August 1860, while Andrew Henry Dibble was living in Camden, he returned to Charleston to secure the necessary papers he needed to verify his being a descendant of a free person, his great-grandmother, Catherine Cleveland (c.1759-1859) who had migrated to the British Colony of South Carolina in 1764, prior to the American Revolution and the establishment of these United States of America. Thus, the family had passed down these important papers that Andrew H. Dibble carried during the turbulent years prior to and during the years of the

Great War between the North and the South. These faded, yellowed folded papers had inscribed on the outside *"Certificate of Freedom of Andrew H. Dibble."* There were three pages to this document. The first page had the South Carolina State Seal and was signed by the Secretary of State, with the date of August 24, 1860. The second page read in part:

> *"The Bearer of this, a native of Africa, was born free on the Island of the Bannanoes, and baptized by the Name of Catherine Cleveland by the Reverend Mr. Hockley, Rector of St. John Parish Berkeley County, was brought to into this State in the year one-Thousand seven hundred and sixty-four, by Elizabeth Clevland now Hardcastle, in the ship Queen of Barrow. Capt. Alexander Taylor, Commander, Col. James Twee...."*

> *Eliz. Hardcastle*
> *Thos Palmer*

This affidavit was signed by Daniel James Ravenel and recorded in the court records on December 9, 1807. (This Daniel James Ravenel, (wife, Katherine) who signed this 1807 document, is the same person whose home Martha was living in Charleston in the early 1820s.) This old document told me that Andrew Henry Dibble was a direct descendant of Catherine Cleveland, who came into the British Colony of South Carolina as a free person, in 1764. It also told that Catherine arrived as a passenger on the ship, *Queen of Bara*, and told of her baptism at the old historic Saint John's "Biggin" Anglican Church, Berkeley County. This important document also gave information on the mother, grandmother, and the great-grandmother of Andrew Henry Dibble. The third page was issued by Governor William A. Gist, of the State of South Carolina, prepared by Francis N. Beckman, a South Carolina State Magistrate, who took a sworn statement from one Charles Kanapaux, on August 24, 1860, which stated: *"Andrew Dibble, a free person of color, age Thirty-Six years, a Tailor, now residing in the town of Camden, in this State, . . ."* Col. Charles Kanapaux also stated that he had known both, Andrew's grandmother, Rebecca and his mother, Martha for years past, *"(and up until the time of her death) the guardian of Martha Smith."* These papers were to document three generations of the ancestors of Andrew Henry Dibble, and enable the author to validate his maternal heritage.

As noted in *Elizabeth Clevland Hardcastle, 1741-1808, A Free Lady of Color in the South Carolina Low County:*

> *"...The Charleston wealthy planters were no longer in control. The working-class white population and the people from the rural communities were now determined to rid the state of all free persons of color. This white working-class resented the position and prosperity of the free persons. By December 1860, at the gathering in Columbia, it was decided, "We the people of the State of South Carolina in Conventions assembled do declare and ordain ... that the union now subsisting between South Carolina and the other States under the name of the 'United States of America' is hereby dissolved. Ordnance of Secession, December 20, 1860.*

> *"Andrew Dibble had no choice but to seek these freedom papers in August 1860. Several factors contributed to the deterioration of conditions in South Carolina. Because of the impending war, South Carolina legislators became fearful of the "free person of color." Andrew, while living in Camden, probably was aware of the discussion on enslaving free persons of color, that was debated in*

*the South Carolina House of Representatives in December1859. During this same session, the legislature contemplated more than twenty new bills that would impose additional limitations and confinements on the free persons of color. One such bill was called "A Bill to provide for the temporary sale of vicious and vagrant free persons of color" This bill stipulated that all free persons would be enslaved if they did not leave the state by March 1, 1860. However, **none** of these bills were passed; they were left pending for the next session. With the outbreak of the war between the states, which occurred in April 1861, the passing of these bills was lost to more important issues related to the war."*

White men of the church or business community usually served as guardians for many of the free persons of color. Therefore, many of these free persons of color depended on these aristocratic and respectable white men of their community to testify or serve as their guardian. Many times, these white men were related to the "free mulatto" or the free persons of color. According to Johnson and Roark in *No Chariot Let Down*:

"Free people of color shared the personalism of the dominant Culture; they understood it and they exploited it. In Charleston the mulatto elite established personal, face-to-face relationships with powerful whites—at work, at church, and in their neighborhoods. Leading white men were often the legal guardians of free person so color, and in some cases, they were men linked by blood. Crowded together on the small peninsula, the white and free colored aristocracies intertwined.

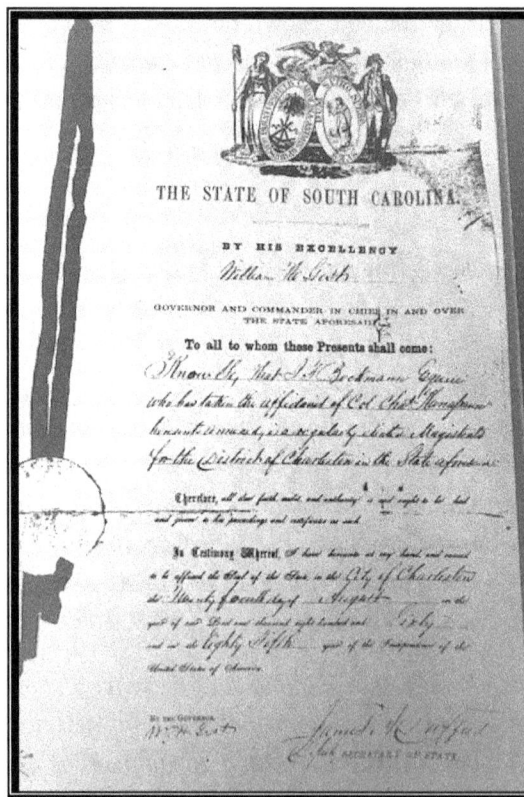

Andrew Henry Dibble Freedom Papers, p.1

Andrew Henry Dibble Freedom Papers, p. 2 Catherine Cleveland's Section, December 1807

Andrew Henry Dibble Freedom Papers, p. 3, August 24,

Family oral history mentioned that Andrew made uniforms for the Confederate military during the Civil War. Andrew Henry Dibble was not only a Tailor, but also a community leader and a businessman who purchased and sold property in the Camden area after the Civil War. In 1867, he was engaged in a contract with a John K. Witherspoon and John D. Johnson, agents of the Southern Relief Association of Philadelphia. These men were investing in Andrew's agricultural business where he grew corn and cotton on his farm. On February 11, 1870, Andrew sold property consisting of ten lots in Camden. These lots bounded on the north by Meetings Street, on the south by Wateree Street, on the east by Littleton Street, and on the west by Market Street, which was one square block.

According to Joan A. Inabinet and L. Glen Inabinet in *A History of Kershaw County, South Carolina:*

> From the 1872 newspapers…. *"The town council passed a resolution on April 15 to divide Camden into four wards. The intendant was Jno. M. Davis, and the wardens were John D. Kennedy, John Kershaw, William Deas, and **Andrew Dibble**."*

According to Lon D. Outen in his book, *Camden Police Department,* he states:

> *"In May 1867, Ammon Reynolds, Don Carlos, **Andrew H. Dibble**, and Frank Carter organized the Camden Union Republican Club and were officers of this club. In 1870, Camden, elected three persons of color for Wardens, which included Henry Cardozo (Republican for the State Senate), E. J. Conway (Reform), **Andrew H. Dibble** (Reform) and Frank Carter (Republican)."*

From this information, it appears that Andrew Henry Dibble was very much involved in the community in which he lived and participated in the political aspects of the community, serving as one of four persons on the "Camden Town Council, in 1872." "Supervisors of Elections" for the county's nine presents indicated representation by both Democrats and Republicans. During this time, the newspapers referred to the Democrats as "Conservative" and the Republicans were referred to as "Radical."

Andrew Henry Dibble. Sr. and his wife the former Ellie Naomi Naudin purchased the family home, lot number 748, on Campbell Street in 1863, where they built their home and lived the remainder of their lives. According to Kershaw County records, this property, "… *front on One Hundred feet West on Campbell Street of said City and extending back – East of uniform width to a depth of Five Hundred Seventy-Three fee (573) more or less.*" They became the parents of twelve (12) children, with ten children living to adulthood and two children (one female and one male) died as infants. Of the twelve children, three daughters married and had families, and three sons married and likewise had families. (A fourth son had a daughter, recently discovered.) Their remaining three sons did not marry and do not have any known descendants.

Andrew and Ellie's seven sons were all involved in the mercantile business starting with their eldest son, John Moreau (1848-1877), who purchased lot number 1043 on the east side of Broad Street on 28 January 1873, he purchased 18 lots on King Street, between Campbell and Church Streets. The Broad Street property stayed in the family until after his mother, Ellie's death in 1920, sixty years later. According to Asa H Gordon, in *Sketches of Negro Life and History in South Carolina*: "…*some of the early Negro business men is that of the Dibble Family of Camden. The family is known all over the state, and its achievements in the mercantile business is of historic importance…*" Between 1900 and 1940, the Dibble family sold 24 lots on Campbell Street. They acquired a vast amount of real estate in Kershaw County and Camden over the years, becoming among the early businessmen in the development of Camden.

Andrew Henry Dibble died on 29 September 1873, while his youngest child, Harriet Catherine, was only an infant. Andrew's Last Will and Testament states: *"... being of sound mind and disposing memory ...Should any of my said children die before the time for the distribution, ... and leave heirs of their body, living at the time of the said distribution, it is my desire and will that such heirs shall take among themselves share and share alike such share or shares of my said property as their parent or parents would receive if living."* His Will, also, give us the name of his wife and the full names of his ten living children (the other two children's names are found in the Family *Bible*). Andrew Henry Dibble died at age 48 years, nine months. His wife, Ellie Naomi Naudin Dibble lived for another forty-seven years, dying at age 92, in 1920. Ellie appeared to be the strong force in this large family, where she was able to guide them and give some direction to her sons in their businesses.

Andrew Henry Dibble, Sr.
1825-1873

Ellie Naomi Naudin
1828-1920

Of the seven children (three daughters and four sons) of Andrew Henry Dibble and Ellie Naomi Naudin, who married and had families, all stayed in South Carolina, except one. The eldest daughter Martha Louisa moved and raised her family in Sumter; the two younger daughters Ella Naudin and Harriet Catherine both settled in Orangeburg. Three sons, Andrew Henry, Jr., Euguene Heriot and Rufus Dennis, all remained in South Carolina with their families. One son, James Laurence ventured to Saint Louis, Missouri, where he lived for several years, and died there. However, his body was brought back to Camden and buried along aside his parents and other brothers, in the Dibble Plot.

This Dibble Store on lower Broad Street, remained in Ellie Naomi Naudin Dibble's possession until her death on May 18, 1920. It was sold as part of her estate in 1923, more than fifty years after the business was started. These early free people of color of Camden, South Carolina lived a rather complex life-style among the dominant community, yet separated from those of the dominant culture and those of the enslaved population.

ANDREW HENRY DIBBLE and ELLIE NAOMI NAUDIN are the parents of:

Martha Louisa DIBBLE (1846-1923)
married Senator Henry J. MAXWELL, Sr. (1837-1906), of Edisto Is.

John Moreau DIBBLE (1848-1877)
died at 29 years old (never married)

Andrew Henry DIBBLE, Jr. (1850-1934)
married Elizabeth LEVY of Camden

William Smith DIBBLE (1852-1930)
(never married)

Eugene Heriot DIBBLE, Sr. (1855-1934)
married Sarah Rebecca LEE of Camden

Wyatt Naudin DIBBLE (1857-1935)
(never married)

James Laurence DIBBLE (1859-1932)
married Maggie

Thomas DIBBLE (5 Oct 1862-9 Mar 1863)
Died about five (5) months old

Ella Naudin DIBBLE (1865-1913)
married Theodore John LEVY, Jr. of Camden

Rufus Dennis DIBBLE (1867-1961)
married Elizabeth Lee GREENLEE of N.C.

Catherine DIBBLE (5 Jul 1871-12 Feb 1872
Died at seven (7) months old

HARRIET CATHERINE DIBBLE (1873-1918)
married Reverend DR. JOHN B. TAYLOR, SR. (1867-1936), of Orangeburg, S.C.

Will of Andrew Henry Dibble, Sr.

The State of South Carolina ⟩
Kershaw County ⟩

In the name of God, Amen!

I, Andrew H. Dibble of the Town of Camden in the State aforesaid, being, by the Grace of God, of Sound mind and disposing memory, do make, ordain, and publish the following to be my last Will and Testament:

Sec. I. To my beloved wife, Elly N. Dibble, for and during the period of her natural life, and no longer, I devise the lot of land upon which I now reside, including the buildings thereon; the same lying and being on the East side of Campbell Street in the said town of Camden and being known and distinguished in the plan of the said town as lot number Seven hundred and forty eight.

Sec. II. From and immediately after the death of my said wife, I devise the said property to my children, viz: — Martha L., John M., Andrew H. Jr., William S., Eugene H., Wyatt N., James L., Ella N., Dennis R., and Harriet C. Dibble; the same to have and to hold unto their own use and behoof, until the youngest of them, my said children, who may be then living shall have attained the age of twenty-one years; and then the same to sell, and distribute the proceeds of such cash among them, my said children, share and share alike.

Sec. III. Should any of my said children die before the time for the distribution, herein before provided for, shall have arrived, and leave heirs of their body, living at the time of the said distribution, it is my desire and will that such heirs shall take among themselves share and share alike such share or shares of my said property as their parent or parents would receive if living.

Sec. IV. I nominate, constitute, and appoint my beloved wife, Elly N. Dibble, Executrix of this my last Will and Testament.

Signed   A. H. Dibble, L.S.

ELLIE NAOMI NAUDIN DIBBLE
1828-1920

Spouse of Andrew Henry Dibble, Sr.

ELLIE NAOMI NAUDIN (1828-1920) (Moreau, John) was born on June 26, 1828, and died on May 18, 1920, in the town of Camden, South Carolina. She was the daughter of Harriet Conway who was born in Camden on July 1, 1797 and died on January 5, 1854 and her father Moreau Naudin, born about 1801 and died March 16, 1856 in the Camden Community. Ellie's father, Moreau was a Clerk of the Court, in Camden. Ellie's grandfather, John Naudin (c.1865-1822), a native of France, came to the Kershaw County area around 1790. He married Louisa Naomi Evans (c. 17?? - c.1814), daughter of Captain Charles EVANS (1745-1807), a Revolutionary War Patriot, who descended from an early Quaker Family who settled in this area of Kershaw County.

Ellie had an older half-sister and half-brother, whose names are Mary Jane E. V. (born on May 23, 1816 and died after the 1880 Census and before 1893), and Ebenezer Conway P. Hodges (March 19, 1819 and died October 18, 1858). Ellie also had three younger brothers, whose names were Wyatt Ebenezer Naudin (1831-1881), James Laurence Naudin (1835-1907) and John Moreau Naudin, who was born April 13, 1837 and died October 8, 1844. The little seven-year-old John Moreau Naudin is buried beside his mother Harriet Conway in Cedar Cemetery in Camden. The *Dibble Family Bible,* gives us these birth and death dates for these earlier generations of the Naudin and Dibble ancestors. This *Bible* has been preserved these many years in the R. Dennis Dibble Family, who is the youngest son of Andrew Henry and Ellie Naudin Dibble.

Ellie was taken to Charleston to attend a school for free people of color, during the early 1840s. Her father, Moreau Naudin took her to Charleston on a stage coach, and as the family lore tells us, *"Because the stagecoach was crowded, and because Ellie was a person of color, the driver asked Ellie to sit up top with him. Her father protested, and stated that "if anyone must give up a seat, he would. Therefore, Moreau and Elle completed their trip in comfort,..."* While attending school in Charleston, Ellie met Andrew Henry Dibble, who she married in 1845. After their marriage and the birth of their eldest child, Martha Louisa Dibble, Ellie and Andrew returned to Camden, where they lived the remainder of their lives.

Ellie, as an industrious and energetic lady who raised this large family, instilled in them strong work-ethics and the importance of education. With her husband's early death in September 1873, and her eldest son's death in 1877, only four years after her husband, she had to be strong and wise to guide these numerous children by herself. She operated the General Merchandise Store on Broad Street, which was left to her in 1877 by her eldest son John Moreau. Ellie, assisted by several of her sons, operated this store until her death in 1920. As stated in the Kershaw County Court records:

> *"Eugene H. Dibble was authorized and directed [by his*
> *mother] to erect certain brick store building upon the said lot*
> *and to use therefor the entire personal estate and the proceeds*
> *of all of the stock of goods and horse of John M. Dibble, being*
> *all of the personal property mentioned in the said Will of John*
> *M. Dibble."*

This business remained in Ellie Naomi Naudin Dibble's possession until her death on May 18, 1920. It was sold as part of her estate in 1923, more than fifty years after the business was started. These early free people of color of Camden, South Carolina lived a rather complex life-style among the dominant community, yet, separate, where they formed a small community within the community, where they could survive. Ellie lived a long life, witnessing the Civil War and World War I, and all the changes this country and South Carolina had brought forth, outliving her eldest son, John Moreau, and her two youngest daughters, Ella Naudin and Harriet Catherine, who both had families. I feel proud and humbled to know that I descend from Ellie Naomi Naudin, my Great-Grandmother, who was strong and wise as she nurtured her children during her 92 years.

Andrew Henry Dibble and Ellie Naudin Dibble
Cedar Cemetery, Camden, S.C.

Andrew Henry Dibble Plot

ANDREW HENRY & ELLIE NAOMI NAUDIN DIBBLE'S
CHILDREN WHO HAVE DESCENDANTS

Martha Louisa Dibble (1846-1923)
Henry Johnson Maxwell, Sr. (1837-1906)
Lawyer, S.C. State Senator

Andrew Henry Dibble, Jr. (1850-1935)
Postmaster
Elizabeth Levy (1856-1933)

Eugene H. Dibble, Sr. (1855-1934)
S. C. State Representative, Merchant
Sarah Rebecca Lee (1862-1955)

James Laurence Dibble
(1859-1932)

Ella Naudin Dibble (1865-1913)
Theadore J. Levy, Jr. (1862-1917)
Barber

Rufus Dennis Dibble (1967-1961)
Merchant
Elizabeth Lee Greenlee (1889-1969)

Harriet Catherine Dibble (1873-1918)
J. B. Taylor, Sr., A.B., A.M., D.D. (1867-
1936) *Methodist Episcopal Minister*

CHILDREN

MARTHA LOUISA DIBBLE (1st child) *(Andrew H., Andrew C., Samuel, Samuel, John, Wakefield, Ebenezer, Thomas, Robert).* Martha was born in Charleston, South Carolina on 5 March 1846, the first child of Andrew and Ellie Naudin Dibble. Martha died on 20 August 1923, in a hospital in Florence, South Carolina. Martha married Senator Henry J. Maxwell at Grace Episcopal Church in Camden, on September 13, 1870. Martha's early education was in Charleston, prior to the Civil War. Martha is seen in the Freedman's Bank Record Number 8051, of 7 June 1871, where she mentions she is married and has no children. Martha taught school during those early years and was working for the Freedman's Bureau in Marlboro County, when she met her husband, who was a South Carolina State Senator, at that time.

Martha Louisa Dibble
(1846-1923)

Senator Henry J. Maxwell
(1837-1906)

Her husband, Henry J. Maxwell (1837-1906), was born on Edisto Island, South Carolina, the son of free people of color, Stephen Johnson, and Thurston Johnson Maxwell. Henry had a law practice in Bennettsville and Sumter, after he received his Certificate to practice Law in South Carolina on 5 March 1872. Henry and Martha raised their family of eight children on a large farm of 42.4 acres on Manning Road, in Sumter County, South Carolina where the younger Maxwell children were born. Martha purchased land, in her name, to build a home in town, on 12 June 1905. This was probably because they were both aging and needed to be in the city. It was a sizeable lot of 163 ft., 6 in, on Council; 172 ft., deep on the northern line; 169 ft., 4 inches, on the southern; 162 ft., 4 inches. on the western line. Although Henry was still living, but probably not well, for he died on 21 August 1906, about a year after they moved in town. She built a large two-story southern style home, at 12 Council Street. Martha lived there until her death in 1923. Neither one of these homes remain standing, today. However, we are very fortunate to have photographs of both homes of Martha, Andrew and Ellie's eldest daughter.

The Maxwell children attended Claflin University for their lower school education, and some attended Claflin for their high school and college education. Their eldest daughter Cassandra received her Normal Certificate in 1889 and taught school in Richmond, Virginia until her early death, in 1893. The daughters Ella and Naomi, also graduates of Claflin, in the classes of 1887 and 1902, respectively, and became teachers, also. Their son Charles Wendell attended Biddle University for his undergraduate work and received his Medical (M.D.) Degree from Howard University, College of Medicine, in 1904. Their son Andrew Dibble Maxwell attended Lincoln University in Pennsylvania for his Bachelor of Science (B.S.) Degree and received his Doctor of Dental Surgery (D.D.S.) Degree from Howard University in 1916. The son John Moreau Maxwell attended Meharry Pharmacy School for a while until he became ill, after which he decided that becoming a merchant was a desired career.

Martha Louisa Dibble and Senator Henry Johnson Maxwell, Sr. are buried in Walker Cemetery in Sumter, South Carolina. Their eldest daughter, Cassandra is also interred there. Martha Louisa Dibble and Senator Henry Johnson Maxwell, Sr., are the parents of eight children:

> Cassandra Jeanette Maxwell (1868-1893),
> > m. …Pope
> Ella Louise Maxwell (1873-1959),
> > m. Rev. James Franklin Page, (1866-1932)
> Henry Johnson Maxwell, Jr. (1876-1954),
> > m. Lilliam Gertrude Pool (1878-1954)
> Charles Wendell Maxwell, MD, (1879-1959),
> > m. Pansy Miller (1885-1976)
> John Moreau Maxwell (1881-1938),
> > m. Katherine Louise Cardozo (1884-1931)
> Naomi Theresa Maxwell (1883-1948),
> > m. George C. Edwards (1882-1952)
> Stephen Lloyd Maxwell, Sr., (1885-1930),
> > m. Ethel May Howard (1890-1959)
> Andrew Dibble Maxwell, Sr., DDS, (1888-1965),
> > m. Florence Parnell (1894-1928)

HONORABLE HENRY JOHNSON MAXWELL, SR.
1837-1906

Attorney
South Carolina State Senator, Union Army Soldier,
United States Postmaster, School Commissioner, Superintendent of Education

Spouse of Martha Louisa Dibble

THE HONORABLE HENRY JOHNSON MAXWELL, SR. (1837-1906) was the fifth of six children born to Stephen J. and Thurston Johnson Maxwell of Charleston. He was born on Edisto Island, South Carolina, on May 3, 1837. Henry died August 21, 1906, in Sumter.

Henry's mother, Thurston Johnson Maxwell (c.1800-post 1880) was the daughter of Harriet Mitchell who was a nurse, and William Johnson who was the son of Hester Johnson (c.1770-), who was the daughter of Soffy (Sophie), who died about 1821, at 91 years of age. Sophie and Hester are documented as Native American women (free) in a 16 February 1824 Charleston document. Hester had five children: William, Susan, Sophie, Benjamin, and Abigail.

Stephen and Thurston Johnson Maxwell had six children: Mary (c.1826), Thurston (c.1827), Stephen J., Jr., (c.1829), Martha (c.1835), Henry J. (c.1837), and Hannah (c.1838). In an 1869 document, Thurston mentions that she is a widow and a nurse, and only mentions four of her children. Therefore, Mary and Martha must be deceased at this time.

Henry and his family moved from Edisto Island to Charleston when Henry was about eight years old. The Maxwell's were free persons of color, and were members of Saint Paul's Episcopal Church, in Charleston. His father had a store, where he sometimes taught grown men to read and write, and his mother taught both white children and children of color on her back porch. Henry's early education included his attending the "Bonneau School" in Charleston, taught by Mr. Seymour. Afterward he attended the "Mood School" on Beaufain Street, in Charleston.

In June 1856, Henry Maxwell left South Carolina, as many other free people of color, during this period, living in New York, Boston and Portland, Maine. He worked in various jobs during this time. By 1857, he settled in Addison, Lenawa County, Michigan. At this time, a convention met to petition the Michigan State Legislature for the right to vote for the State's "people of color" citizens.

Maxwell was appointed to canvass the state for signatures. He visited every county in the state and secured more than 2,000 names on the petition. He then traveled through Indiana, Ohio and a large portion of Canada.

In 1863, when Massachusetts called for colored troops, Henry J. Maxwell volunteered in the Massachusetts Colored Troops, but was later rejected for health reasons. He later assisted in recruiting volunteers for the Fifth and Sixth Pennsylvania Colored Regiments, and went with Major Stearns to Tennessee. He was stationed at Gallatin, Tennessee and assisted in raising the Fourteenth, Fifteenth and Seventeenth Regiments of United States Colored Troops, which were later known as "Morgan's Brigade." He resigned from being a recruiting officer and volunteered for the third time and served as First Sergeant in the Second United States Light Artillery, in Nashville, Tennessee, under Captain J. V. Meggs. He served this Country as a Union Solider until he mustered out as a First Sergeant in 1866. He later served as a Colonel in the South Carolina 6th Regular National Guard.

After leaving the service, Henry J. Maxwell returned to Charleston. Around January 1867, he became Superintendent of Education of the Freedman's Bureau in Chesterfield District. In October 1867, Maxwell was transferred to Bennettsville, (Marlboro County), by the Freedman's Bureau, where he was to organize schools in the Bennettsville area. In 1868, he was elected the first School Commissioner of Marlboro County. He established and taught school in Bennettsville until 1871. He was a great promoter of education for all people, regardless of ethnicity. Also, in March 1871, he was admitted to the bar and began his law practice in the Fourth Congressional District of South Carolina. On March 6, 1872, he was admitted to practice law before the South Carolina Supreme Court.

Senator Maxwell was elected to the South Carolina Senate representing Marlboro County in the Forty-eighth through the Fifty-second General Assemblies (1868-1878). While serving in the Senate, he was a member and Chairman of the Committee on Education (1870-1877); Chair (1874-1877), Chairman of the Committee on Mines and Mining (1869, 1874-1877); Chair, 1876-1877), and Chairman of the Committee on Enrolled Bills (1870-1874); Chair, (1870-1872). Senator Maxwell served on the committees on military (1868-1872 & 1876-1877); public lands (1870-1872); incorporations (1870-1872); printing (1870-1874); claims (1872-1877); the judiciary (1872-1877); and the penitentiary (1872-1877).

On March 16, 1869, Henry J. Maxwell was appointed the first colored Post Master in the United States. He served at Friendship Junior College in Rock Hill. He was also a Colonel in the South Carolina Sixth Regiment

National Guard (1870-1871), and Brigadier General of the First Brigade, First Division of the National Guard (1873-1877).

Maxwell served as Chairman of Marlboro County Republican Party (1870-1874). He was a delegate to the National Republican Convention, in Philadelphia, in 1872, which nominated President Grant and Wilson. He was a devout Christian, and devoted many years to the betterment of his fellow man, and held many positions of distinction during his long career of public service. His impressive career included work as a tradesman, postmaster, lawyer, politician, union soldier and statesman.

In 1877, Maxwell like other "men of color" who held elected positions in the State during Reconstruction came under investigation for alleged corruption, by the Democrats. Many of the men received letters asking that they vacate their positions. Maxwell resigned his Senate position on October 4, 1877. He was charged and arrested, to be later released on bond, October 13, 1877. According to W. Lewis Burke in his book, *At Freedom's Door*, as he quotes Walter Edgar, these Democrats made a *"systematic attempt...to blacken the reputation of those who governed the State from 1968 to 1877."*

Maxwell married Rebecca Sass Cooper, a native of Charleston and daughter of Paris Cooper (1808-1861), of Philadelphia, on October 20, 1868. Henry J. and Rebecca had one son, both wife and son died in 1869. Senator Maxwell, Sr. married Martha Louisa Dibble of Camden, South Carolina on September 13, 1870 at Grace Episcopal Church in Camden. They became the parents of eight children, mentioned above.

There are approximately sixty-seven descendants of Henry J. and Martha Louisa Dibble Maxwell, as of 2018. There are numerous great-grandchildren, and great great-grandchildren. Henry J. Maxwell's last living grandchild, was The Honorable Stephen Lloyd Maxwell, Jr., who retired from the Ramsey County District Court Bench, in Saint Paul, Minnesota, and died on August 31, 2009, at age 88.

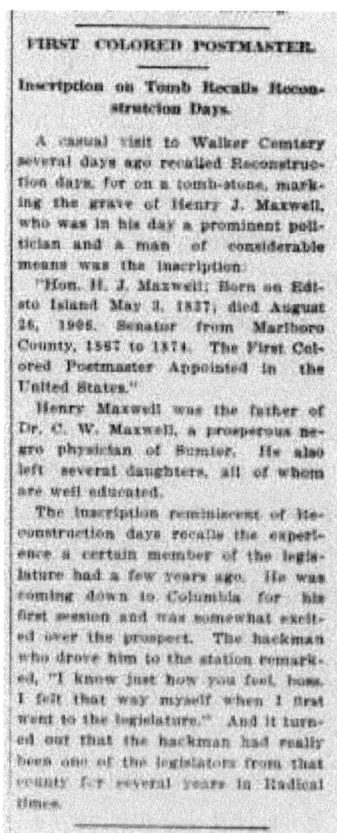

FIRST COLORED POSTMASTER.

Inscription on Tomb Recalls Reconstruction Days.

A casual visit to Walker Cemetery several days ago recalled Reconstruction days, for on a tomb-stone, marking the grave of Henry J. Maxwell, who was in his day a prominent politician and a man of considerable means was the inscription:

"Hon. H. J. Maxwell; Born on Edisto Island May 3, 1837, died August 26, 1906. Senator from Marlboro County, 1867 to 1874. The First Colored Postmaster Appointed in the United States."

Henry Maxwell was the father of Dr. C. W. Maxwell, a prosperous negro physician of Sumter. He also left several daughters, all of whom are well educated.

The inscription reminiscent of Reconstruction days recalls the experience a certain member of the legislature had a few years ago. He was coming down to Columbia for his first session and was somewhat excited over the prospect. The hackman who drove him to the station remarked, "I know just how you feel, boss. I felt that way myself when I first went to the legislature." And it turned out that the hackman had really been one of the legislators from that county for several years in Radical times.

The Southern Watchman Newspaper, 22 June 1910, p. 3

Walker Cemetery, Sumter, South Carolina

MARTHA LOUISA DIBBLE
Wife of
H. J. MAXWELL

Born in Camden, S. C.
MAR 3, 1846
Died in Florence, S.C.
AUG. 20, 1923

A LOVING WIFE' AND
AFFECTIONATE MOTHER
A LIBERAL FRIEND TO THE LESS FORTUNATE

HON. H. J. MAXWELL
Born: EDISTO ISLAND, MAY 3 1837
Died: AUG 21, 1906

A LOVING HUSBAND
A KIND AND AFFECTIONATE FATHER
A CONSISTENT CHRISTIAN

SENATOR OF MARLBORO Co.
1968-1877
FIRST COLORED POSTASTER
APPOINTED IN THE U. S.

WITH A CHERRY SMILE
AND A WA E OF HIS HAND
HE HAS WANDERED INTO AN UNKNOWN LAND

JOHN MOREAU DIBBLE (1848-1877) (*Andrew H., Andrew C., Samuel, Samuel, John, Wakefield, Ebenezer, Thomas, Robert*). John Moreau Dibble was born on 7 March 1848 in Camden, South Carolina, the 1st son and 2nd child of Andrew Henry Dibble and Ellie Naomi Naudin. He evidently was named for his mother, Ellie's father, Moreau and her grandfather, John Naudin. He died on 16 January 1877, at 28 years and 10 months, a very young man, only three years after his father.

John Moreau Dibble purchased Lot Number 1043 on 28 January 1873, on the east side of Broad Street, in downtown Camden, where he owned and operated a general store on what was then called Main Street. In 1888, a store advertisement stated: *"General Merchandise, Heavy and Fancy Groceries, Boots, Shoes, Hats, Etc., Fruit and Confectionery… Polite Attention to all Customers."* After his early death, his mother Ellie ran the store with the help of several of her sons. In 1875, John Moreau was one of the early businessmen of Camden, purchased 18 lots on King Street, between Campbell and Church.

His Last Will and Testament states: *"being of sound mind but of feeble and decaying health…I bequeath to my mother, Ellie Dibble and to my two younger sisters, Ella, and Hattie and my younger brother Rufus all of my rightfully and interest in all my property both real and personal…"* Signed the 15th January 1877. His Will also tell us that he knew he was seriously ill. His will further mentions the property on Broad Street, which states:

> *"Eugene H. Dibble was authorized and directed [by his mother] to erect certain brick store building upon the said lot and to use therefore the entire personal estate and the proceeds of all of the stock of goods and the horse of John M. Dibble being all of the personal property mentioned in said Will of John M. Dibble."*

This business remained in Ellie Naomi Naudin Dibble's possession until her death on May 18, 1920, and sold as part of her estate in 1923, more than fifty years after the business was started. John Moreau Dibble is buried with a sizeable marker, in the Dibble Family Plot in Cedar Cemetery in Camden.

John Moreau Dibble Store (c.1892) Broad St., Camden, S.C.

John Moreau Dibble Marker

Andrew Henry Dibble, JR. (1850-1935)
Postmaster, Bennettsville, S. C.

Elizabeth J. Levy
(1854-1933)

ANDREW HENRY DIBBLE, JR. (1850-1935) (*Andrew H., Andrew C., Samuel, Samuel, John, Wakefield, Ebenezer, Thomas, Robert*). Andrew, Jr., was born on 15 July 1850, in Camden, South Carolina, the 3rd child and 2nd son of Andrew Henry Dibble, (1825-1873) and Ellie Naomi Naudin (1828- 1920). Andrew died 9 August 1935. He married Elizbeth Levy, daughter of Theodore John Levy, Sr., (1820-1862) and Charlotte Johnson (1833-1898), of Camden. Andrew's wife Elizabeth was born 21 July 1853 in Camden and died on 20 March 1834 in Chester, South Carolina. Elizabeth had three siblings: Sarah Levy (1856-1936), who married Reverend Wilson Williams; Prudence Levy (1861-post-1920), who married Henry C. Elliott; and her brother Theodore John, Jr., who married Ella Naudin Dibble, the sister of her husband.

In the 1880 U.S. Census, we see Andrew with his wife and 7-years-0ld daughter Catherine living in Bennettsville. He worked as a carpenter and was appointed a United States Postmaster for Marlboro County on 7 January 1873. He is living in Sumter for the 1900, 1910 and 1920 Censuses, working as a carpenter. According to his granddaughter Catherine Martin Means, Andrew and Elizabeth lived at 6 Oakland Avenue and had his store on Main Street, at the corner of Oakland Avenue, in Sumter. She remembers spending many summers there. The 1930 Census shows he is living with his only daughter and her family in Chester, South Carolina, where his son-in-law, Dr. James D. Martin is President of Brainer Institute, a private Presbyterian school.

Andrew Henry, Jr., married a second wife, Della Bell, shortly after his wife Elizabeth's death in 1934, although his deceased wife objected to such a quick marriage. Andrew, Jr.'s Will is filed in Chester County, Book E, p. 412, dated 18 December 1936, although his death certificate has date of death, 9 August 1935. Andrew had another daughter named Minnie Dibble (1875-1947), daughter of Fannie Quick (1861-1934) of Bennettsville, which has become known to the family, very recently. Minnie Dibble married Columbus Fletcher (1875-), and had two daughters and two sons. Andrew lived only about one year after his first wife's death. Andrew, Jr. and his first wife Elizabeth are buried in the Dibble Family Plot in Cedar Cemetery, in Camden. His wife has a sizeable marker with a very nice epitaph. His marker was added about 1982.

Andrew Henry Dibble, Jr., and Elizabeth J. Levy Dibble are the parents of:
Catherine Cleveland Dibble (1872-1947),
m. James Daniel Martin, Ph.D.

Andew Henry Dibble, Jr. is the father of:

Minnie Dibble (1875-1947),

m. Columbus Morgan Fletcher

Elizabeth Levy Dibble
A devoted wife, a loving mother, a true friend…
Safe in the Arms of Jesus
Safe on His gentle breast.

Andrew Henry Dibble, Jr.,

Cedar Cemetery, Camden, S.C.

WILLIAM SMITH DIBBLE (1852-1930) *(Andrew H. Andrew C., Samuel, Samuel, John, Wakefield, Ebenezer, Thomas, Robert).* William was born in Camden the 4th child of Andrew Henry Dibble and his wife, Ellie Naomi Naudin (1828-1920). He never married and lived with his brother Rufus Dennis, after his mother died in 1920. William helped his brothers with their grocery store businesses. Bubba Will was generously kind and thoughtful, when he remembered the nieces and nephews of his three sisters in his Last Will and Testament, as well as his five brothers. William is buried in the Dibble Plot in Cedar Cemetery in Camden.

Honorable Eugene Heriot Dibble, Sr.
(1854-1934)
S.C. Representative, Kershaw County

Sarah "Sallie" Rebecca Lee
(1862-1955)

EUGENE HERIOT DIBBLE, SR. (1855-1934*) (Andrew H., Andrew C., Samuel, Samuel, John, Wakefield, Ebenezer, Thomas, Robert).* Eugene was born on 12 May 1854 in Camden, the 4th son and 5th child of Andrew Henry Dibble and Ellie Naomi Naudin, Eugene died on 27 December 1934.

Eugene's early education was obtained from Mather Academy in Camden. According to the *Catalogue of the Officers and Students of Howard University, District of Columbia, 1871-1872,* Reed & Woodward, Printers (1872), Eugene is listed as a student in the Preparatory Department, Junior Class, which had 129 students, during the 1871-1872 school year. Eugene attended Bridgewater State College in Bridgewater, Massachusetts in the early 1870s, majoring in business. After his return to Camden on 2 February 1874, he received his Certificate to teach school by the South Carolina Board of Examiners for Kershaw County. During the Reconstruction, Eugene was a South Carolina Representative from Kershaw County in the South Carolina House of Representatives from 1876-1878.

Eugene is seen in an early photograph made at the Albumen Print, Johnson Bros., at 457 & 489 Pennsylvania Avenue, in Washington, D. C., about the 1872, which was probably made while he was attending Howard University in their Preparatory Department. Another early photograph of Eugene was made at Wurst Art Studio, at 180 Sixth Avenue, New York City, about 1889. This photograph was made when he took his younger sister, Harriet to New York to see and eye doctor. His sister Harriet had a professional photograph made at this same time.

Eugene married Sarah Rebecca Lee (1862-1955) on 14 April 1888, in Mecklenburg County, North Carolina. Sarah (Sallie) R. Lee is the daughter of William States Lee (1840-1907), and Dorcas Elizabeth Conway (1837-1894), and was the granddaughter of Peter Conway (1811-1865). The *Camden City Directory, 1913-1914* and *1914-1915,* lists their residence as 652 10th Avenue (Rutledge and Market), in Camden. By 1925, they had built a home at 808 Lafayette Avenue, and lived there until their deaths in 1934 and 1955, respectively. Their youngest daughter, Miss James Laurence Dibble (1902-1976), lived in the home until her death.

The Honorable Eugene Heriot Dibble was a businessman, educator, and South Carolina State Representative, in 1876-1878, representing Kershaw County. He, along with his brother, James Laurence Dibble founded the *"E. H. Dibble & Brother Grocers and Crockery*," according to the *"1900 Camden Business Directory."*

This store was founded on the corner of Broad and DeKalb Street in 1887, in Camden. According to Asa H. Gordon, in *Sketches of Negro Life and History in South Carolina*: *"... some of the early businessmen is that of the Dibble Family of Camden. The family is known all over the state, and its achievement in the mercantile business is of historic importance...."* This structure is still standing, today, with a historic marker that was placed there by Eugene's grandson, Edmund Perry Palmer, II, on April 20, 2002. Eugene was considered one of the early successful businessmen in South Carolina. Eugene and his wife became the parents of six children; three sons and three daughters.

All their children attended Atlanta University for their high school and normal education. His son Eugene, Jr., graduating in 1915 from Howard University Medical School and son Andrew Henry, graduating from Meharry Medical School, in 1924, and son, Harold Leonidas became a businessman. His three daughters, Josephine, Ellie, and James Laurence, all became teachers. Eugene and his wife Sarah "Sallie" are buried in the Eugene Dibble Plot in Cedar Cemetery, in Camden, along with their son, Andrew Henry Dibble, III, MD, and the youngest daughter Miss James Laurence Dibble.

Eugene Heriot Dibble, Sr., and Sarah R. Lee are the parents of six children:

> Josephine Heriot Dibble (1888-1974)
> > m. Harry Sanders Murphy, Sr. (1884-1975)
> Eugene Heriot Dibble, Jr., MD, (1893-1968)
> > m. Helen Anita Taylor (1900-1980)
> Harold Leonidas Dibble (1897-1982)
> > m. Jessie Cornelia Moorer (1897-1972)
> Ellie Naudin Dibble (1898-1973)
> > m. Edmund Perry Palmer, Sr., (1896-1949)
> Andrew Henry Dibble, III, MD (1900-1946)
> > m. Thelma A. West (1908-2007)
> Miss James Laurence Dibble (1902-1976) (never married)

SARAH "SALLIE" REBECCA LEE
1862-1955

Spouse of Eugene Heriot Dibble, Grandson

SARAH REBECCA LEE (1862-1955), was born on 1 August 1862, in Camden, South Carolina, the daughter of Dorcas Elizabeth Conway (1837-1895) and William States Lee (1940-1907). Sarah died on 21 December 1955, in Camden. Sarah, "Sallie" as she was called, was the granddaughter of Peter Conway and Great-granddaughter of Bonds Conway (1763-1843), of Virginia, and later Camden.

Sarah is seen in the 1870 U. S. Census, while living in Charleston, with her mother, Dorcas and siblings: Amelia Elizabeth Bulkley, age 16, sister, Thaddeus Lee, age 13, brother, Josephine H. Lee, age 6, sister and herself, age 8 years. The 1880 Census, she is back in Camden, teaching school at age 17 years. The 1900 Census, she is seen with her husband, Eugene and the four oldest children, with her niece, Ida J., age 20 years. Ida was the daughter of her sister Amelia. By the 1910 Census, Sallie is seen with all six of her children ranging in ages 21 years to 7 years, with I. J. Lee, listed as adopted daughter, age 30 years, and Mary, age 12, listed as a servant. Eugene is listed as a merchant and they have been married for 23 years. Their six children are listed above. Sallie is buried beside her husband in Cedar Cemetery in the Eugene H. Dibble Plot, in Camden, South Carolina.

Eugene Heriot Dibble (1854-1934)
May 12, 1854 – Dec. 27, 1934

Sallie Rebecca Lee
Aug. 1, 1862—Dec 21, 1955

Eugene H. Dibble Plot
Cedar Cemetery
Camden, S. C.

Wyatt Naudin Dibble
(1857-1935)

WYATT NAUDIN DIBBLE (1857-1935) *(Andrew H., Andrew C., Samuel, Samuel, John, Wakefield, Ebenezer, Thomas, Robert)* was born in Camden, the 6th child and 5th son of Andrew Henry Dibble and Ellie Naomi Naudin. Wyatt died on February 27, 1935, in Camden.

It appears that Wyatt Naudin Dibble became a barber very early, as we see he is barbering in several places, including Georgetown and Lancaster, South Carolina. By 1888, we see him living at 215 Broad Street, in Lynn, Massachusetts, where he lived for several years. In 1895, he is living in Norwalk, Connecticut, working as a barber. Wyatt Naudin Dibble had a first cousin, John Moreau Naudin (1856- 1919), the son of his uncle Wyatt Naudin, who also was born in Camden, who had also migrated to Lynn, Massachusetts about this same time.

Bubba Wyatt had been away from Camden for many years before returning shortly before his mother's death in May 1920. Wyatt never married and is buried alongside his five brothers and his parents, in the Dibble Family Plot, in Cedar Cemetery, in Camden, S.C.

James Laurence Dibble
(1859-1932)

JAMES LAURENCE DIBBLE (1859-1932) *(Andrew H., Andrew C. Samuel, Samuel, John, Wakefield, Ebenezer, Thomas, Robert)* was born in Camden, the 7th child and 6th son of Andrew Henry Dibble and Ellie Naomi Naudin. He died on 5 September 1932 in Saint Louis, Missouri.

On 9 November 1878, James Laurence is seen receiving his certificate to teach school from the South Carolina Board of Examiners for Kershaw County. He and his brother Eugene were in business together for a number of years before he left Camden. He is seen in Topeka, Kansas in 1900 and by the 1910 Census, he is living in St. Louis, Missouri. According to the census records, he worked for the City of St. Louis, as a janitor. He married Maggie, in 1904, in St. Louis, who is deceased by the 1930 United States Census, when he states he is a widower. James Laurence is buried in the Dibble Family Plot in Cedar Cemetery, alongside his five brothers, in Camden.

He left a sizeable estate, including the following:

> *"...bequeath unto my nieces, Ellie N. Thompson and Elizabeth Davis, and my nephew, Eugene Levy, all now residing in the city of Washington, D.C, the sum of One thousand Dollars ($1,000.00), each, ... I bequeath unto my nephew, John M. Maxwell, of Orangeburg, Elizabeth Dibble, wife of my brother, Andrew H. Dibble, ... and Bessie Dibble, wife of my brother R. D. Dibble, ...the sum of Five Hundred ($500.00), each. ..."*

James Laurence also left $2,000.00 in the Mercantile Trust Company, of Saint Louis, in Trust for his brother William S. Dibble, to be paid in annual installments. The remainder of his estate was to be divided among his five brothers, who were to receive five-eights (5/8th), each; and the nieces and nephews of his three sisters, which included seven Maxwells, three Levy's and three Taylors, all receiving One-eighth (1/8), each. His thoughtfulness and generosity is evident in his giving spirit. It is interesting that he included the wives of two of his brothers and the nieces and nephew of his three sisters.

Probably, unknown to him, he had one biological daughter, Estelle E. Hoskins (1892-1996), who was born in Camden, the daughter of Sarah "Sallie" English (1859-1910), who had about seven children, according to the 1900 census, with Estelle being the youngest, at 8 years old. (A DNA match of 2017 with a granddaughter of

83

Estelle R. Hoskins, which indicated that one of the Dibble men fathered Estelle. With the process of elimination and looking at the possibilities, it was determined that James Laurence Dibble was the father.) The Daniel and Sallie English Hoskins' family moved to Charlotte, North Carolina while Estelle was a youngster. Estelle married Dr. Hardy Liston, Sr. (1889-1956), President of Johnson C. Smith University, in Charlotte, N.C. Estelle and her husband had six children: three sons and three daughters, and have numerous descendants.

James Laurence Dibble is the father of one daughter:

>Estelle R. Hoskins (1892-1996)
>>married Hardy Liston, Ph.D. (1889-1956)

James Laurence Dibble
(1859-1932)

THOMAS DIBBLE (1862-1863) *(Andrew H., Andrew C., Samuel, Samuel, John, Wakefield, Ebenezer, Thomas, Robert)* was born in Camden the 8th child and 7th son of Andrew H. Dibble and Ellie Naomi Naudin, living only about five months. According to the Family *Bible,* he was born on 5 October 1862, and died 9 March 1863. He is probably buried in the Dibble Family plot, but does not have a marker.

Ella Naudin Dibble
(1865-1913)

Theodore John Levy, Jr.
(1862-1917)

ELLA NAUDIN DIBBLE (1865-1913) *(Andrew H., Andrew C., Samuel, Samuel, John, Wakefield, Ebenezer, Thomas, Robert)* was born in Camden the 9th child and 2nd daughter of Andrew Henry Dibble and Ellie Naomi Naudin. Ella was born on 30 May 1865 and died on 1 June 1913, in Orangeburg, South Carolina, dying at 48 years, 2 months.

Ella married Theodore John Levy, Jr. (1862-1917), of Camden, on 6 April 1887, and moved to Orangeburg, South Carolina, where they raised their family of three children. They lived in a very comfortable two-story home at 114 Amelia Street, near the corner of Treadwell, in Orangeburg. The *1900 Census* tells us that they had been married 13 years, had five children, with three living, at that time. They also had a servant living with them, Mattie Clifton, age 20 years, and Fred Carter, a barber, age 18, who was a cousin to Ella. The *1910 Census,* tells us that the three children were still living at home, Ella, age 22, Elizabeth, age 21 and Eugene, age 19. Theodore is seen as early as 1900 in the *Business Directory for Orangeburg,* but was living there prior to that time. Their home was destroyed by fire in the 1960s.

Ella and Theodore had three children to live to adulthood, two daughters, Ellie Naomi (BS Degree, 1909) and Elizabeth Catherine (BS Degree, 1910), are both graduates of Claflin University. Their son Eugene Dibble Levy also attended Claflin, became a barber. The three Levy siblings relocated to Washington, D. C. area shortly after their father died in 1917. Ella Naudin Dibble and her husband Theodore John Levy (1862-1917) are buried in the Orangeburg Cemetery. Within a wrought iron fence and gate, standing high above all other markers in the cemetery is a beautiful angel looking down on those who are resting here. Her epitaph reads: *"SHE WAS TOO GOOD, TOO GENTLE, AND FAIR"*

Ella Naudin Dibble and Theodore John Levy Jr., are the parents of:

> Ellie Naomi Levy (1888-1943),
>> married Wesley Hamilton Thompson (1877-1920)
> Elizabeth Catherine Levy (1889-1954),
>> married Harry Winfred Davis (1892-1975)
> Eugene Dibble Levy (1890-1958),
>> married Idalean Elizabeth McLain (1894-1982)

Josephine Levy (1893-1893) (Orangeburg Cemetery.

THEODORE JOHN LEVY, JR.
1862-1917

Spouse of Ella Naudin Dibble, Granddaughter

THEODORE JOHN LEVY, JR., (1862-1917), the son of Theodore John Levy, Sr., (1830- 1862), and his wife the former Charlotte Johnson (1833-1898), of Camden. His siblings were Elizabeth (1854-1934), Sara (1856-1936), and Prudence (1861-post 1920). He died on 20 January 1917, in Spartanburg, South Carolina.

Theodore moved to Orangeburg and began purchasing property as early as 1886, and continued to purchase property until 1914. He married Ella Naudin Dibble, of Camden on 6 April 1887. He learned the skill of barbering as a young teen as an apprentice working in the *"George McLain & Sons Barbershop,"* in downtown Camden. George W. McLain (1847-1917), was a skilled barber, operating a barbershop on Main Street for more than seventy years. Theodore and George were first cousins, their mothers were sisters. He gained the professional experience needed to serve all people, including the affluent society of Orangeburg. Theodore became an early entrepreneur, having one barber shop for the white clientele and one for the people of color, situated next door to each other, in downtown Orangeburg. The 1900 and 1910 Census, indicates he owned his building and had enough business to warrant his employing others to work in the barbershops, also training a new generation of barbers to service his clientele. Frederick Carter, who was a native of Camden and a relative of his wife, Ella, worked as a barber in his shops. The 1909-1910 *Business Directory, Orangeburg,* and the *1912 City Directory, Orangeburg,* tells us that Theodore operated these barbershops at 20 South Middleton Streets, *i*n downtown Orangeburg.

After his wife Ella Naudin Dibble's death in 1913, Theodore evidently relocated to Spartanburg, where we see him in 1916: seen as the *"T. J. Levy Undertaker & Co."* at 138 Liberty Street. Theodore John Levy married Natalie McLain, on 7 July 1915, in Camden. She was the daughter of George McLain, of Camden. Theodore John died in Spartanburg on 20 January 1917, and is buried in the Orangeburg Cemetery besides his first wife, Ella Naudin Dibble Levy, and young daughter Wilhelmina, who was born and died in May 1893. This magnificent monument with the angel standing at the top looking down is a great tribute to Theodore and Ella Naudin Dibble Levy.

Marriage Certificate, April 6, 1887
Ella Naudin Dibble and Theodore John Levy

Orangeburg Cemetery, Orangeburg, South Carolina

THEODORE J. LEVY

**BORN AT CAMDEN, S. C.
MAR. 28. 1862
DIED: ORANGEBURG, S. C.
JAN. 20, 1917**

ELLA N. DIBBLE

Wife of T. J. LEVY

**BORN AT CAMDEN, S. C.
MAY 30, 1865
DIED AT ORANGEBURG, S. C.
JUNE 6, 1913**

"SHE WAS TOO GOOD, TOO GENTLE AND FAIR"

Rufus Dennis Dibble
(1867-1961)

Elizabeth "Bessie" Lee
Greenlee (1888-1969)

RUFUS DENNIS DIBBLE (1867-1961) *(Andrew H., Andrew C., Samuel, Samuel, John, Wakefield, Ebenezer, Thomas, Robert)* was born in Camden, the 10th child and 8th son of Andrew Henry Dibble and Ellie Naomi Naudin. Rufus was born 5 November 1867 and died 27 January 1961. He out lived all his siblings, with five of his brothers dying during the 1930s, and his three sisters all died earlier. He married Elizabeth "Bessie" Greenlee who was born on 30 November 1889, in Marion, North Carolina and died on 11 December 1969, in Dallas, Texas. She came to Camden to work as a teenager.

During his early years, Dennis worked along-side his brothers in the Dibble Store on Broad (Main) Street. Dennis had lived with his mother, until her death in 1920, after which he built his home at 719 Lafayette Avenue (corner of Campbell), in the early 1920s. According to the *Camden City Directory, 1925-1926*, he owned and operated a store at 1206 Campbell Avenue with his brother William S. Dibble working as a clerk. Dennis and Bessie's only daughter, Wilhelmina graduated from Howard University with a Bachelor of Science Degree in 1929. In 1930, she received her Master's Degree in Mathematics from Columbia University in New York.

"Bubba Den," as he was known to us of the next generation was a kind and caring uncle to my father and aunt. He always remembered my siblings and myself at Christmas time. He lived a long life and is the only one, of the original Dibble siblings that I knew. Rufus Dennis Dibble is buried in the Dibble Family Plot in Camden, along with his other five brothers. His brother Eugene is buried in a plot across the walkway from the original Dibble Plot. His wife is buried in Dallas, Texas, where she went to live with her daughter after her husband's death, in 1961.

Dennis Rufus Dibble and Elizabeth "Bessie" Greenlee are the parents of:

Wilhelmina Lee Dibble (1908-1984)
m. (1) Dr. William Alonzo Warfield
m. (2) Eolus Von Rettig, Sr.

Rufus Dennis Dibble
1867-1961
Cedar Cemetery
Camden, S. C.

Elizabeth "Bessie" Lee Greenlee
1887-1969
Restland Memorial Park, Garden of Ascension
Dallas, Texas

CATHERINE "KATIE" DIBBLE (1871-1872) *(Andrew H., Andrew C., Samuel, Samuel, John, Wakefield, Ebenezer, Thomas, Robert)* was born the 11th child and 3rd daughter of Andrew Henry Dibble and Ellie Naomi Naudin. According to the Dibble Family *Bible*, she was born on 5 July 1871 and died on 12 February 1872, living only seven months. She is probably buried in Cedar Cemetery, but there is no marker for her.

Harriet Catherine Dibble
(1873-1918)

Rev. Dr. John B. Taylor, Sr.
(1867-1936)

HARRIET CATHERINE DIBBLE *(Andrew H., Andrew C., Samuel, Samuel, John, Wakefield, Ebenezer, Thomas, Robert). (12th child, and 4th daughter)* Harriet was born in Camden, on 16 April 1873, the youngest child of Andrew an Ellie Naudin Dibble. She died on 24 September 1918, in Florence, South Carolina, at age 45 years, and five months. Harriet Catherine was named for her maternal grandmother Harriet Conway and her paternal aunt Catherine Smith Springs (1828-1895) and great-great-grandmother, Catherine Cleveland (c.1759-1859).

For her early education, Harriet attended Browning Home, which was founded for people of color in 1867 by the Methodist Episcopal minister, Reverend James Mather and his wife Sarah. Browning Home later became known as Mather Academy. Harriet then attended Claflin University in Orangeburg, graduating from the Normal Program in 1889, along with her nieces Catherine Cleveland Dibble and Cassandra Jeanette Maxwell, who were the daughters of her brother Andrew and sister Martha. According to Claflin history, she was among several students considered a "music scholar," playing the violin and piano. The earliest photograph of Harriet, as a young girl about twelve or thirteen, she is wearing glasses. Evidently, she had trouble with her eyes since she was a youngster. Her brother, Eugene, took her to New York City, to see an eye doctor, about 1889. We have a photo of both Harriet and her brother, Eugene, made at the Wurst Art Studio, on Sixth Avenue, New York. She is elegantly dressed in this studio photograph.

Harriet married the Reverend Dr. John Benjamin Taylor, Sr., a native of North, South Carolina, on 22 October 1902, in the home of her sister Ella Naudin Dibble Levy, who lived at 144 Amelia Street in Orangeburg. She met her husband while a student at Claflin University, during the 1880s. Oral history tell us she had a ten-year courtship, prior to her marriage at age 29 years old. Reverend Taylor purchased a lot at 385 North Boulevard (earlier known as North Railroad Avenue) on 25 September 1900, with the home built shortly thereafter, and home was deeded to his wife, the former Harriet Catherine Dibble on 6 March 1903. We are very fortunate that the home is still standing and has a historic marker to be placed in front of the home.

Harriet Catherine Dibble and her husband, Reverend Doctor John Benjamin Taylor, Sr., are buried in the Taylor Plot, in the Orangeburg Cemetery, with a sizeable marker ad epitaph along with their young son, Naudin Dibble Taylor (1905-1906) and daughter Harriet Louise Taylor (1910- 1937). Also buried in the plot, is their eldest son John B. Taylor, Jr. (1903-1980), and his wife, Amanda Felicia Allen and their daughter Catherine Allen Taylor McConnell (1929-1996).

The Reverend Doctor John Benjamin Taylor, Sr. and his wife, Harriet Catherine Dibble Taylor became the parents of four children:

> John Benjamin Taylor, Jr. (1903-1980)
> > m. Amanda Felicia Allen (1907-2004)
> Naudin Dibble Taylor (1905-1906)
> Catherine Springs Taylor (1907-1991)
> > William Walter Humphrey; m.2. Oscar Hanna
> Harriet Louise Taylor (1910-1937)

REVEREND DR. JOHN BENJAMIN TAYLOR, SR.
A.B., A.M., D.D.
1867-1936

Educator, Minister, Businessman and Trustee

Spouse of Harriet Catherine Dibble

REVEREND DR. JOHN BENJAMIN TAYLOR, SR., (1867-1936) *A.B., A.M., D.D.* was born on 26 December 1867, in Orangeburg County. He was raised by his mother Beulah Taylor and his stepfather Taylor, with numerous Taylor half-brothers and sisters. He was aware that he was not a full sibling and was often reminded of such. while growing up. He died in Orangeburg on 31 December 1936. It has been determined through Y-DNA/Autosomal DNA analysis that his biogeological father is Reverend William Brooker (c.1807-1879), who was a Baptist Minister from the nearby community of Barnwell District.

My grandfather John grew up in the rural community near the present town of North, with the desire to seek not only educational opportunities and an intellectual environment, but also a chance to attain economic security, to build and to serve God. He realized early in his life that he did not want to work on a farm, and ventured into Orangeburg as a teenager, where he would seek an education, graduating from the College Preparatory Program at Claflin University in 1890. He continued his education, graduating with the distinct honor of being Valedictorian of his Class, receiving his Bachelor of Arts Degree in 1894.

By 1892, he was serving as a teacher and prior to 1900 he had been appointed as the first Principal of the Sterling School, which was the only elementary school for African Americans in Orangeburg during this period. Early education for youngsters in Orangeburg was started in 1865 as a Freedman's School No. 1. By 1867, the teachers were Thaddeus K. Sasportas and Henry Frost. By 1888 the name of the school had been changed to Sterling School, closing in 1922. According to the newspaper, *Times and Democrat*, dated Sunday, June 21, 1987, Mr. Hugo Ackerman stated:

> *"The Principal of the Sterling School for Blacks for several years had been the **Rev. J. B. Taylor**. His assistants in 1903 were Misses Bessie Brown, Mamie M. Dickson and E. V. Jackson. At this time, the Sterling School enrolled 582 pupils...220 males and 362 females... The building being used at this time was rented at a cost of $160.00 per year...*

This was a distinct position for any person, this early in the history of South Carolina. He was able to give back to the community and to the young children who had not had the opportunity to attend school prior to this time. He was a dedicated servant of God as he worked tirelessly for the betterment of the youth of Orangeburg.

Reverend John B. Taylor, Sr., first became a Baptist Minister in the Orangeburg community, and later prepared himself to serve the Methodist Episcopal Church community, which was a better fit for him. In 1892, Reverend Taylor was also serving as a minister, and by 1902-1903, he served as pastor of Trinity Methodist Episcopal Church, in Orangeburg, during which time he hosted the annual District Conference.

In 1903-1907, he served as pastor of Trinity Methodist Episcopal Church in Camden. The site where Trinity stands today was purchased in 1828 by a white Methodist Church. This church, as all others, was originally known as a Methodist Episcopal Church, but with a change in the church structure in 1972, the name became Trinity United Methodist Church. A congregation of people of color began worshipping at this site in 1872. In November 1875, Trinity was purchased from the Methodist Episcopal Church South. Trustees at Trinity negotiating for the sale included John Moreau Dibble (1848-1877), who later becomes Reverend Taylor's brother-in-law. Church records state:

> *"Many improvements were made on the Church, Under the pastorage of J.B. Taylor (1903-1907), e.g. the building was covered with shingles, the stairway was moved to the front of the church and lighting was replaced by electricity and a chandelier was purchased. All these things were done in preparation for the Annual Conference scheduled for Trinity in 1907."*

Reverend Taylor was appointed District Superintendent of the Charleston District of the Methodist Episcopal Church, where he served from 1907 until 1913. In 1914, he went to Florence, where he served for four years, and guided Cumberland Church in completing the payment for their new church. After spending one year in Greenville, at John Wesley Methodist Episcopal Church, he moved to Bennettsville, in 1919 to pastor at St. Michael's. Here he was to spend five years, resulting in the building of a new and beautiful church and parsonage, which were dedicated on October 23, 1923. A beautiful cornerstone stands today to honor Reverend Taylor:

> *"Notwithstanding, the fact that the other ministers did well, the realization of the building of the new church was due to **Rev. J. B. Taylor's** zeal, enthusiasm, dynamic leadership, and sacrificial giving. We were able to enter and hold our first service on October, 1923."*

In 1924, he was appointed District Superintendent of the Orangeburg District of the Methodist Episcopal Church, where he served until 1929. According to the *Trinity United Methodist Church Homecoming Souvenir Booklet, 1866-1984*, The Quarterly Conference which was held on October 19, 1926, passed the following:

> *"...Whereas the Trustees have entered into a tentative agreement with Mr. W. E. Atkinson that they would convey to him all of the property owned on Amelia Street and Pittman Alley for an in consideration of all that part and parcel of property owned by The Trustees of State College and Mr. W. A. Livingston, and others fronting on North Boulevard and Amelia Street and $5,000.00. Be it resolved that it is the sense of this Quarterly Conference assembled this 19th day of October, 1926, that the Trustees have made a wise deal and it speaks for the best interest of the church and all concerned. Be it further resolved that this Quarterly Conference do now and here authorize the Board of Trustees To make the legal conveyance of this property to Mr. W. E. Atkinson for the above consideration mentioned."*

Signed: **J. B. Taylor**
Chairman of Quarterly Conference

While serving as Orangeburg District Superintendent of the Methodist Episcopal Church, he presided over the annual conferences held in Bennettsville, Greenville, Hartsville, Charleston, Cheraw, and Anderson, South Carolina. He served as Treasurer of the S. C. Conference, 1934-1936 and delivered the Memorial Address at the 66th Session of the Annual Conference in 1933. In order to better serve both the Methodist Church and Claflin University, he attended the General Conferences of the Methodist Episcopal Church during these years in Des Moines, Iowa, Boston and Cape Cod, Massachusetts. He served as a Methodist Episcopal Church leader, for forty-four years. My father remembers well his father's travels to these many conferences to cities and places across the country.

Reverend J. B. Taylor served as a United States Enumerator for the *1910 U. S. Census* for Orangeburg, South Carolina. This was the first-time minorities were recruited to take the Census in their own communities. He is seen in the 1910 Census for Orangeburg City, Supervisor District No. 7, Enumeration District No. 61, in April 1910.

While attending Claflin, Reverend Taylor met his soon to be wife, Harriet Catherine Dibble (1873-1918), the youngest daughter of Andrew Henry Dibble, Sr. (1825-1873), of Charleston and later Camden, and his wife,

Ellie Naomi Naudin (1828-1920), of Camden. They were married on October 22, 1902, in Orangeburg in the home of her sister Ella Naudin Dibble Levy and her husband Theodore John Levy, who lived at 114 Amelia Street.

Rev. J. B. Taylor, the efficient principal of the colored graded school in this city, will be married next Wednesday to Hattie Dibble, of Camden, S. C. He is a good man, and has the best wishes of his many white friends for a long and happy married life.

The Times and Democrat Newspaper, October15, 1902

Claflin University and the community of Orangeburg benefited from the contributions made by the Reverend Doctor Taylor who served and constantly sought monetary and scholastic support for his Alma Mater in order that the young men and women of the college would be successful and give back, once they had completed their education. He recognized the importance of both business and economics in the growth and development of the school and the education of all South Carolinians. Because of his strong interest in education, he was appointed a Trustee of Claflin University in 1908, and was to serve in that capacity for twenty consecutive years, through 1928. As a Methodist Episcopal Minister and a Trustee of Claflin, he was able to serve dual roles as he sought support for Claflin from the business, educational, and religious communities of South Carolina. For his strenuous efforts in support of his Alma Mater, he was awarded the Degree of Doctor of Divinity in 1910. Claflin was very much in need of strong leadership and financial aid, and he was there to lead in this effort.

According to Thaddeus K. Bythewood, *"...on October 19, 1926, the Quarterly Conference passed ... property owned by the Trustees of State College and others ... fronting on North Boulevard and Amelia Street...."* *"Signed by J. B. Taylor, Chairman of Quarterly Conference."* This passage is in reference to the purchase of the property at 185 Boulevard Street, where Trinity Methodist Episcopal Church was built, beginning in 1927 and where it stands today. (Mentioned earlier.)

"The J. B. Taylor Offices and Stores," located in the unit hundred block of North Boulevard, were designed to have six stores on the ground level and six offices above. Reverend Taylor, completed the building of this structure in January 1929, and according to *The 1935 City Directory for Orangeburg*, *"T. H. Best, Dentist, H. D. Rowe, Physician, Health and Life Insurance Company"* and others occupied the office spaces. The first level was occupied by East End Café, East End Shoe Shop, Breeland's Café, People's Barber Shop and Oliver's Barber shop. Reverend Taylor owned this commercial property, contributing to the development of businesses in this downtown area, near the colleges.

The Reverend Doctor Taylor Family lived at 385 North Boulevard (formerly 147 North Railway Avenue). (Except when he was assigned to other locations in the State of South Carolina under the direction the Methodist Episcopal Conference, to serve as pastor to other churches.) The Taylor property was purchased September 25, 1900 where he built a home. He deeded the home to his wife on March 6, 1903, and raised his children here. The home remained in the family until the death of Reverend Taylor's second wife, Daisy McLain Bulkley Taylor, in 1965.

Orangeburg Cemetery, Orangeburg, South Carolina

"UNTIL THE DAY BREAKS AND THE SHADOWS
FLEE AWAY"

HATTIE DIBBLE TAYLOR
April 16, 1873 – September 24, 1918

*"THE INFLUECE OF THY LIFE WAS AS
SWEET PERFUME TO ME,
IT LINGERS STILL, THROUGH THE DAYS,
WEEKS AND YEARS,
PASS INTO LIFE'S DEEP SEA,
BUT SWEETER FOR IT WILL BE TO ME,
WHERE WITH US PARTING SHALL NEVER BE."*

REV. JOHN B. TAYLOR
December 26, 1867 – December 31, 1936

*"WHAT MEMORIES OF UNSELFISH DEEDS
AND SACRIFICIAL SERVICE OF
KIND WORDS SPOKEN,
AND WEARY STEPS TAKEN AND
SUFFERING IN SILENCE AND OF
HEARTBREAK TURNED INTO JOY AND
MOURNNG TURNED INTO IMMORTAL HOPE,
GATHER ABOUT THE LIFE OF THIS
OUR FATHER AND HUSBAND."*

The epitaph is on the rear of the marker

GRANDCHILDREN OF
ANDREW HENRY DIBBLE, SR. AND ELLIE NAOMI NAUDIN

Neither citizen nor slave, Free Negroes dangled awkwardly in the middle of the Southern caste system. They shared some of the privileges of whites and were burdened with many of the liabilities of slaves, yet the stood apart from both.

Ira Berlin, 1974

Andrew Henry Dibble, Sr. and his wife Ellie Naomi Naudin produced numerous, interesting and remarkable descendants. However, we must always consider the conditions of persons of color living in the South during the late nineteenth and early twentieth centuries. These early family members faced adversity discrimination and prejudices, as they tried to map out a good life for their families. Then there were those who were able to succeed with great determination, sacrifices, and hard work who overcame many of these obstacles to become valued members of their community, and oftentimes, leaders. Many times, this was accomplished mainly by stressing the importance of education. They evidently instilled in their children, very early, the importance of education and they in turn, passed this desire and determination down to the many generations thereafter. All of Andrew and Ellie's children received an education either in Charleston, Orangeburg, or at home in Camden.

Andrew Henry and Ellie Naudin Dibble had twelve children and approximately 409 known descendants, as of 2018. (Not including those recently discovered.) With ten of their children living to adulthood, seven sons and three daughters, born between 1846 and 1873, only six of these children producing descendants.

There were twenty-three grandchildren, the eldest born in 1871 and the youngest born in 1910. Of these twenty-three grandchildren, twenty-one attended schools of higher learning, with three grandsons becoming physicians, one becoming a dentist, two barbers, two became businessmen and twelve teachers. Most of the grandchildren attended Claflin University, a Methodist Episcopal school, in Orangeburg, South Carolina. At this time, Claflin had a varied educational program which consisted of a high school, normal program, and a university program. However, the children of their son Eugene, mostly attended Atlanta University for their normal program and some college work.

There were several grandchildren who became teachers, before the turn of the twentieth century, with most of them being female. The oldest granddaughters, Ella Louise, and Cassandra Jeanette Maxwell, receiving their Teacher's Certificates from Claflin University in 1887 and 1889, and their brother Henry, received his Certificate in 1890, and sister Naomi, in 1902. Catherine Cleveland Dibble, daughter of their son, Andrew H. Dibble, Jr., also received her Teacher Certificate from Claflin in 1889. Becoming a teacher was one of the main occupations for the female, at this early time, and therefore, many of Andrew and Ellie's granddaughters choose this profession.

After the turn of the twentieth century, many of the female granddaughters of Andrew and Ellie, continued in the field of education. Ellie Naomi and Elizabeth Catherine Levy, both received their Bachelor of Science (B, S.), Degrees, from Claflin University in 1909 and 1910, respectively, and became teachers. Other granddaughters who also became teachers are the three daughters of their son Eugene: Josie, Ellie and Jimmie, and granddaughters

Wilhelmina Dibble who received a B.A. Degree from Howard University in 1929, and Catherine Taylor, who received her Teacher's Certificate from Claflin University, in 1926.

Many of these grandchildren moved to other locations across the country, and experienced a way of life, different from what they had known in South Carolina. Some of these grandchildren lived or settled in places such as Alabama, Georgia, Kentucky, Maryland, Minnesota, New Jersey, New York, Oklahoma, Pennsylvania, Texas, Virginia, Washington, D.C., and Wisconsin.

All the grandchildren of Andrew and Ellie Naudin Dibble, persevered and believed in an education that would provide for them and their families. These grandchildren taught on the elementary, high school and college levels, from as early as 1887 when the first teacher's certificate was issued to their oldest granddaughter through to the 1970s, when their last granddaughter retired, in Dallas, Texas.

Included in this section, are the biographical sketches of some of these grandchildren. It is impossible to have developed a detailed sketch on all these grandchildren because of the lack of available documentation. Many of these grandchildren lived so early, when records were not being collected and preserved, as we see, today, and naturally, some of the sketches are more detailed and lengthier than others, depending on available information.

Cassandra J. Maxwell
1871-1893

Ella L. Maxwell
1873-1959

Henry J. Maxwell, Jr.
1876-1954

C. Wendell Maxwell, MD
1879-1959

John M. Maxwell
1881-1938

Naomi T. Maxwell
1883-1948

Stephen L. Maxwell
1885-1930

Andrew D. Maxwell, DDS
1888-1958

Josephine H. Dibble
1888-1974

E. H. Dibble, Jr., MD
1893-1968

Harold L. Dibble
1896-1982

Ellie N. Dibble
1898-1973

A. H. Dibble, III, MD
1900-1946

Ms. James L. Dibble
1902-1975

Ellie N. Levy
1888-1943

Elizabeth C. Levy
1889-1954

Eugene D. Levy
1890-1958

Grandchildren of:
Ellie Naomi Naudin
1828-1920 &
Andrew Henry Dibble
1825-1873

Catherine C. Dibble
1873-1947

Wilhelmina L Dibble
1908-1984

John B. Taylor, Jr.
1903-1980

Catherine S. Taylor
1907-1991

Cassandra Jeanette Maxwell
1871-1893

CASSANDRA JEANETTE MAXWELL
1871-1893
Granddaughter of Andrew Henry Dibble, Sr.

CASSADRA JEANETTE MAXWELL (1871-1893) *(Martha Dibble, Andrew H., Andrew C., Samuel, Samuel, John, Wakefield, Ebenezer, Thomas, Robert).* Cassandra Jeanette Maxwell was born on 17 December 1871, in Bennettsville, South Carolina, the eldest daughter of Martha Louisa Dibble and her husband Senator Henry Johnson Maxwell, Sr. Cassandra died on 27 December 1893, in Richmond, Virginia. Cassandra received her early education at Browning Home (later Mather Academy) a Methodist Episcopal School, in Camden. Cassandra attended Claflin University for her high school and college education, receiving her Normal Degree (Teacher's Certificate) in the Class of 1889 from Claflin. Cassandra moved to Richmond, Virginia to begin her teaching career, dying there at an early age of 20 years. She is buried in the Maxwell Family Plot in Walker Cemetery in Sumter, South Carolina.

Ella Louise Maxwell 1873-1959

ELLA LOUISE MAXWELL PAGE

1873-1959

- **Granddaughter of Andrew Henry Dibble, Sr.**

ELLA LOUISE MAXWELL PAGE (1873-1959) (*Martha Dibble, Andrew H. Andrew C., Samuel, Samuel, John, Wakefield, Ebenezer, Thomas, Robert).* Ella Louise Maxwell was born on 19 December 1873 in Bennettsville, South Carolina and died on 14 June 1959 in Sumter, South Carolina. She was the daughter of Martha Louisa Dibble and her husband Senator Henry Johnson Maxwell, Sr. Ella attended Browning Home (later Mather Academy), a Methodist Episcopal school, in Camden, South Carolina for her early education. Ella attended Claflin University for her high school education and received her Normal (Teacher's Certificate) Degree in 1887 from Claflin, in Orangeburg. Ella taught for many years in the Sumter County School System. She died at 85 years and six months.

REVEREND DR. JAMES FRANKLIN PAGE (1866-1932)

Spouse of Ella Louise Maxwell, Granddaughter

Reverend James Franklin Page, born on September 16, 1866, in Marion, South Carolina, was the second son of Eliza and Daniel Page. There were three brothers, Wallace, Harry and Henry and one sister, Catherine. In 1887, he graduated from Claflin Normal School, but continued his studies, obtaining a Bachelor of Divinity Degree (B.D.) and still later a Doctor of Divinity Degree (D.D.). In 1889, he entered the South Carolina Conference of the Methodist Episcopal Church, and admitted in 1891, at age 25 years old.

Ella Louise Maxwell married Reverend James Franklin Page (1866-1932) on 12 February 1906. He pastored at many of the Methodist Episcopal Churches in the South Carolina Conference. He served as a Trustee to his Alma Mater, Claflin University from 1909 until 1932. He attended all the General Conferences between 1912 and 1932. He was elected to serve as a Presiding Elder from 1906- 1908. Later, he served as a District Superintendent during the following years: 1908-1910, 1915-1920, 1923, and 1930-1931. Reverend Page hosted the Annual Conference while pastoring at Trinity Methodist Episcopal Church on November 19, 1913. He also presided over the Annual Conference held in Sumter on December 9, 1930 and in Camden on December 8, 1931. Reverend Pages' attendance at the 1932 General conference was to be is last official assignment, for he suffered a fatal heart attack while returning home and died in McKinney, Virginia on May 17, 1932. They made their home in Sumter, South Carolina. Ella Maxwell, her husband and son James Wendell Page are buried in the Page Family Plot in the Walker Cemetery in Sumter, S.C.

Ella Maxwell and Reverend Dr, James Franklin Page became the parents of one son:

> James Wendell Page (1911-1965)
>> married Angeline Evans (1912-1973). He attended Voorhees College.

"At Rest From Sight, To Memory, Dear."

Henry Johnson Maxwell, Jr.
1876-1954

HENRY JOHNSON MAXWELL, JR.

1876-1954

Grandson of Andrew Henry Dibble, Sr.

HENRY JOHNSON MAXWELL, JR. (1876-1954*) (Martha Dibble, Andrew H., Andrew C., Samuel, Samuel, John, Wakefield, Ebenezer, Thomas, Robert)* was born on Friday, 14 January 1876 in Columbia, South Carolina. (According to the Maxwell Family Bible, he was originally named Henry Dibble Maxwell, but later his name was changed to Henry Johnson Maxwell, Jr.) He is the son of Martha Louisa Dibble and her husband Henry Johnson Maxwell, Sr., who was an attorney and South Carolina State Senator, representing Marlboro County, South Carolina, during Reconstruction. Henry died on 4 February 1954, in Saint Paul, Minnesota, and is buried in the Oakland Cemetery, St. Paul, Minnesota.

Henry attended Claflin University, graduating during the 1890s. During December 1898 and January 1899, while a student at Claflin, he along with other Claflin students, travelled throughout New England with the Claflin University Singers, to raise money for Claflin.

102

He migrated to Massachusetts, where he met and married Lillian Gertrude Pool of Providence, Rhode Island on 28 October 1902, in Boston, Massachusetts. His sister Ella, from Sumter, South Carolina, and brother Stephen, from Saint Paul, attended this wedding. He and his wife moved to Saint Paul, Minnesota in 1906. Henry is seen in the 1910 U.S. Census living in Saint Paul with his wife and brother Stephen. He worked as a waiter, for the Northern Pacific Railroad Company, which states, his height was 5 feet, 4 inches and weighed 130 pounds.

LILLIAN GERTRUDE POOL MAXWELL
1878-1954

Spouse of Henry Johnson Maxwell, Jr., Grandson

Lillian Gertrude Pool (1878-1954) was born on 27 September 1878, in Providence, Rhode Island the daughter of C a r o l i n e   Lela Howland Poole of Rhode Island and Samuel Henry Poole, formerly of Virginia. Her grandfather was Sergeant Major Zebedee Howard who served in the Rhode Island 14th Regiment of Heavy Artillery during the Civil War. She married Henry Johnson Maxwell on 28 October 1902, in Boston, Massachusetts. Lillian was a dressmaker. Lillian died on 3 May 1954, three months after her husband. Henry and Lillian made their home in Saint Paul, Minnesota, where they both died. They had no children. They are interred in the Oakland Cemetery, Saint Paul, Ramsey County, Minnesota.

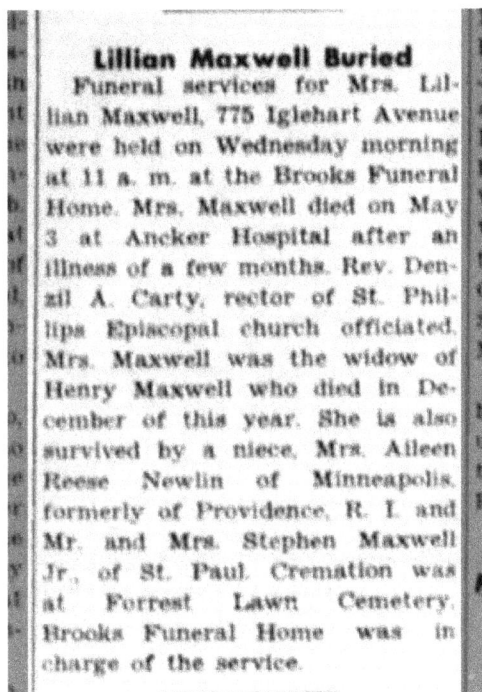

Lillian Maxwell Buried

Funeral services for Mrs. Lillian Maxwell, 775 Iglehart Avenue were held on Wednesday morning at 11 a. m. at the Brooks Funeral Home. Mrs. Maxwell died on May 3 at Ancker Hospital after an illness of a few months. Rev. Denzil A. Carty, rector of St. Phillips Episcopal church officiated. Mrs. Maxwell was the widow of Henry Maxwell who died in December of this year. She is also survived by a niece, Mrs. Aileen Reese Newlin of Minneapolis, formerly of Providence, R. I. and Mr. and Mrs. Stephen Maxwell Jr., of St. Paul. Cremation was at Forrest Lawn Cemetery. Brooks Funeral Home was in charge of the service.

Charles Wendell Maxwell, M.D.
1879-1959

CHARLES WENDELL MAXWELL, M.D.

1879-1959

Grandson of Andrew Henry Dibble, Sr.

CHARLES WENDELL MAXWELL, M.D., (1879-1959) *(Medical Physician)* *(Martha Dibble, Andrew H., Andrew C., Samuel, Samuel, John, Wakefield, Ebenezer, Thomas, Robert).* Charles Wendell was born on 2 March 1879 in Bennettsville, South Carolina, the son of Senator Henry Johnson Maxwell, Sr.

and his wife the former Martha Louisa Dibble of Camden. He died in Philadelphia, Pennsylvania on 28 June 1959. His World War II Registration states he is 5 feet, 10 inches, grey eyes, grey hair and weighs 205 pounds.

He attended Claflin University for his early education, and graduated from Biddle University (now Johnson C. Smith University) and graduated from Howard University College of Medicine in 1904. He returned to Sumter that same year and set up his practice and practiced medicine in downtown Sumter for eighteen years. On June 24, 1908, Dr. Maxwell married Pansy E. Miller, daughter of Thomas Ezekiel Miller,, United States Representative of Beaufort and Charleston, who later became President of South Carolina State University, in Orangeburg.

I first met Cousin Wendell in the mid-1940s, while visiting Philadelphia. He later visited our family in Washington on several occasions. I was so moved with the stories he told of growing up with my paternal grandmother, who was his aunt, and near his age. His stories made an indelible impression, which resulted in my naming my eldest son for him.

Wendell migrated to Philadelphia in July 1922 and set up his practice at 616 South 15th Street, where he built and maintained a lucrative practice. Dr. Maxwell was appointed the Police Surgeon in September 1936, becoming the second person of color to be appointed to this position. Dr. Maxwell was appointed along with a white physician. Dr. Maxwell was awarded a *Certificate of Merit* for completing fifty years in the medical profession by the Philadelphia County Medical Association, in October 1954. He has made numerous contributions to his profession. The most outstanding was in 1924 with the discovery of the drug "condurango" that aids in controlling hemorrhages of women, which today is used very extensively in the profession. Dr. Maxwell' findings have been published in several medical journals including the "Medical World" and "Sorjous Encyclopedia of Practical Medicine." At the time of Dr. Charles Wendell Maxwell's death, he had practiced medicine for 55 years with 37 years spent in Philadelphia.

PANSY E. MILLER MAXWELL
1885-1976

Spouse to Charles Wendell Maxwell, MD, Grandson

PANSY E. MILLER (1885-1976) was born in Charleston, South Carolina, the daughter of The Honorable Thomas Ezekiel Miller (1849-1938) and his wife, the former Anna M. Hume (1853-1936), of Charleston. Thomas and Anna had a very large family of about nine children. Pansy married Dr. Charles Wendell Maxwell on 24 June 1908. Dr. and Mrs. Maxwell celebrated their 50th Wedding Anniversary at the Waldorf-Astoria on 28 June 1958. They had no children.

John Moreau Maxwell
1881-1938

JOHN MOREAU MAXWELL, SR.

1881-1938

Grandson of Andrew Henry Dibble, Sr.

JOHN MOREAU MAXWELL, Sr. (1881-1938) (*Martha Dibble, Andrew H., Andrew C., Samuel, Samuel, John, Wakefield, Ebenezer, Thomas, Robert*), was born on 29 June 1881 in Augusta, Georgia. He died in Philadelphia, Pennsylvania on 25 July 1938, where his physician brother lived. He was the son of South Carolina State Senator Henry Johnson Maxwell (1837-1906) and his wife the former Martha Louisa Dibble (1846-1923), of Camden and Sumter.

John Moreau grew up in Sumter County and in 1890, was one of the first boys to attend Mather Academy, which had previously been a female academy, for his primary education. He attended Claflin University for his

Preparatory education and probably for his college education. He also attended Meharry Dental School for a portion of his post-college education, until he became ill and had to suspend his education there.

John Moreau Maxwell worked in the grocery business of his maternal uncle, "*John Moreau Dibble's General Merchandise*" store in Camden. This Camden business was started in 1873 and operated in downtown Camden for over fifty years. Camden had been a winter resort for wealthy northern families, who ventured south during the winter season. The clientele of customers who patronized the Dibble Store were from the highest social and economic classes and the store stocked gourmet and fancy groceries that were not found at other Camden stores. During their busy season they employed fifteen clerks and had counter service and delivery service. This is where young John Moreau Maxwell apprenticed as a youth, and developed the interest and desire to open his grocery business in Orangeburg. Because of the kinship, experiences, and close relationship with his relatives in Camden, he was able to develop the qualities and business sense needed to become a very successful businessman.

He started his first, small business in Orangeburg, in 1904, along Railroad Avenue. Within three-years, he had expanded and moved his business: "*Maxwell's Staple and Fancy Groceries*," to 189-191 East Russell Avenue between Railroad Avenue and Treadwell Street. At this location, he and his wife developed a prominently, productive business that he operated for thirty-four years, until his death in 1938. After his death the store was operated another thirteen years, by several of his children, until 1951. According to an article written in March 1940, in the *Opportunity Journal of Negro Life,* published by the National Urban League, the Maxwell Store: "*Six people are employed as clerks, one as a bookkeeper, four as delivery boys, and in addition, several part-time workers are hired during holiday periods and week-end.*"

The *1909-1910 City Directory of Orangeburg* shows that Andrew Dibble Maxwell (1888-1958) was working in his brother's store. The Maxwell Store had two large display windows and had a warehouse for storage of 80- to 90-percent of the merchandise received directly from the manufacturers. The clientele included those "*from both racial groups… some of the oldest and most substantial citizens of Orangeburg purchase their groceries here,*" according to Fitchett. During the 1920s John Maxwell's store was considered among the finest in the state according to Asa H. Gordon in *Sketches of Negro Life and History in South Carolina.* The First Annual Meeting of Negro Business League of South Carolina was held in July 1928, in Orangeburg, where John M. Maxwell was one of the speakers.

John Moreau married Katherine Louise Cardozo about 1909, according to the 1910 U. S. Census Report, for Orangeburg. The John Moreau Maxwell Family lived at 53 North Boulevard (formerly, North Railroad Avenue).

John and Katherine Cardozo Maxwell became the parents of six children:

> John Moreau Maxwell, Jr. (1908-1964)
> Cassandra Elizabeth Maxwell (1910-1974), (J.D.),
>> married Dr. James Hope Birnie (1909-1974)
> Nunez Cardozo Maxwell (1913-1916)
> Katherine Louise Maxwell (1914-1988),
>> married:
>> (1) George Morris Kersey, MD (1912-1947);
>> (2) Henry N. Vincent, Jr. (1908-1984)
> Dr. Charles Wendell Maxwell, II (1916-1966)
>> married Cecilia Yoshiko Segawa

Henry Cardozo Maxwell (1922-1993),
married:
(1) Gloria Martin, Ph.D.
(2) Beatrice Cowdery

John Moreau Maxwell and his wife the former Katherine Louise Cardozo are interred in the Orangeburg Cemetery with their young son, Nunez Cardozo Maxwell, their son, Charles Wendell Maxwell, II and son-in-law, Dr. George M. Kersey.

KATHERINE LOUISE CARDOZO MAXWELL
1884-1931

Spouse of John Moreau Maxwell, Sr., Grandson

KATHERINE LOUISE CARDOZO (1884-1931) *(Isaac N. II, Henry, Isaac N. I, David)* Katherine Louise Cardozo was born on 13 August 1884, in Charleston, South Carolina, the daughter of Reverend Isaac Nunez Cardozo, II (1856-1898), an early pastor of Trinity Methodist Episcopal Church and Professor at Claflin University and the State College and his wife Elizabeth Williamson (1860- 1935). Katherine died on 30 August 1931, in Orangeburg.

Katherine's father Reverend Isaac Nunez Cardozo was born in Charleston the son of South Carolina State Senator Henry Weston Cardozo and his wife Catherine. Reverend Henry (1830-1886) was one of the early pastors of Old Bethel United Methodist Church, the oldest United States Methodist Church, still standing, in Charleston. Henry later moved to Kershaw County, where he served as County Auditor and a member of the Board of Examiners. Also serving as State Senator from 1870-1874. In 1858, the family moved to Cleveland, Ohio, with the impending Civil War and the threat of enslaving free people of color. He returned to Charleston after the war. He also served as one of the early Trustees at Claflin University, Henry was one of six children born to Isaac Nunez I (1792-1855), and Lydia Weston (1805-1864), a free person of color. Reverend Isaac. II. graduated from Claflin University in 1886, with a Bachelor of Arts Degree in Classical Studies and Religion. He became Minister of Trinity Methodist Church from 1886 through 1888. He was also Professor of Historical Theology at The Baker Theological Institute, at Claflin at this same time.

Katherine's great-grandparents are Lydia Weston and Isaac Nunez Cardozo, I, a Jewish Customs Officer, in Charleston, who was the son of Rabbi David Nunez Cardozo, I (1753-1835), was born in New York and died in Charleston. Rabbi David was a patriot of the American Revolution, fighting at the battle of Beaufort in February 1779. In 1880, he helped defend Charleston against the British and was taken prisoner at the capture of Charleston.

Katherine grew up in Charleston and Orangeburg where her father pastored and taught school. The 1900 Census, we see her as a student at Scotia Seminary, in Johns River, Cabarrus, North Carolina. The *1909 Orangeburg City Directory*, Katherine is teaching in Orangeburg. The 1910 United States Census, she has been married to John Moreau Maxwell for one year, with her five-month-old son, John Moreau, Jr. The John Moreau Maxwell Family lived at 53 Boulevard, in Orangeburg. They are buried in the Orangeburg Cemetery.

John Moreau Maxwell Plot, Orangeburg Cemetery

Naomi Theresa Maxwell
1883-1948

NAOMI THERESA MAXWELL EDWARDS

1883-1948

Granddaughter of Andrew Henry Dibble, Sr.

NAOMI THERESA MAXWELL PAGE (1883-1948) *(Martha Dibble, Andrew H., Andrew C., Samuel, Samuel, John, Wakefield, Ebenezer, Thomas, Robert)* was born on Sunday, 11 March 1883, in Sumter, South Carolina, the third daughter and sixth child of Martha Louisa Dibble and Senator Henry Johnson Maxwell, Sr. Naomi died on 31 July 1948, after a lengthy illness. She is buried in the Denison Cemetery in Swoyersville, Luzerne County, Pennsylvania.

Naomi attended Claflin University for her high school, graduating from the Preparatory Program in the Class of 1899, and receiving her Normal Certificate in 1902. She is seen in the1900 U.S. Census, still living at home as a seventeen-year-old. The 1910 Census, we see her living in Wilkes-Barre, Pennsylvania with her husband George Christopher Edwards (1882-1957), which tells us she has been married two years.

She was active with the Inter-Racial Committee of the YMCA and the women's Auxiliary of the South Branch YMCA. She was employed as a social worker with the Luzerne County Board of Public Assistance. She was a member of the Bethel AME Church and chairman of its Stewardess Board.

Naomi Theresa Maxwell and George C. Edwards are the parents of two children:

> Christopher Maxwell Edwards (1915-1976)
> Selina Louise Edwards (1921-1988)
> > married George Warren Reed, Ph.D. (1920-2015)

GEORGE CHRISTOPHER EDWARDS
1882-1957

Spouse of Naomi Theresa Maxwell, Granddaughter

GEORGE CHRISTOPHER EDWARDS (1882-1957) was born on January 26, 1882, in Sumter, South Carolina, the son of Julius and Sally Legere Edwards, of Charleston and Sumter. George is one of 18 children born to Sally and Julius with 10 living in the 1900 U.S. Census. George died on December 7, 1957, in Chicago, Illinois, where he had gone to live with his daughter, after his wife's death.

He graduated from Wilkes-Barre High School and lived in Wilkes-Barre for more than 60 years. He served forty-four years with the U.S. Post Office, starting in 1904 and retiring in December 1948. He was active in numerous civic organizations in Wilkes-Barre, including the Postal Employees Credit Office, the Welfare Association, as a member of the executive board. He was also active with the Bethel AME Church where he served in many capacities, including superintendent of the Sunday School and president of church board.

George Christopher Edwards and his wife the former Naomi Theresa Maxwell are buried in the Denison Cemetery, Swosville, Luzerne County, Pennsylvania.

Year's Illness Fatal To Mrs. Naomi Edwards

Mrs. Naomi Edwards, 65, of 19 Orchard Street, died Saturday morning in Jefferson Medical College Hospital, White Haven, where she had been a patient for a year. She was the wife of George C. Edwards, a post office clerk.

Mrs. Edwards was a graduate of Claflin College, Orangeburg, S. C., and formerly had taught school.

She was active with the Inter-Racial Committee of the YMCA and the Women's Auxiliary of the South Branch YMCA. For a while she was employed as a social worker with the Luzerne County Board of Public Assistance.

Deceased was a member of Bethel AME Church and chairman of its Stewardess Board.

In addition to her husband, she is survived by two children, Maxwell and Mrs. George Reed, Chicago; sister, Mrs. Ella Page, Sumter, S. C.; brothers, Dr. C. W. Maxwell, Philadelphia; Dr. Andrew Maxwell, Paterson, N. J.; Henry Maxwell, St. Paul, Minn.

Funeral will be held from Bethel AME Church Tuesday at 2 with Rev. S. D. Lancaster officiating. Interment will be in Denison Cemetery.

Remains will lie in state from noon until funeral time.

Friends may call at Luther M. Kniffen Funeral Home, Monday night from 7 to 10.

Stephen Lloyd Maxwell, Sr.
1885-1930

STEPHEN LLOYD MAXWELL, SR.

1885-1930

Grandson of Andrew Henry Dibble, Sr.

STEPHEN LLOYD MAXWELL, SR., (1885-1930) *(Martha Dibble, Andrew H., Andrew C., Samuel, Samuel, John, Wakefield, Ebenezer, Thomas, Robert)* was born on Thursday, 28 May 1885, in Sumter, South Carolina, the seventh child of Martha Louisa Dibble and her husband the Honorable Henry Johnson Maxwell (1837-1906). Stephen died on Christmas Day, 1930, in Saint Paul, Minnesota.

His early education was at Claflin University, in Orangeburg. He ventured to Minnesota when working on the railroad, in the early 1900s. On 22 June, 1910, he married Ethel Mae Howard, of Saint Paul. He later worked as a barber for his father-in-law and later operated his own barber shop.

Stephen and his wife Ethel Mae became the parents of three sons:

> Lloyd Howard Maxwell, born 28 March 1911, died 21 December 1911.
>
> Ramon Howard Maxwell (adopted)
>
> Justice Stephen Lloyd Maxwell, Jr., (1921-2009), of Saint Paul.

ETHEL MAY HOWARD MAXWELL
1890-1959

Spouse of Stephen Lloyd Maxwell, Sr., Grandson

ETHEL MAY HOWARD (1890-1959) was born in Saint Paul, Minnesota the daughter of Obadiah D. Howard (1859-1938), who was born in Tennessee, and Elizabeth B. Hyde (1863-1927), who was born in Missouri, both spending most of their adult life in Saint Paul, Minnesota. They married on 26 September 1888, in Iowa.

Obadiah (1859-1938) owned and operated a barbershop in Saint Paul, and is later seen as an osteopath. He is seen living in Tennessee in the earlier census reports, and in 1900 U.S. Census, he and his family are living in Saint Paul, Minnesota. Ethel had one sister, Olive who became a pharmacist and businesswoman. Ethel received her Master's Degree from the University of Minnesota. She taught at Atlanta University's School of Social Work during the 1830s, returning to Minnesota and continuing her career in social work.

Andrew Dibble Maxwell, Sr., D.D.S.
1888-1958

ANDREW DIBBLE MAXWELL, D. D. S.

1888-1958

Grandson of Andrew Henry Dibble, Sr.

ANDREW DIBBLE MAXWELL, D.D.S., (1888-1958) (*Dental Surgeon*) (*Martha Dibble, Andrew H., Andrew C., Samuel, Samuel, John, Wakefield, Ebenezer, Thomas, Robert)* was born on 13 July 1888 in Sumter, South Carolina, the son of South Carolina State Senator Henry John Maxwell, Sr., of Charleston and his wife the former Martha Louisa Dibble of Camden. He died on 1 February 1958, in Morris Plains, New Jersey, after a long illness.

Andrew grew up in Sumter County and attended Claflin University for his primary education where he is listed in the Preparatory Class of 1908. Andrew attended Lincoln University in Pennsylvania, where he received his Bachelor of Arts Degree (B.A.) in 1913. He received his Doctor of Dental Surgery Degree (D.D.S.) from the Howard University College of Dentistry, in 1916. He married his first wife, Florence, in Washington D.C., on 1 March 1917, before returning to Sumter. They had two sons, mentioned below.

Andrew returned to Sumter where he practiced dentistry for several years before his move to Patterson, New Jersey. He lived and practiced Dentistry in Patterson for 44 Years, until his death in 1958. He married a second wife Camille Carrol Levy, on 30 December 1930, daughter of James Levy, a native of Camden and Florence. He married his third wife, Wilhelmina L. Dingle Shackleford, a native of South Carolina in 1947. Wilhelmina died in 1970, in New Jersey.

FLORENCE "FLOSSIE" ESTELLE PARNELL
1894-1928
Spouse of Andrew Dibble Maxwell, Grandson

FLORENCE ESTELLE PARNEL (1894-1928), a native of Washington, D. C., was the daughter of Ada V. Barnett who married a Parnell and then Harry C. Reeler. Florence married Andrew Dibble Maxwell on 1 March 1917, in Washington. They lived in Sumter, where both of their children were born. Their son Henry Johnson Maxwell, III (1918-1919), is buried in the Walker Cemetery, in Sumter, South Carolina.

Andrew Dibble Maxwell, Sr. and Florence became the parents of two sons:

> Henry Johnson Maxwell, III (1918-1919)
> Andrew Dibble Maxwell, Jr., D.D.S. (1920-1992)

Henry Johnson Maxwell, III (1918-1919)
Walker Cemetery, Sumter, S.C.

Josephine Heriot Dibble
1888-1974

JOSEPHINE "JOSIE" HERIOT DIBBLE MURPHY

1888-1974

Granddaughter of Andrew Henry Dibble, Sr.

JOSEPHINE HERIOT DIBBLE MURPHY (1888-1974) *(Eugene, Andrew H., Andrew C., Samuel, Samuel, John, Wakefield, Ebenezer, Thomas, Robert)* was born on 31 July 1888, in Camden, South Carolina, the eldest child of Eugene Heriot Dibble, Sr., (1855-1934), and his wife Sarah (Sallie) Rebecca Lee (1862-1955). She died in October 1974, in Atlanta, Georgia. They made their home on Fair Street, in Atlanta.

Her early education was at Mather Academy, a private Methodist School in Camden. She later attended school in Concord, North Carolina before attending Atlanta University, from which she graduated in elementary education, in 1909. Following her graduation, Josephine worked with the United States Census Bureau in

Washington, D. C., for the 1910 Census. She later went to Miles Memorial College in Birmingham, Alabama, to become head of the home economics department, and Fort Valley State College.

Cousin Josie worked at Atlanta University as Hostess to Diplomats from all around the world, for more than twenty-two years. During these years, she became friends with many well-known personalities, including the former First Lady, Mrs. Eleanor Roosevelt. She served as President of the National Alumni Association of the College for fifteen years, and left the office in 1966. She was an active member of and one of its founders of the local branch of the *Women's International League for Peace and Freedom*. She dedicated her life to helping young people from all parts of the world to obtain a college education in the United States. Mrs. Murphy travelled extensively, to Sweden, Denmark Moscow Leningrad, to name a few. In 1966, she took a three-month tour around the world, with her husband and two sisters: Ellie Dibble Palmer, and Miss. James Laurence Dibble. Cousin Josie was involved with our family research, very early, and was the first to share the "Andrew H. Dibble Freedom Papers" with me in the 1960s.

HARRY SAUNDERS MURPHY, SR.
1884-1975

Spouse of Josephine Heriot Dibble, Granddaughter

HARRY SAUNDERS MURPHY (1884-1975) was born in Camden, South Carolina, the nephew of Benjamin Murphy. He graduated from Hampton Institute, 1910 and received his Bachelor's Degree in Journalism in 1916 from the University of Wisconsin. Harry taught at Langston University in Oklahoma and Alabama State College before moving to Atlanta, as Vice President of Standard Life Insurance Company. Harry was one of the early businessmen of Atlanta, and in 1926, he founded *The House of Murphy Printers,* which he operated for more than forty years, retiring in 1969. Harry Saunders Murphy, Sr., married Josephine Heriot Dibble, who he had grown up with in Camden, on 3 September 1913, in Chicago, Illinois. She went with him while he attended the University of Wisconsin.

Josephine Heriot Dibble and her husband, Harry Saunders Murphy, Sr., became the parents of four children:

Doris Theodora Murphy (1915-2004)
married Maurice A. Coates
Sarah Elizabeth Murphy (1916-2015), married
(1) Atty. James G. Lemon
(2) Ernest Palmore
Mabel H. Murphy (1918-2006), married
(1) Ambassador Hugh H. Smythe, Ph.D.
(2) Robert Haith
Harry Saunders Murphy, Jr. (1927-1991)

Eugene Heriot Dibble, Jr, M.D.
1893-1968

EUGENE HERIOT DIBBLE, JR., M.D. LT. COL. U.S. ARMY, M.C.

1893-1968

Grandson of Andrew Henry Dibble, Sr.

EUGENE HERIOT DIBBLE, JR., MD (1893-1968) *(Eugene, Andrew H., Andrew C., Samuel, Samuel, John, Wakefield, Ebenezer, Thomas, Robert).* Eugene, a Physician, Coronel, U.S. Army, Medical Corps, was born in Camden, South Carolina, on 14 August 1893, the son of Eugene Heriot Dibble, Sr., and his wife Sarah "Sallie" Rebecca Lee of Camden, South Carolina. He died on 1 January 1968, in Tuskegee, Alabama.

His early education was obtained from Mather Academy in Camden, after which he graduated from Atlanta University in 1915. He received his Medical Doctor Degree (M.D.) from Howard University in 1919, followed by his Internship at Freedman's Hospital in 1920, in Washington, D. C. He moved to Tuskegee, Alabama, to do a surgery residency program at John Andrew Hospital at Tuskegee Institute. In 1923 he was appointed Surgeon-in-Chief at the Veterans Administration Hospital in Tuskegee. In 1925, he was appointed medical director of the John Andrew Memorial Hospital for the first time. In 1936, he returned to the Veterans Hospital as manager and medical director, with the rank of Colonel in the U.S. Army Medical Corps. Except for when he served as the medical directory of the Veterans Hospital, during World War II, he served as medical director at John Andrew Hospital from 1923 until his retirement. From 1935 until 1968, he served on the Board of Trustees of Meharry Medical College, in Nashville, Tennessee. Dr. Dibble sponsored annual J. A. Andrews Clinics, in which many well-known persons in the medical field came to Tuskegee. Dr. Dibble spent more than forty years at Tuskegee where he is known for the many contributions he made to field of medicine. He was a dedicated servant in his field.

He married the former Helen Anita Taylor, the daughter of Robert Robinson Taylor, the architect who designed many of the buildings, at Tuskegee Institute. Dr. Eugene Heriot Dibble, Jr., and his wife, the former Helen Anita Taylor had five children.

HELEN ANITA TAYLOR DIBBLE
1900-1980

Spouse of Eugene Heriot Dibble, Jr., M.D., Grandson

HELEN ANITA TAYLOR (1900-1980) *(Robert, Henry)* was born on 14 October 1900 in Cleveland, Ohio, the daughter of Robert Robinson Taylor (1868-1942) and his wife, the former Beatrice Frances Rochon (1874-1909). Her father, Robert R. Taylor was an architect and educator and the first African American to graduate from the Massachusetts Institute of Technology (MIT). With Booker T. Washington's encouragement, he settled at Tuskegee Institute, in 1892, where he designed numerous buildings between 1903 and 1932, including the library and Chapel. Robert R. Taylor was honored with a United States postage stamp in 2015. Helen spent most of her life at Tuskegee, dying in January 1980, in Washington, D. C., where she had gone to be with her children.

She married Dr. Eugene Heriot Dibble, Jr. in 1926, at Tuskegee, Alabama. They became the parents of five children: Helen, Eugene III, Robert, Ann, Clarice.

Eugene Heriot Dibble, Jr., MD & Helen A. Taylor Dibble
Tuskegee University Campus Cemetery
Tuskegee, Alabama

Harold Leonidas Dibble
1897-1982

HAROLD LEONIDAS DIBBLE

1897-1982

Grandson of Andrew Henry Dibble, Sr.

HAROLD LEONIDAS DIBBLE (1897-1982) (*Eugene, Andrew H., Andrew C., Samuel, Samuel, John, Wakefield, Ebenezer, Thomas, Robert*) son of Eugene Heriot Dibble, Sr. (1855-1934) and Sarah (Sallie) Rebecca Lee (1862-1955), was born on 29 May 1897, in Camden, South Carolina. He died in Oak Park, Michigan on 1 January 1982.

He attended Mather Academy in Camden for his primary education and Atlanta University for his high school and college education. During his early years, he was known as "Saul" by family members, and later was called "H. L," by those of the next generation. During the 1920s, he worked in his father's store, located at the corner of Broad and Dekalb Streets in Camden, South Carolina. He also worked in the Maxwell Grocery Store, which was owned and operated by his first cousin, John Moreau Maxwell, Sr., in Orangeburg, South Carolina. John M. Maxwell was the son of his Aunt Martha Louisa Dibble Maxwell, of Camden and later Sumter, S.C.

On 11 July 1922, he married Jessie Cornelia Moorer, of Orangeburg, South Carolina. H. L. (as he was affectionately called) and his wife Jessie lived in Patterson, New Jersey for several years before relocating to Washington, D. C., where he lived the remainder of his life. H. L. died in Oak Park, Michigan, while visiting with his only daughter, Carol. His daughter married The Honorable Julian Abele Cook, Jr. (1930-2017), of Washington, D. C., and Oak Park, Michigan. Julian is the grand-nephew of the distinguished architect Julian Francis Abele (1881-1950), who contributed to numerous buildings at Duke University, during the early 1900s.

H. L. served as Resident Manager of the Suburban Gardens Apartments, in Washington, D. C., from 1940 until his retirement in 1963. He was Vice President of York Services Mechanical Contracting Company of Washington, from 1963 until 1972. Harold Leonidas Dibble is buried beside his wife Jessie C. Moorer Dibble (1897-1972), in Fort Lincoln, Brentwood, Prince George County, Maryland. Harold and Jessie are the parents of one daughter.

JESSIE CORNELIA MOORER DIBBLE
1899-1972

Spouse of Harold Leonidas Dibble, Grandson

JESSIE CORNELIA MOORER 1899-1972) was born in Orangeburg, South Carolina, the daughter of Dr. Daniel Moorer (1855-1941) and Alice Louise Jackson (1865-1954), of Orangeburg. Dr. Moorer is a graduate of Claflin University and Meharry Medical School, in Nashville, Tennessee. He is the first person of color to practice medicine in Orangeburg, South Carolina. Jesse along with her siblings are also graduates of Claflin University, in Orangeburg. Jessie's early career including teaching and later worked alongside her husband in the Suburban Gardens Apartments, in Washington, D.C.

Harold L. Dibble and Jessie C. Moorer Dibble
Fort Lincoln Cemetery, Prince George County, Marland

Ellie Naudin Dibble
1898-1973

ELLIE NAUDIN DIBBLE PALMER

1898- 1973

Granddaughter of Andrew Henry Dibble, Sr.

ELLIE NAUDIN DIBBLE PALMER (1898-1973) *(Eugene, Andrew H., Andrew C., Samuel, Samuel, John, Wakefield, Ebenezer, Thomas, Robert)* was born on 12 November 1898, in Camden, South Carolina the daughter of Eugene Heriot Dibble, Sr.(1855-1934) and his wife Sarah "Sallie" Rebecca Lee (1862-1959), of Camden. Ellie died in Sumter on 15 May 1973.

Her early education was at Mather Academy, a private Methodist School in Camden. She later attended Atlanta University for her high school and normal training. She married Edmund Perry Palmer, Sr., of Columbia. Ellie worked alongside her husband who owned and operated the Palmer Funeral Home, in Sumter that was established in 1923.

Ellie Naudin Dibble and Edmund Perry Palmer became the parents of four sons:

> Robert John Palmer, II (1926-1995)
> James Laurence Dibble Palmer, MD (1928-2009)
> Edmund Perry Palmer, II (1935-2010)
> Andrew Dibble Palmer (1939-1960)

EDMUND PERRY PALMER, SR.
1896-1949

Spouse of Ellie Naudin Dibble, Granddaughter

EDMUND PERRY PALMER, SR. (1896-1949) *(Robert)* was born on 26 June 1896 in Columbia, South Carolina, the son of The Honorable Robert John Palmer (1849-1928), and his wife the former Adelaide Perry. His father served in the South Carolina State House in 1876-1878, representing Richland County. Edmund was the second son and had eight sisters. Edmund died on 5 November 1949, in Tuskegee, Alabama, where he had gone for medical treatment with his brother-in-law, Dr. Eugène Heriot Dibble, Jr., who was medical director there.

Edmund is a graduate of Claflin University in Orangeburg. He married Ellie Naudin Dibble of Camden. He was the first person of color Funeral Director and Embalmer in Sumter County. He founded the Palmer Funeral business in 1923, in Sumter County. He and his wife Ellie worked together, over many years to grow and develop this business, until his death in 1949.

Andrew Henry Dibble, III, M.D.
1900-1946

ANDREW HENRY DIBBLE, III, M.D.

1900-1946

Grandson of Andrew Henry Dibble, Sr.

ANDREW HENRY DIBBLE, III (1900-1946) *(Eugene, Andrew H., Andrew C., Samuel, Samuel, John, Wakefield, Ebenezer, Thomas, Robert)* was born on 14 June 1900 in Camden, South Carolina, the son of Eugene Heriot Dibble, Sr., and his wife, Sarah (Sallie) Rebecca Lee, of Camden. He died from a sudden heart attack, on 30 May 1946, Jefferson, Kentucky.

Andrew graduated from Mather Academy, in Camden in 1918, and attended Atlanta University for his high school and college work, graduating with a Bachelor of Science (B.S.) Degree from Atlanta University, in 1924. In 1928, Andrew graduated from Maharry Medical School in Nashville, followed by his internship at Freedman's Hospital in Washington. D. C. from 1929-1930. He practiced medicine in Warrenton, Virginia from 1931 to 1941. He then took a Post graduate Course, U. S. Public Health Service in venereal diseases at Freedman's Hospital, in Washington, in 1941, after which he took another Post Graduate Course for three months, at the U. S. Public Health Service in Bethesda, Maryland. In January 1942, he worked for the U. S. Public Health Service in Louisville, Kentucky. In January 1946, he became director of the Central Louisville Health Center.

Andrew married Thelma A. West on 3 May 1933, in Washington, D. C. He is seen in the *City Directory* for Washington, D. C., in 1930 and 1933. They are seen in the 1940 Census, where he and Thelma are living in Warrenton, Virginia. By 1945, Andrew is working for the United States Public Health Service, and assigned to the Central Louisville Health Center. Andrew Henry Dibble, III, died two weeks before he was to turn 46 years old, in Louisville, Kentucky, of a heart attack. He is buried in the family plot of his father, Eugene H. Dibble, Sr., in Cedar Cemetery, in Camden.

Miss James Laurence Dibble
1902-1975

MISS JAMES LAURENCE DIBBLE

1902-1975

Granddaughter of Andrew Henry Dibble, Sr.

Miss JAMES LAURENCE DIBBLE (1902-1975) (*Eugene, Andrew H., Andrew C., Samuel, Samuel, John, Wakefield, Ebenezer, Thomas, Robert*) was born on 4 September 1902, in Camden, South Carolina, the daughter of Eugene Heriot Dibble, Sr., (1855-1934), and his wife Sarah "Sallie" Rebecca Lee (1862-1959), of Camden. James Laurence died in Camden on 31 July 1976, in Camden.

Her early education was at Browning Home/Mather Academy, a private Methodist school in Camden. She later attended Atlanta University for her high school and normal training. She taught school in Camden for many years, and lived in the family home, that her father built.

Retired Teacher
Miss Dibble Dies

CAMDEN — Miss James L. Dibble of 808 Lafayette St. died Saturday at the Kershaw Memorial Hospital.

Born in Camden, she was a daughter of the late Eugene H. and Sallie Rebecca Lee Dibble. She was a retired public school teacher in Camden.

Surviving are a brother, H. L. Dibble of Washington, and many nieces and nephews.

Services will be 5 p.m. today at Trinity United Methodist Church, with burial in Cedar Cemetery.

The family suggests that those who wish may make memorials to Trinity United Methodist Church.

Collins Funeral Home is in charge.

Catherine Cleveland Dibble
1875-1947

CATHERINE CLEVELAND DIBBLE MARTIN

1872-1947

Granddaughter of Andrew Henry Dibble, Sr.

CATHERINE CLEVELAND DIBBLE MARTIN (1872-1947) *(Andrew H., Andrew H., Andrew C., Samuel, Samuel, John, Wakefield, Ebenezer, Thomas, Robert)* was born on 18 November 1872, in Camden, SC, the only child of Andrew Henry Dibble, Jr. (1850-1934) and his wife Elizabeth Levy (1856-1933), of Camden. Catherine Cleveland Dibble Martin died on 18 December 1947, at her home at 130 Martin Street in Charlotte, North Carolina.

Catherine attended Browning Home, Mather Academy in Camden, for her primary education. Catherine attended high school and graduated from the Normal Program at Claflin University, as salutatorian of her class in 1889. Claflin is a Methodist Episcopal School in Orangeburg, South Carolina Catherine became a teacher. In 1893 she married Dr. James Daniel Martin (1864-1941), of Mechanicsville, South Carolina. Catherine taught high school for many years in North Carolina, They lived at 130 Martin Street, (named for Dr. Martin), which was adjacent to Johnson C. Smith University campus.

JAMES DANIEL MARTIN, A.B., A.M., Ph.D.
1864-1941

Spouse of Catherine Cleveland Dibble, Granddaughter

JAMES DANIEL MARTIN (1864-1941), A.B., A.M., Ph.D. was born on 9 May 1864, the son of John and Eliza Porter Martin, of Mechanicsville, Sumter County, South Carolina. He died on 12 May 1941 in Charlotte, North Carolina.

James received his A.B. Degree from Biddle University, in 1888. He received his Master's (A.M.) Degree, in 1911, and his Ph.D. Degree, also from Biddle University, which is today, Johnson C. Smith University, in Charlotte. He did graduate work at Columbia University where he became a Latin Scholar. He was active with the Presbyterian Church where he held numerous positions and traveled to numerous places, such as, Louisville, Kentucky, in 1908, Chicago in 1914, Washington, D. C. in 1919 and to Zurich, Switzerland in 1913.

He served as Assistant Principal of the State Normal School in Salisbury, North Carolina and in 1891, he was elected principal of the State Normal School in Goldsboro, N.C. He then returned to Biddle University in 1892, as professor Latin and history, where he remained for 36 years, retiring in 1928. In 1928, he became President of Brainerd Institute, in Chester, South Carolina, where he remained until 1934, when he again retired and returned to his home at 130 Martin Street, in Charlotte.

Catherine Cleveland Dibble Martin and James Daniel Martin are the parents of nine children:

        Andrew Dibble Martin, MD (1894-1918)
        James Daniel Martin, Jr. (1896-1897)
        John Franklin Martin, DDS (1897-1949)
        James Dwight Martin, DDS (1900-1980)
        Elizabeth Bernice Martin (1903-1967)
        Catherine Beatrice Martin (1905-2001)
        Louise Wendella Martin (1907-2000)
        Beauregard Langford Martin (1911-1991) & twin sister Mary Panella Martin (1911-1911)

Pinewood Cemetery, Charlotte, North Carolina

James Daniel Martin Family

Ellie Naomi Levy
1888-1947

ELLIE NAOMI LEVY THOMPSON

1888-1947

Granddaughter of Andrew Henry Dibble, Sr.

ELLIE NAOMI LEVY THOMPSON (1888-1947) *(Ella Dibble, Andrew H., Andrew C., Samuel, Samuel, John, Wakefield, Ebenezer, Thomas, Robert),* was born the eldest daughter of Ella Naudin Dibble and her husband, Theodore John Levy, Jr., of Camden and Orangeburg, South Carolina. She died in Washington, D.C., on 15 June 1947. Ellie attended Claflin University for her high school and college training, graduating with a Bachelor of Science Degree (B.S.) in 1909. She taught at South Carolina College in Orangeburg. Ellie married Wesley Hampton Thompson, a native of Columbia, on September 14, 1910, at Trinity Methodist Episcopal Church, in Orangeburg. He was born on 7 December 1877 and died on 26 July, 1920, in Columbia, as the result of a fire. He worked for the postal service.

Ellie relocated to Washington, District of Columbia, about 1919. In the 1920's, and is seen in the city directories during the 1920's working for the National Benefit Insurance Company, in Washington. Ellie is seen in the 1930 and 1940 censuses living with her sister and family on Randolph Place in Washington, D. C. By 1940, Ellie is seen as a saleswoman and her son James is a salesman for an insurance company. Her son James served in the United States Army as a First Lieutenant. Ellie and Wesley had one son, James Lewis Thompson (1914-1947), who was born in Columbia, S.C., and raised in Washington, D.C. His sudden death was on 19 November 1947, after suffering from the loss of his mother, a few months earlier. She is interned at Lincoln Memorial Cemetery, Prince George County, Maryland.

131

Elizabeth Catherine Levy
1889-1955

ELIZABETH CATHERINE LEVY DAVIS

1889-1955

Granddaughter of Andrew Henry Dibble, Sr.

ELIZABETH CATHERINE LEVY DAVIS (1889-1955) *(Ella Dibble, Andrew H., Andrew C. Samuel, Samuel, John, Wakefield, Ebenezer, Thomas, Robert)*, was born the second daughter of Ella Naudin Dibble and her husband, Theodore John Levy, Jr., of Camden and Orangeburg, South Carolina. She died in Washington, D.C., on 23 May 1955.

Ellie attended Claflin University for her high school and college training, graduating with a Bachelor of Science Degree (B.S.) in 1910. She married Harry Winfred Davis (1892-1975), a native of Hampton, Virginia, who was working at South Carolina State University, in Orangeburg, when they met.

The 1910 Census, we see Elizabeth living at home with her parents in Orangeburg, and teaching at South Carolina State College. The enumerator for this census is the Reverend Dr. J. B. Taylor. This is the first United States Census where minorities are used as enumerators. On 4 January 1920, the date of the 1920 Census, we now see Elizabeth and Harry living in Washington with their young son John who was born in Orangeburg, and was now one year and two months.

Elizabeth is working as a clerk for an insurance company and we see her sister Ella and her son James, are now living with her on Randolph Place. By the 1940 Census, Ellie and James are still living with the Davis family. Elizabeth "Lizzie," along with her sister Ellie relocated to Washington, District of Columbia about 1919. The 1930, 1940 and 1950 Censuses, Harry is working as a waiter for the railroad. Elizabeth and her husband are interred at Lincoln Memorial Cemetery.

Elizabeth Catherine Levy and Harry W. Davis became the parents of three children:

John Dibble Davis, 25 October 1918, S. C.- 9 April 1989, D. C. m. Martha L. Steele
Ella Naomi Davis, 19 December 1922 - 27 Oct 2002 m. Thomas A. Jordan
Nancy Elizabeth Davis, 19 August 1924 - 15 March 2004

HARRY WINFRED DAVIS
1892-1975

Spouse to Elizabeth Catherine Levy, Granddaughter

HARRY WINFRED DAVIS (1892-1975) was born on 3 October 1892, the son of Andrew Davis (1858-1949) and his wife the former Frances Nash (1866-1955), of Hampton, Virginia. Harry was one of seven sons and one daughter. He died on October 1975, in Washington D. C. He and his family lived on Randolph Place, N. W. Washington, D.C., for many years, and this is where they raised their family. He spent his later years living with his eldest daughter, Ella Naomi Davis Jordan.

His World War II Registration, states that he is 5 feet, 7 inches, weighs 160 pounds and has brown hair, hazel eyes. He is working for the Railroad Company on his World War I and II, Registrations.

DAVIS, ELIZABETH LEVY. On Monday, May 23, 1955, ELIZABETH LEVY DAVIS of 143 Randolph pl. n.w., devoted wife of Harry W. Davis, mother of John Dibble Davis, Ella Davis Jordan and Nancy E. Davis; sister of Theodore Levy. She also is survived by five grandchildren and many other relatives and friends. After 4 p.m. Wednesday, May 25, friends may call at the Frazier Funeral Home, 389 Rhode Island ave. n.w., where services will be held on Thursday, May 26, at 10:30 a.m. Rev. C. Shelby Rooks officiating. Interment Lincoln Memorial Cemetery.

Eugene Dibble Levy
1890-1958

EUGENE DIBBLE LEVY

1890-1958

Grandson of Andrew Henry Dibble, Sr.

EUGENE DIBBLE LEVY (1890-1958) (*Ella Dibble, Andrew H., Andrew C., Samuel, Samuel, John, Wakefield, Ebenezer, Thomas, Robert),* was born on 3 September 1890, in Orangeburg, South Carolina the son of Ella Naudin Dibble (1865-1913) and her husband Theodore John Levy, Jr. (1865-1917), of Camden and Orangeburg. He died on 20 January 1958, in District Heights, Prince George County, Maryland.

Eugene attended Claflin University, in Orangeburg, for his lower school and high school education. He married Idalean Elizabeth McLain on 30 September 1912, in Camden, Kershaw County, South Carolina. He is seen in the 1910 Census, in Orangeburg, working as a nineteen-year-old barber, and by 1916, he and his wife are living in Spartanburg, where he is working as a barber. In 1920-1922, Eugene and Idalean are living Columbia, South Carolina. According to the *City Directories* of 1924 to 1927 he is seen working in Washington, D. C., as a barber and by the 1930 Census he is living in Fairmont Heights, Prince George County, Maryland, where he owns his own home. His World War II Registration, gives the following information: race: white; 5 foot-3 inches; 135 pounds; eyes, brown; hair, red; complexion, light.

Eugene Dibble Levy and Idalean Elizabeth McLain Levy are the parents of four children:

> Theodore John Levy, III (1913-1980)
>> married Ida Beatrice Mosley (1918-)
> Elizabeth McLain Levy (1915-2004)
>> married Lester N. Porter (1906-2004)
> Dennis Dibble Levy (1917-1996)
> Idalean Helen Levy (1925-1982)

IDALEAN ELIZABETH MCLAIN LEVY
1894-1982

Spouse of Eugene Dibble Levy, Grandson

IDALEAN ELIZABETH McLAIN (1894-1982) was born on 16 September 1894, in Camden, Kershaw County, South Carolina, the daughter of George Weston McLain (1846-1917) and his second wife, Elizabeth Calcock Lloyd (1858- 1951). She died in September 1982, in Prince George County, Maryland.

Idalean was one of seventeen children born to George W. McLain. His first wife, Anna Rebecca (1849-1889) was the mother of twelve children, and his second wife was the mother of five children. There were three sons and fourteen daughters. They all grew up in Camden and had their home at 1413 Lyttleton Street. They attended Browning Home/Mather Academy. Idalean married Eugene Dibble Levy on 30 September 1912, in Camden. Idalean is mentioned in several United States Census Reports and city directories, alongside her husband, Eugene. Idalean is seen as a seamstress and in the 1930 Census working in a hotel in Washington, D.C.

Eugene and Idalean are interred the Maryland National Memorial Park, in Price George County, Maryland.

Wilhelmina Lee Dibble
1907-1984

WILHELMINA LEE DIBBLE WARFIELD RETTIG

1907-1984

Granddaughter of Andrew Henry Dibble, Sr.

WILHELMINA LEE DIBBLE WARFIELD RETTIG (1908-1984) (*Dennis, Andrew H., Andrew, C., Samuel, Samuel, John, Warfield, Ebenezer, Thomas, Robert*) was born in Camden, South Carolina the only child of Rufus Dennis Dibble and his wife the former Elizabeth (Bessie) Lee Greenlee. She died on 8 January 1984, in Dallas, Texas.

She attended Mather Academy in Camden for her primary education, and Atlanta University for her High School education. She attended Howard University, in Washington, District of Columbia, where she received her Bachelor of Science (B.S.) Degree, in 1929. Wilhelmina received her Master of Science (M.S.) Degree at Columbia University, in New York, in 1930. She married William Alonzo Warfield, of Washington, D. C., on 31 December 1928, in Bishopville, South Carolina. He graduated from the Howard University College of Medicine, in 1930.

Wilhelmina's teaching career began at Bethune Cookman College in Daytona Beach, Florida. Later, she moved to Tyler, Texas, where she taught mathematics at Butler College and then at Texas College. After moving to Dallas, Texas, Wilhelmina taught mathematics at Booker T. Washington High School and was one of the original members of the faculty at Lincoln High School. While working in the Dallas Independent School District, she earned a Master of Science (M.S.) Degree in Counseling from North Texas State University and became the first person of color to serve as a counselor in the district. She was acclaimed as an outstanding Counselor at James Madison High School, Pinkston High School, Booker T. Washington High School, and North Dallas High School. Wilhelmina retired in 1974.

Wilhelmina (sometimes called "Willie" and sometimes "Billie") was a member of the Alpha Kappa Alpha Sorority, Inc., Hamilton Park United Methodist Church where she served with the Altar and Flower Guild, and was a faithful and talented member of the Royal Art Club. She was known as a great humanitarian who received her greatest joy in doing for, and helping others

Wilhelmina later married Eolus Von Rettig, Sr. (1908-1983), of Texas, who preceded her in death, on 29 April, 1983. They are interred in Rest Land Memorial Park, Dallas. Wilhelmina is the mother of two children:

> Wilhelmina Dibble Warfield (1932-2004)
> > married Van Buren McClellan (1930-1962)
> Eolus Von Rettig, Jr. (1946-2005)

WILLIAM ALONZO WARFIELD, M.D.
1902-1969

Spouse of Wilhelmina Lee Dibble, Granddaughter

WILLIAM ALONZO WARFIELD, MD (1902-1969) was born in Washington, D.C., the son of Dr. William A. Warfield, Sr., and his wife, the former Violet B. Thompson. He graduated the Howard University College of Medicine in 1929. He practiced medicine in Washington, D. C. He married Wilhelmina L. Dibble, on 31 December 1928, in Bishopville, S.C. He had one daughter, Wilhelmina Dibble Warfield (1932-2004). He later married a second wife in Washington, D.C.

John Benjamin Taylor, Jr.
1903-1980

JOHN BENJAMIN TAYLOR, JR.

1903-1980

Grandson of Andrew Henry Dibble, Sr.

JOHN BENJAMIN TAYLOR, JR. (1903-1980*) (Harriet Dibble, Andrew H., Andrew C., Samuel, Samuel, John, Wakefield, Ebenezer, Thomas, Robert)*. John was born on 26 July 1903, in Orangeburg, South Carolina, the eldest of four children born to the Reverend Dr. John Benjamin Taylor, Sr, and his wife Harriet Catherine Dibble, of Camden. John Benjamin Taylor, Jr. died in Washington, D. C. on 10 December 1980, at age 77.

As a youth, he spent most of his summers visiting his grandmother, Ellie Naomi Naudin Dibble in Camden, where he played with many of his first cousins. His grandfather, Andrew Henry Dibble, Sr., had died while his mother was still an infant and John's mother also died while he was a youth.

When the first family reunion was held in July 1979, he was most excited. Several years prior to this reunion, my sister Catherine and I had uncovered numerous small things concerning our family research. Dad was extremely excited and fascinated about the many discoveries, concerning his heritage. Much of the information discovered, only confirmed, and substantiated many of the family stories that had been passed down for several generations. At this first reunion, he was able to see his two living first cousins and many other relatives that he had not seen for many years, as well as meet new relatives that he had only heard about. This was one of the highlights of his life, to be able to be a part of this reunion, which celebrated his grandfather, Andrew Henry Dibble's maternal heritage, documenting when Andrew's Great-Grandmother, Catherine Cleveland entered the British Colony of South Carolina, in 1764. (Bennie died the next year, only experiencing one reunion.)

John, who was called "Bennie" most of his life, attended Claflin University for his elementary school education, graduating from the Preparatory Program in 1923, and receiving his Teacher's Certificate in 1926. It was understood that he would attend Claflin, as did both his father and mother. He experienced the dormitory life and was an academically strong student, who also excelled in all the sports of his school. During his high school and college years, he played football, baseball, and tennis. In 1927-1928, he attended South Carolina State College where he also played football. He became a determined and seasoned athlete, who loved the game of all sports.

While at Claflin, he met and later married a college schoolmate, Amanda Felicia Allen, and they became the parents of four daughters and one son. After graduating from Claflin, he worked numerous jobs that were available for people of color, during this period in the south, due to segregation and then the depression, which affected most people in the country. During the early years of his marriage, he and his wife taught school in several South Carolina rural communities, including Saint George. He worked in Greenville, S. C., Ashley, Kentucky, and Asbury Part, New Jersey. The family relocated to the Nation's Capital during the World War II era when many persons left their homes in the south, to obtain jobs that were available elsewhere.

Bennie had a lighthearted and easy-going personality, and was always happy and jovial about most things. He loved to kid and joke around and tease his fellow man. He had a hardy laugh and would laugh harder than anyone else, at his own jokes. Playing cards was where he got the most enjoyment, although he was an avid checker player during those earlier years. Bennie and his sister, Catherine, often had regular meetings to play pinochle with their friends and card partners. He and his sister were very close, especially after their father and sister died a few months apart. He was avid reader, spending hours at a time reading almost anything, including newspapers, magazines, keeping abreast of what was going on in the world.

On November 26, 1978, Bennie and Felicia celebrated their 50th Wedding Anniversary, with their children, grandchildren and many relatives and friends in attendance. Bennie's first cousin Harold L. Dibble, (who lived in Washington) was among those attending. As a grandfather, he spent time with his grandchildren, when they came along. He took time out to play ball with his grandsons, and to take them to a baseball game. When Wendell and Will, both at age 14, received their *Eagle Scout Awards*, from the Boy Scouts of America, he was there, to celebrate along with his grandsons, as a proud grandfather. When his granddaughter Felicia received her Bachelor of Arts Degree (B.A.) from George Washington University in 1978 and when his grandson, Wendell received his M.D. Degree in 1979, from Howard University College of Medicine, he was able to attend both graduations as a proud grandfather.

AMANDA FELICIA ALLEN TAYLOR
1907-2004

Spouse to John Benjamin Taylor, Jr., Grandson

Amanda Felicia Allen Taylor was born on 12 June 1907, in Seneca, South Carolina, a small town in the most western part of South Carolina. She was the youngest daughter of five children born to Amanda Stegall Allen. Felicia's step-father was Alexander Allen. Amanda Felicia died on 9 November 2004, at 97 years, 5 months, in Columbia, SC.

Felicia's maternal grandfather is Spencer Soorcher Stegall (1818-1898), and her earliest Stegall ancestor, William (1577-1650) came to America, from London on May 16, 1635, arriving in Williamsburg, Virginia. William's descendant, Richard (1754-1836), who was born in Virginia, was the first Stegall to settle in Pendleton District, South Carolina. This Richard had numerous children and three wives.

Amanda Felicia's early education was in Seneca, later enrolling in grades 4th through 8th grades, at Allen Home, a Methodist Boarding School in Asheville, North Carolina. In 1922, she entered Claflin University Preparatory School for her high school and earned her Normal School Degree in 1928. Felicia was reserved and a very serious person, about each task she undertook, and this demeanor continued the remainder of her life. While attending Claflin, she met and later married a college schoolmate, John Benjamin Taylor, Jr. Bennie, and Felicia became the parents of four daughters and one son.

Feleicia was employed for more than thirty years working as a cartographer for several federal government agencies, in the Washington D. C. area. She retired from the United Stated Naval Oceanographic Office in 1972. She loved her work drafting maps as they pertained to military bases, small, uninhabited islands across the globe, as well as charting many waters, including the oceans for hurricanes, iceberg, and other atmospheric conditions. She was an expert in world geography and was knowledgeable of many small places, unknown to the average person. She developed and drew these much-needed maps and charts. She received numerous citations and awards for her dedicated and devotional work in a male dominated field. Oftentimes, she was the only female working in her immediate area.

Felicia, like her mother, was an adventurous and inquisitive person, who began traveling early in her life and continued to do so up until the late 1990s, when she was in her late eighties. Among her many travels, was her six-week trip to Europe in June 1963, aboard the *Queen Elizabeth I*, and returning to the United States on the *Queen Mary*. She visited ten western European countries, and was able to see many fascinating and interesting places and sites she had read about for many years.

Felicia was a Charter Member of the Washington Chapter of the Claflin Alumni Association. In 1991, she was Founder's Day Honoree at Claflin University, in recognition of her contributions to her alma mater. In 1993, Amanda Felicia moved back to South Carolina after more than seventy years, to live with her daughter.

Felicia and Bennie are the parents of five children: Catherine, Joan, Dorothy, Elsie, and John.

TAYLOR

John Benjamin, Jr.
July 26, 1903
In Orangeburg, SC
Dec. 10, 1980, in DC

Amanda Felicia
Allen
June 12, 1907 in Seneca, SC
Nov. 9, 2004 in Columbia, SC
Born: Seneca, SC
Died: Columbia, SC

Taylor Plot
Orangeburg Cemetery
Orangeburg, South Carolina

Catherine Springs Taylor
1907-1991

CATHERINE SPRINGS TAYLOR HUMPHREY

1907-1991

Granddaughter of Andrew Henry Dibble, Sr.

CATHERINE SPRINGS TAYLOR HUMPHREY (*Harriet Dibble, Andrew H., Andrew C., Samuel, Samuel, Lt. John, Wakefield, Ebenezer, Thomas, Robert***).** Catherine was born on 1 May 1907 in Camden, South Carolina, the daughter of Harriet Catherine Dibble (1873-1918), and her husband Reverend Dr. John Benjamin Taylor, Sr. (1867-1936), of North and Orangeburg, South Carolina. She was the third child born to this union. Catherine had two brothers and one sister, John B. Taylor, Jr. (1903-1980), Naudin

Dibble Taylor (1905-1906) and Harriet Louise Taylor (1910-1937). Catherine died on February 12, 1991, in Washington, District of Columbia.

Catherine Springs Taylor was named for the sister of her grandfather Andrew Henry Dibble who was Catherine Smith Springs (1828-1895), of Charleston and Summerville. Catherine S. Springs was the Godmother, and aunt to her mother, Harriet Catherine Dibble.

Catherine's early life was spent in several parsonages of the South Carolina Methodist Church where her father served several districts as Pastor, Presiding Elder and Superintendent. Following the death of her mother in 1918, when Catherine was only 10 years old, she attended school at Allen Home, a Methodist boarding School in Asheville, North Carolina. Although the family had a home in Orangeburg, she was able to experience the dormitory life along with other young girls, when she attended Claflin University for her high school and college work. She graduated from high school at Claflin in the Preparatory Program, in 1924, and received her Teacher's Certificate from Claflin University in 1926.

She began her professional career by teaching in elementary schools in Orangeburg County, South Carolina, from the late 1920s until about 1940. She married William Walter Humphrey, a school principal in Orangeburg School District, in 1927. She relocated to New York City in the early 1940s, prior to her moving to Washington, D.C. in the late 1940s. She worked for several Federal agencies prior to her retirement in 1972 from the Army Division of the Department of Defense.

Catherine was an active person with many interests. She was an avid reader, and enjoyed doing handiwork such as crochet, knitting, etc. She was active with the Claflin University Alumni Association and was an active member of Mount Olivet Lutheran Church in Washington. She travelled extensively, and enjoyed playing cards with several Pinochle groups.

When the *Naudin-Dibble Family Reunion* was started in 1979, she was one of four surviving grandchildren of Ellie N. Naudin and Andrew H. Dibble. Because she possessed a very keen memory for details, she was a key resource person in helping to develop the family history. In 1989, she helped to unveil a plaque in front of the Bonds Conway House, in Camden, S.C., honoring her great-great- grandfather, who was an early businessman in Camden.

Catherine was the last surviving granddaughter of Andrew and Ellie. Catherine Springs Taylor Humphrey is interred at Fort Lincoln Cemetery, Brentwood, Maryland.

Catherine had three daughters:

> Emma Hattie Humphrey, Ph.D., J.D.
> > m. Major Bailey P. Pendergrass, Jr. (USAF, Ret.)
> Wilhelmina, and Joanne

Great-Grandchildren
of
Andrew Henry Dibble, Sr. and Ellie Naomi Naudin

*Through the will of the majority is in all cases to
prevail, that will, to be rightful, must be reasonable;
the minority possess their equal right, which equal
laws must protect, and to violate would be oppression.*

Thomas Jefferson
Inaugural Address, 1801

Great-Grandchildren of
Andrew Henry Dibble and Ellie Naomi Naudin

Andrew Henry Dibble and his wife, Ellie Naomi Naudin had about fifty-three Great-Grandchildren, born between 1894 and 1942. (Not including those recently found.) The oldest of these great-grandchildren are the children of their granddaughter Catherine Cleveland Dibble Martin, who had nine children, with seven living to adulthood, and only the three great-granddaughters having descendants.

Andrew and Ellie's eldest daughter, Martha Louisa Dibble Maxwell (1846-1923), had eight children, which included three daughters and five sons. These eight grandchildren, had thirteen great-grandchildren, with ten reaching adulthood. These ten great-grandchildren included three females and seven males.

Their son Eugene Heriot Dibble, Sr. (1855-1934), had six children: three daughters and three sons. Of these six children, four married and had families, two daughters and two sons, which resulted in fourteen great-grandchildren, which are seven females and seven males.

Andrew's second daughter, Ella Naudin Dibble Levy (1865-1913), had two daughters and one son. These three grandchildren produced eight great-grandchildren, which consists of four females and four males.

Rufus Dennis Dibble (1867-1961), the youngest son of Andrew Henry Dibble, Sr., had one daughter, Wilhelmina Lee Dibble, who had two children. These two great-grandchildren are one son and one daughter.

Harriet "Hattie" Catherine Dibble (1873-1918), the youngest daughter of Andrew Henry Dibble, Sr. had four children, (her son Naudin Dibble Taylor died as an infant, and daughter Harriet Louise, died as a young adult.), with one son and one daughter reaching adulthood, marrying, and having families. Therefore, this daughter produced eight great-grandchildren: seven female, and one male.

Of these fifty-three great-grandchildren, about forty-eight lived to adulthood and lived and prospered in the twentieth century. They pursued many different careers that were available to them, including several attorneys, businessmen, dentists, judges, physicians, social workers, career military, with one United States Ambassador, and more than twenty in the field of education, with several receiving a Doctor of Philosophy (Ph.D.) Degree. Today, only ten (10) of this generation are still with us, with all of them in their eighties and nineties. Most of these great-grandchildren lived full lives during the twentieth century, with a few living into the twenty-first century.

With this generation of the descendants of Andrew and Ellie Naudin Dibble, most of them had left the South and were now living all over the country and some living abroad. They were working in all types of jobs, businesses, and professions.

In this section, I will not discuss all forty-eight of the great-grandchildren, but will try to highlight some of these of this generation who descend from each of the six children who had families. I have used numerous documents, materials, and other information that is available in the public domain for this generation, which includes interviews, funeral programs, newspaper articles and obituaries and of course, the internet. I have not included any of this generation who are still living.

Great-Grandchildren of Andrew Henry Dibble, Sr., and Ellie Naomi Naudin:

James Wendell Page (1912-1966)

John Moreau Maxwell (1909-1962)

Cassandra Elizabeth Maxwell Birnie, LLB (1910-1974)

Nunez Cardozo Maxwell (1913-1916)

Catherine Louise Maxwell Kersey Vincent (1914-1985)

Charles Wendell Maxwell, II, D.Litt. (1915-1965)

Henry Cardozo Maxwell (1923-1995)

Christopher Maxwell Edwards (1915-1876)

Selina Louise Edwards Reed (1921-1985)

Lloyd Howard Maxwell (1911-1911)

Justice Stephen Lloyd Maxwell, Jr., LLB (1920-2009)

Henry Johnson Maxwell (1918-1919)

Andrew Dibble Maxwell, Jr., DDS (1920-1992)

Andrew Dibble Martin, MD (1894-1918)

James Daniel Martin, Jr., (1896-1897)

John Franklin Martin, DDS (1897-1949)

James Dwight Martin, DDS (1900-1980)

Elizabeth Bernice Martin Richardson (1903-1967)

Catherine Beatrice Martin Means (1905-2001)

Louise Wendella Martin White (1907-2000)

Beauregard Langford Martin (1911-1991) and his twin Mary Panella Martin (1911-1911)

Doris Theodora Murphy Coates (1915-2004)

Sarah Elizabeth Murphy Lemon Palmore (1916-2015)

Mabel Hancock Murphy Smythe Haith, Ph.D. (1918-2006)

Harry Saunders Murphy, Jr. (1927-1991)

Helen Beatrice Dibble Cannaday (1927-1996)

Eugene Heriot Dibble, III (1929-2014)

Robert Taylor Dibble, M.D.

Ann Janice Dibble Cook Jordan

Clarice Anita Dibble Walker

Carol Annette Dibble Cook

Robert John Palmer (1926-1995)

James Laurence Dibble Palmer, M.D. (1928-2009)

Edmund Perry Palmer, Jr., (1935-2010)

Andrew Dibble Palmer (1939-1960)

Lieutenant James L. Thompson, (U.S. Army) (1913-1947)

John Dibble Davis (1918-1989)

Ella Naomi Davis Jordan (1922-2002)

Nancy Elizabeth Davis (1924-2004)

Theodore John Levy, III (1913-1980)

Elizabeth McLain Levy Porter (1915-2004)

Dennis Dibble Levy (1917-1996)
Idalean Helen Levy Jackson (1925-1982)

Wilhelmina Lee Warfield McClelland (1932-2004)
Eolius Von Rettig, Jr., (1946-2005)

Catherine Allen Taylor Howard McConnell (1929-1996)
Joan Felicia Taylor Jackson Lee
Dorothy Bennie Taylor Howard
Elsie Louise Taylor Goins
John Benjamin Taylor, III
Emma Hattie Humphrey Pendergrass, Ph.D., J.D. (1928-2022)
Wilhelmina Palmer Humphrey Franklin
Joan Suzanna Hanna Johnson

Great-Grandchildren of Andrew Henry Dibble, Sr.

Great-Grandchildren of Andrew Henry Dibble, Sr.

Elizabeth Bernice Martin

1903-1967

ELIZABETH BERNICE MARTIN RICHARDSON

1903-1967

Great-Granddaughter of Andrew Henry Dibble, Sr.

ELIZABETH BERNICE MARTIN RICHARDSON (1903-1967) *(Catherine Dibble, Andrew H., Jr., Andrew H., Andrew C., Samuel, Samuel, John, Wakefield, Ebenezer, Thomas, Robert)* was born on 5 February 1903, in Charlotte, North Carolina, the fifth child and first daughter of Catherine Cleveland Dibble, and her husband Professor James Daniel Martin, Ph. D. She died on 30 June 1967, in Charlotte.

Lizzie Bernice, as she was called during her early years, grew up on the campus of Biddle University, which later became Johnson C. Smith University, where her father was Latin professor, for 36 years. Elizabeth "Lizzie" was a student at Biddle University when she met her husband to be, Paul Hamilton Richardson (1896-1943).

Paul was born 31 December 1896, in Cameron, North Carolina, the son of George and Annie Sinclair Richardson. He entered Biddle University in 1919, where he was a roommate to Emory Lewis Means, who later married Elizabeth's sister Catherine. Paul graduated from Johnson C. Smith University. Lizzie and Paul married 5 November 1921, in Beaufort, North Carolina. It appears he enlisted in the service during World War I, and was assigned to a Training Detachment at Biddle University, in 1918. His Honorably Discharge papers are dated December 7, 1918.

Paul owned and operated his barber shop in Charlotte, North Carolina. According to the *Charlotte Observer* newspaper obituary, Monday, December 20, 1943: "*Proprietor of West Fourth Street Barber Shop… many prominent businessmen of Charlotte were regular customers of his."*

The 1930 U.S. Census, we see Lizzie, Paul and their three daughters, Annie, age 7, Catherine, age 5, and Emily, age 4. He is working as a barber and owns his home. The 1940, Census, shows the three daughters still at home and Paul is again, listed as a barber. By the 1950 Census, Lizzie is listed as an enumerator, with only the oldest daughter Annie, at home, teaching science, in the city high school. Her brother, Beauregard is living with her. Lizzie's husband is now deceased. Elizabeth Bernice and Paul became the parents of three daughters, Dr. Annie Louise Richardson (1923-1983), Catherine Elizabeth (1924-), and Emily Marie (1925-2008). She married Lawrence Harrison Bullock on 9 September 1956, after Paul Richardson's death in 1943.

Lizzie Bernice and her first husband are interned in the Pinewood Cemetery, in Charlotte, NC., probably in the same family plot with her parents, Dr. and Mrs. James Daniel Martin.

Martin Plot
Pinewood Cemetery, Charlotte, NC

Catherine Beatrice Martin Means
1905-2001

CATHERINE BEATRICE MARTIN MEANS

1905-2001

Great-Granddaughter of Andrew Henry Dibble, Sr.

CATHERINE BEATRICE MARTIN MEANS (1905-2001) *(Catherine Dibble, Andrew H., Jr., Andrew H., Andrew C., Samuel, Samuel, John, Wakefield, Ebenezer, Thomas, Robert)* was born the sixth child of Catherine Cleveland Dibble and her husband, Professor James Daniel Martin, Ph.D. She was born on 3 February 1905, on the campus of Johnson C. Smith University, in Charlotte, North Carolina, where her father taught Foreign Languages for 36 years. Her mother was the only child of Andrew Henry Dibble, Jr., and Elizabeth Levy, of Camden and Sumter, South Carolina. She died on 16 March 2001, in Chicago, Illinois.

Catherine attended the public schools of Charlotte and finished Columbia Heights High School in Winston Salem, N.C. She continued her education and graduated from Johnson C. Smith University with honors of Magna Cum Laude as an Education major, in 1946. Her first teaching job was in Monroe, N.C., and later continued her teaching profession in the Charlotte Public School System for five years.

Catherine married Emory Lewis Means on January 4, 1930, in Chester, South Carolina. Emory was born on July 17, 1896, in Pine Bluff, Arkansas. In 1919, he entered Biddle University, in Charlotte, graduating in 1923. He met Catherine while a student there, marrying eleven years later. He began his teaching career at the Black Metolius High School, in Illinois, later moving to Paducah, Kentucky, to teach at Lincoln High School. He remained there as a Latin, history, and government teacher until his death in 1962, totaling 39 years.

Catherine and Emory moved to Paducah, Kentucky where she made her home for the next sixty years. Catherine worked as a Home Economics Specialist for Kentucky Utilities Company, after which she worked for the Paducah Board of Education, where she remained until her retirement, in 1974. She received her post-graduate studies at Murray State University, University of Missouri at Kansas City and University of Kansas.

Catherine was an active member of Burks Chapel A.M.E. Church, where she was a member for over fifty years. She was a Trustee for many years, and held numerous other positions in the church during these many years. Catherine was a member of Alpha Kappa Alpha Sorority, Inc.; Founder of the Gamma Pi Chapter of the National Sorority of Phi Delta Kappa, in 1971; Civic-Mu-So-Lit-Club, Las Amigas Club and the City of Paducah Beautification Board. In 1974, she received the honor of receiving "Outstanding Teacher of the Year Award"; she was honored by the Mayor of Paducah as a Duchess of Paducah and the Governor of Kentucky as a Kentucky Colonel. In 1998, she received a jacket from the Governor with the Kentucky State Emblem.

In 1989, Catherine moved to Kansas City, Kansas to be near her daughter, Mildred, and in 1997, she moved to Park Forest, Illinois, to live with her youngest daughter Emily. She attended our first Family Reunion in 1979 and has continued to be supportive and has contributed much information on the early family. Catherine had two daughters: Mildred Means Lassiter and Emily Means-Willis.

Emory and Catherine Beatrice Martin Means
Oak Grove Cemetery
Paducah, KY

Louise Wendella Martin
1907-2000

LOUISE WENDELLA MARTIN WHITE

1907-2000

Great-Granddaughter of Andrew Henry Dibble, Sr.

LOUISE WENDELLA MARTIN WHITE (1907-2000) *(Catherine Dibble, Andrew H., Jr., Andrew H. Andrew C., Samuel, Samuel, Lt. John, Wakefield, Ebenezer, Thomas, Robert)*, was born, the seventh child of Catherine Cleveland Dibble and her husband Professor James Daniel Martin, Ph.D. She was born on 17 April 1907, on the campus of Johnson C. Smith University, where her father taught Foreign Languages for 36 years. Her mother, Catherine Cleveland Dibble was the only child of Andrew Henry Dibble, Jr., and Elizabeth Levy of Camden and Sumter, South Carolina. Louise Wendella died on 28 February 2000, in Atlanta, Georgia.

Louise, along with her eight siblings, grew up on the campus of Johnson C. Smith. She attended public schools of Charlotte and finished Columbia Heights High School in Winston Salem, North Carolina, which was part of the Slater Normal School Program. She continued her education and attended Howard University receiving her Bachelor of Arts Degree in Education, in 1929, and did graduate studies at Columbia University, in New York City. Louise became a member of Alpha Kappa Alpha Sorority, in 1927, while attending Howard University.

Louise taught at Hillside High School in Durham, North Carlina for two years before her marriage in August 1931, to Dr. Herbert Nathaniel White, who was born on December 31, 1896, in Asheville, N. C. He died on February 22, 1962. He received his Bachelor's Degree from Bennett College in Greensboro, North Carolina and his Doctor of Medicine Degree (M.D.) from Howard University School of Medicine, in 1929. He was a Veteran of World War I, with a rank of Lieutenant. He was classmate of Louise's brother James Dwight Martin, D.D.S., at Howard University. He practiced medicine in Asheville for 37 years.

She was always "Cousin Louise," to me, living across the street from me and my family, and her knowing me since I was born, as well as, I, having her name and she being my "God Mother." She was always very special to me. When her mother, who was my grandmother's niece and my father's first cousin, visited Asheville, I along with my siblings, were always excited about seeing family.

Louise continued her teaching career, in Asheville, North Carolina, where she retired from the Public School System, with forty-three years service. Many summers, she managed the Walton Street Park and taught swimming. In 1987, she was honored by receiving a Special Humanitarian Award from the Asheville-Buncombe Commission on the Status of Women, for her services to the community as a founder of the Good Neighbor Community Club and the "Daughter's of Wesa." Louise was a fun loving, and caring person who gave to many. Louise attended our first *Naudin-Dibble Family Reunion* in 1979, and continued to be one of senior supporters. Louise had one daughter Choquita.

Dr. Herbert Nathaniel and Louise Martin White are interred at Violet Hill Cemetery, Asheville, Buncombe County, NC.

James Dwight Martin, D.D.S.
1900-1980

JAMES DWIGHT MARTIN, D.D.S.

1900-1980

Great-Grandson of Andrew Henry Dibble, Sr.

JAMES DWIGHT MARTIN, DDS (1900-1980) *(Catherine Dibble, Andrew H. Jr., Andrew H., Andrew C, Samuel, Samuel, John, Wakefield, Ebenezer, Thomas, Robert)* was born on 26 May 1900, in Charlotte, North Carolina, the 4th son of Catherine Cleveland Dibble and her husband James Daniel Martin, Ph.D. He grew up on the campus of Johnson C. Smith University. He died on 13 July 1980.

James Dwight graduated from Biddle University (today, Johnson C. Smith University), with a Bachelor of Arts (B.A.) Degree, in 1921. He graduated from Howard University School of Dentistry, in 1929, with a Doctor of Dental Surgery Degree (D.D.S.). He is seen in the 1930 Census living in Brooklyn, New York, working in a dental office. He later returned to Charlotte, where he practiced dentistry for 49 years.

Most of us knew him as "Dwight." He was involved with the community, as a member f the NAACP, the McCrorey Branch of the YMCA. He was president of the state convention of the Old North State Dental Society. He also taught anatomy and physiology at Good Samaritan Hospital for about fifteen years, as a volunteer. Dwight was a devoted member of the First United Presbyterian Church, in Charlotte.

J. Dwight married Ruby Mae Barr (1900-1959), on 14 August 1920, in New York City. She was born 26 September 1900, in South Carolina and died 19 December 1959, in Charlotte, North Carolina. She was the daughter of Spencer and Tillie Barr of Columbia. Ruby worked in New York for some years before she and Dwight returned to Charlotte. Ruby graduated from Johnson C Smith University, summa cum laude in the class of 1948. She worked as a teacher and as an administrator at Barber Scotia College, in Concord, North Carolina.

After Ruby's death, Dwight married Erma.

Dr. James Dwight Martin and his wife Ruby are interned at Pineland Cemetery in Charlotte, NC.

Cassandra Elizabeth Maxwell
1910-1974

CASSANDRA ELIZABETH MAXWELL BIRNIE, LLB

1910-1974

Great-Granddaughter of Andrew Henry Dibble, Sr.

CASSANDRA ELIZABETH MAXWELL (1910-1974) (*John Maxwell, Martha Dibble, Andrew H., Andrew C., Samuel, Samuel, John, Wakefield, Ebenezer, Thomas, Robert*) was born on 20 October 1910, in Orangeburg, South Carolina, the daughter of John Moreau Maxwell, Sr., (1881-1938) and his wife Katherine Louise Cardozo Maxwell (1884-1931). Her father was a merchant in Orangeburg and her mother, a former teacher at South Carolina State College, in Orangeburg. She was the eldest daughter of six children. Cassandra died in August 1974 and her husband, a few months later, in December 1974, at their home in Philadelphia.

Cassandra married Dr. James Hope Birnie on August 1, 1950. Dr. Birnie (1908-1974) was a Phi Beta Kappa scholar and scientist. He received his undergraduate degree from Morehouse College in Atlanta. He received his Master's Degree from Brown University and his Ph.D. Degree from Syracuse University, in 1951. He was professor of biology at Morehouse from 1951-1961. Birnie was the youngest son of Richard Birnie, a prominent Charlestonian. Birnie's two eldest brothers both became medical doctors and sister married Dr. Robert Shaw Wilkinson, President of South Carolina State College.

Cassandra was the granddaughter of South Carolina State Senator Henry Johnson Maxwell (1837-1906) and Martha Louisa Dibble Maxwell (1846-1923). H. J. Maxwell represented Marlboro County from 1868-1878, and was Chairman of the State Committee on Education.

Her maternal grandfather was the Reverend Isaac Nunez Cardozo, a Professor at Claflin University and South Carolina State College and Methodist Minister; and her great-grandfather was Reverend Henry Weston Cardozo (1830-1886), a Methodist Minister and State Senator from Kershaw County, from 1870-1874. He was Auditor for Kershaw County (1868-1869).

Cassandra attended elementary and high school at Claflin University in Orangeburg, graduating from High School in 1928. She attended Spelman College in Atlanta (1928-1930); a Business School and Training (1930-1933); received her LA AB Degree in 1935 from Howard University; received her LW LLB Degree from Howard University in 1938.

Attorney Maxwell was admitted to practice law before the South Carolina Supreme Court in December 1941, giving her the distinction of being the first person of color to be admitted to the South Carolina Bar. She had a well-established law practice when the State of South Carolina refused to admit persons of color to the University of South Carolina Law School, in Columbia. Therefore, in 1947, the State of South Carolina established a law school at South Carolina State College for students of color, and Attorney Maxwell was appointed an instructor. Thereby, giving her the distinction of being the first female to hold a faculty position in a law school in South Carolina. She had an outstanding and successful career as a law professor and as well as a lawyer. In 1939, she was secretary to Supreme Court Justice Thurgood Marshall, in New York City, and assisted him in his work with the NAACP. Cassandra and her husband moved to Philadelphia in 1962, where she lived the remainder of her life.

Cassandra Maxwell Marries Dr. Birnie

Prof. Cassandra E. Maxwell, South Carolina's only Negro woman attorney, has been married to Dr. James H. Birnie, former Orangeburg man, who is now a member of the Cornell University faculty.

The wedding took place Monday, with Dr. Benjamin Mays, president of Morehouse College, Atlanta, officiating.

The couple was expected to leave soon for Europe, where Dr. Birnie will undertake an assignment for the U. S. government.

The woman attorney is a professor of law at State A. & M. College and is an executive of Maxwell's Superette.

Dr. Birnie for several years was a member of the State College faculty here.

Catherine Louise Maxwell
1914-1988

CATHERINE LOUISE MAXWELL KERSEY VINCENT

1914-1988

Great-Granddaughter of Andrew Henry Dibble, Sr.

CATHERINE LOUISE MAXWELL KERSEY VINCENT (1814-1988) *(John Maxwell, Martha Dibble, Andrew H., Andrew C., Samuel, Samuel, John, Wakefield, Ebenezer, Thomas, Robert)* was born on 10 September 1914, the daughter of John Moreau Maxwell (1881-1938), and his wife the former Katherine Louise Cardozo (1884-1931).

Her father, a merchant, who owned the *Maxwell Staple and Fancy Groceries*, and her mother a former teacher at South Carolina State College, in Orangeburg. She was one of six children, who are Cassandra Elizabeth, John Moreau, Jr., Isaac Nunez, Charles Wendell, II, Henry Cardozo Maxwell. Catherine Louise died on 30 December 1988, in Orangeburg.

Her Cardozo heritage in South Carolina dates to the earliest Cardozo who came into New York in 1752, and then moved to Charleston. Her maternal grandfather is Reverend Isaac Nunez Cardozo who was a Methodist Minister and Professor at Claflin University and South Carolina State College. Her Great-grandfather is Reverend Henry Weston Cardozo (1830-1886), a Methodist Minister and State Senator from Kershaw County, from 1870-1874. Catherine Louise's paternal grandfather is the Honorable Henry Johnson Maxwell, Sr. (1837- 1906), who served in the South Carolina State Legislature, during reconstruction. He married Martha Louisa Dibble (1846 - 1923), of Camden and Sumter, South Carolina.

She attended elementary and high school at Claflin University and graduated from West Virginia State University with a Bachelor's Degree in home economics. She was one of the first faculty members at Wilkinson High School when it opened in 1937, as the first public high school for African Americans in Orangeburg. Louise taught in the Orangeburg public schools until her retirement.

Catherine Louise was mostly known as "Louise." She married Dr. George Morris Kersey (1911- 1947), son of Benjamin Franklin Kersey (1878-1960), and his wife the former Leola Predesta, of Richmond, Virginia. George was born on August 2, 1911 and had three brothers, Benjamin, Jr., William Warren, and Frederick F. Kersey. George graduated from Virginia Union University and received his Doctor of Medicine (M.D.) Degree from Meharry School of Medicine, in Nashville, Tennessee, in 1940. Following his internship at Freedman's Hospital, in Washington, D. C., he joined the United States Army Medical Corps, and was stationed at the Veterans Administration Hospital, in Tuskegee, Alabama. He enlisted in the medical corps on June 20, 1944 and was discharged on June 11, 1946, with the rank of Captain. At the time of his early death, he had a private medical practice, in Atlanta Georgia. George died on 16 April 1947.

C. Louise later married Henry N. Vincent, Jr. (1908-1984), a native of Columbia, who was the son of Belle Ellis and Henry N. Vincent, Sr. Henry was a World War II, veteran, who began working at South Carolina State University in 1947, retiring in 1974, as Assistant to the President. Louise and Henry made their home in Orangeburg.

Catherine Louise and George M. Kersey have one daughter: Leola Louise

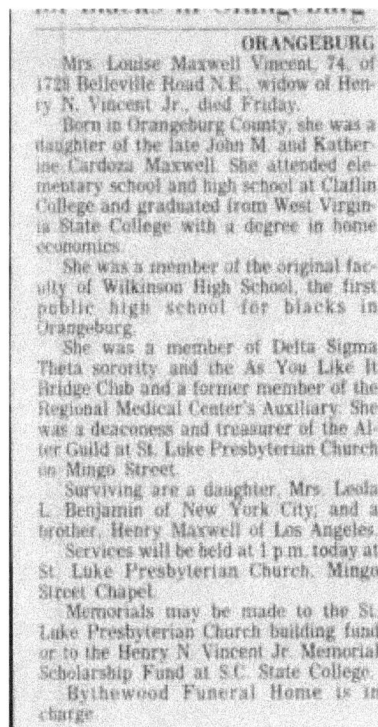

ORANGEBURG

Mrs. Louise Maxwell Vincent, 74, of 1728 Belleville Road N.E., widow of Henry N. Vincent Jr., died Friday.

Born in Orangeburg County, she was a daughter of the late John M. and Katherine Cardoza Maxwell. She attended elementary school and high school at Claflin College and graduated from West Virginia State College with a degree in home economics.

She was a member of the original faculty of Wilkinson High School, the first public high school for blacks in Orangeburg.

She was a member of Delta Sigma Theta sorority and the As You Like It Bridge Club and a former member of the Regional Medical Center's Auxiliary. She was a deaconess and treasurer of the Alter Guild at St. Luke Presbyterian Church on Mingo Street.

Surviving are a daughter, Mrs. Leola L. Benjamin of New York City; and a brother, Henry Maxwell of Los Angeles.

Services will be held at 1 p.m. today at St. Luke Presbyterian Church, Mingo Street Chapel.

Memorials may be made to the St. Luke Presbyterian Church building fund or to the Henry N. Vincent Jr. Memorial Scholarship Fund at S.C. State College.

Bythewood Funeral Home is in charge.

Henry Cardozo Maxwell
1923-1995

HENRY CARDOZO MAXWELL

1923-1995

Great-Grandson of Andrew Henry Dibble, Sr.

HENRY CARDOZO MAXWELL (1923-1995) *(John Maxwell, Martha Dibble, Andrew H., Andrew C., Samuel, Samuel, John, Wakefield, Ebenezer, Thomas, Robert)* was born on 12 January 1923 in Orangeburg, South Carolina, the son of John Moreau Maxwell (1881-1938) and his wife the former Katherine Louise Cardozo (1884-1931), the daughter of Isaac Nunez Cardozo and Elizabeth Williamson, of Orangeburg. Henry died in Los Angeles, California, on 1 May 1995.

His father, a merchant, owned the *Maxwell Staple and Fancy Groceries,* and her mother a former teacher at South Carolina State College, in Orangeburg. He was one of six children, who are Cassandra Elizabeth, John Moreau, Jr., Isaac Nunez, Catherine Louise, Charles Wendell, II,

His Cardozo heritage in South Carolina dates to the earliest Cardozo who came into New York in 1752, and then moved to Charleston. His maternal grandfather, Reverend Isaac Nunez Cardozo, was a Methodist Minister and Professor at Claflin University and South Carolina State College. His Great-grandfather is the Reverend Henry Weston Cardozo (1830-1886), a Methodist Episcopal Minister and State Senator, representing Kershaw County, from 1870-1874, for whom he is named for.

Henry's paternal grandfather is the Honorable Henry Johnson Maxwell, Sr. (1837-1906), who served in the South Carolina State Legislature, during reconstruction. He married Martha Louisa Dibble (1846 -1923), of Camden and Sumter, South Carolina. These early Maxwell's were free people of color, originally from Edisto Island and later, Charleston, South Carolina. Henry's grandfather Henry Johnson Maxwell was appointed the first colored Post Master in the United States, on March 16, 1869.

Henry's early education was at Claflin University and South Carolina State University, in Orangeburg. Henry's World War II Registrations Card, dated 26 June 1942, states that he is five foot 9 inches tall, and weighs one hundred and forty-five (145) pounds, living at 69 North Boulevard, in Orangeburg. He enlisted in the United States Army on March 3, 1942, at Fort Jackson Army Base, in Columbia, South Carolina. He was discharged on January 15, 1946.

Henry attended The Wharton School of Business School of the University of Pennsylvania, in 1955. He was a member of Omega Psi Phi Fraternity. Henry is interred at the Forest Lawn Memorial Park, Hollywood Hills, Los Angeles, California.

Henry married Gloria G. Martin, Ph.D., in Philadelphia, in 1946, and had one daughter, Katherine.

He later married Beatrice Cowdery and had two children: Mark and Monique.

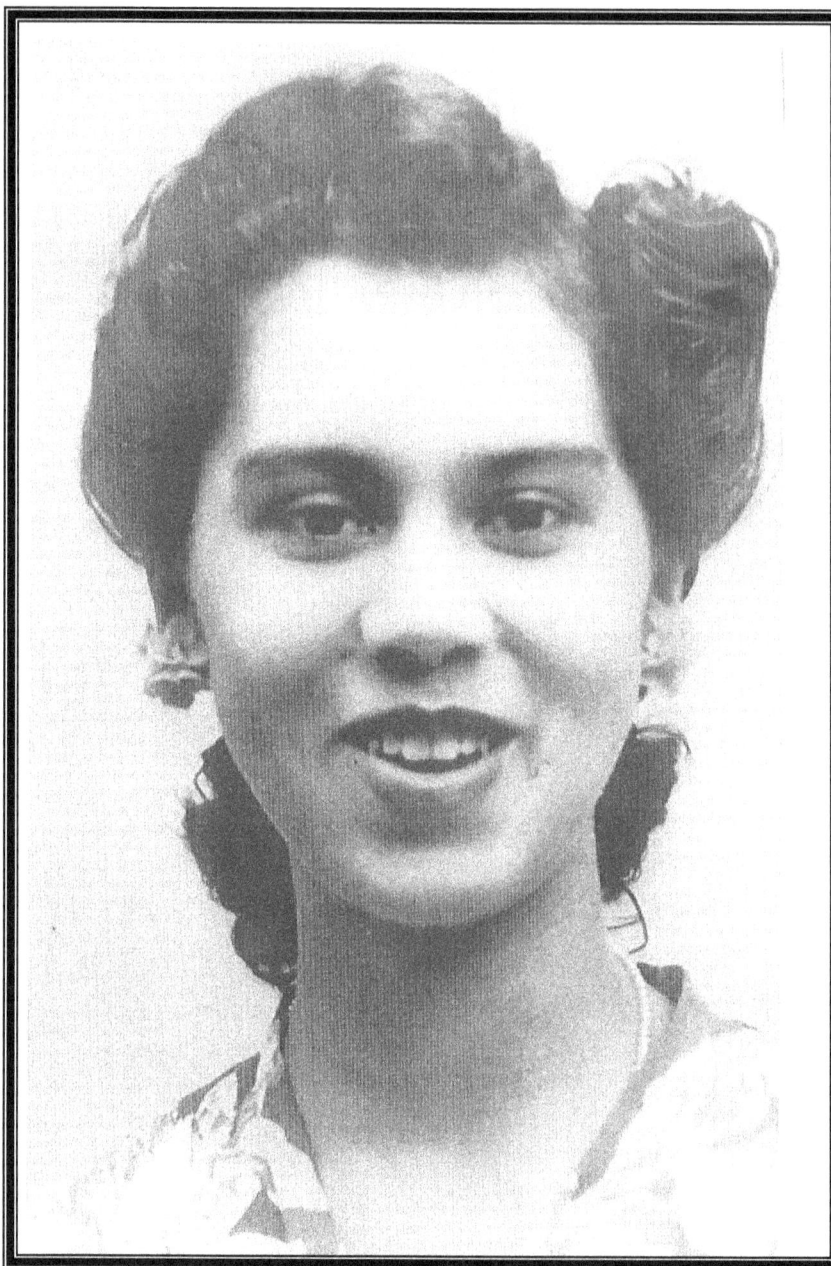

Selina Louise Edwards
1920-1985

SELINA LOUISE EDWARDS REED

1920-1985

Great-Granddaughter of Andrew Henry Dibble, Sr.

SELINA LOUISE EDWARDS REED (1921-1985) *(Naomi, Martha Dibble, Andrew H., Andrew C., Samuel, Samuel, John, Wakefield, Ebenezer, Thomas, Robert).* Selina was born on 28 January 1921 in Wilkes-Barre, Pennsylvania., the second child of George C. and Naomi Maxwell Edwards. She was the Granddaughter of Martha Louisa Dibble (1846-1923), of Camden, and her husband, Senator Henry Johnson Maxwell, Sr. (1837-1906), who served in the South Carolina Legislature during the Reconstruction. Selina died on 15 November 1985, in Chicago, Illinois.

In 1940 Selina received an A.A. Degree from Wilkes College (now Bucknell, Jr. College) and then continued her education at Howard University where she met her future husband George W. Reed, Jr. She graduated in 1942 with a B.A. Degree and went on to matriculate from the University of Pennsylvania with a M.S.W., in 1945.

Selina was a professor at the University of Chicago, and Kennedy King College, among numerous other positions, such as a case worker, teacher, administrator, and therapist. Over the years she worked in many institutions. Among them were the Family Service Bureau, Illinois Childrens Home, and Aid, and the Abraham Lincoln Center. She often went beyond what some would consider her professional duty. For instance, while at Bobs Roberts Hospital, she convened the first group of medical professionals in the Chicago area to address the problem of child abuse.

On June 30, 1945, Selina married George Warren Rood, Jr. (1920-2015), of Washington, D.C. George graduated from Dunbar High School and received his B.S. Degree from Howard University in 1942, and his M.S. Degree, two years later. He then completed his Ph.D. Degree from the University of Chicago, in 1952. He died on August 31, 2015, in Chicago. George was one of many scientists recruited for the Manhattan Project, which produced the atom bomb during World War II. George Reed spent his entire career as a chemist specializing in a variety of fields within the discipline. His training as both a nuclear and geo-chemist would play equally important in his long research career. He was also on the lunar sample planning team with the National Aeronautics and Space Administration (NASA) from 1972 to 1980. After the first moon landing Reed was one of about 140 scientists from around the world chosen to analyze the sample of moon rock from Apollo Space missions, in a nuclear reactor; he eventually concluded that the rock contained minerals not found on earth. Reed published more than 120 scientific papers.

When I met Selina many years ago, she was the most kind and thoughtful person I had ever met. She reached out and welcomed everyone with a genuine and caring demeanor. Her sincerity and kindness were always felt by all who she encountered. I still feel today, that I lost a very close friend and cousin.

Selina and George are interred in the First Unitarian Church Crypt, Chicago, Cook County, Illinois.

Selina and George are the parents of four: Rev. Dr. Mark; Atty. Carol (1953-1998); Philip, Lauren.

The Honorable Stephen Lloyd Maxwell, Jr.
1920-2009

THE HONORABLE STEPHEN LLOYD MAXWELL, JR.

1921-2009

Great-Grandson of Andrew Henry Dibble, Sr.

THE HONORABLE STEPHEN LLOYD MXWELL, JR. (1921-2009) *(Stephen, Martha Dibble, Andrew H. Andrew C., Samuel, Samuel, John, Wakefield, Ebenezer, Thomas, Robert)* was born in Saint Paul, Minnesota, on 12 January 1921 to Stephen Lloyd and Ethel Howard Maxwell. The Honorable Stephen L. Maxwell, Jr., died 31 August 2009. Stephen, Sr. was born in Sumter, South Carolina the son of Senator Henry J. Maxwell and his wife the former Martha Louisa Dibble of Camden. Judge Maxwell followed in the footsteps of his grandfather Senator Henry J. Maxwell, who also became an attorney.

Judge Maxwell's father died when he was 9 years old, and his mother supported her two sons by working as a social worker and teacher. After graduating from St. Paul Central High School in 1939, he attended the University of Minnesota, transferring to Morehouse College in Atlanta, Georgia where he earned a Bachelor of Arts (B.A.) Degree in accounting, in 1942. In 1942, he enlisted in the U.S. Coast Guard and was discharged in 1945. He served as a Hospital Corpsman during World War II. In 1947, he joined the U. S. Naval Reserve and in 1981, retired with the rank of Captain.

Returning to St. Paul after the War, Stephen Maxwell worked as an accountant for several government agencies as an IRS tax collector and auditor from 1945-1948; accountant for the St. Paul Auditorium, 1948-1951; and Special Agent Investigator, for the Office of Price Stabilization, 1951-1953. Judge Maxwell graduated from the Saint Paul College of Law in 1953 (LLB) Degree, and began his private law practice in St. Paul.

Judge Maxwell's career included several firsts in the State of Minnesota during his thirty-four- year career as a jurist. Steve became the first person of color to become a District Court Judge in Minnesota, 1968-1987, and the second person of color to serve as a Municipal Judge in the State of Minnesota, 1967-1968. He also was the first person of color to be St. Paul Corporation Council, the City's Chief Attorney for St, 1964-1966. He was also the first person of color to serve as an Assistant Ramsey Court Attorney, 1959-1966, 1967. Judge Maxwell served as an Acting Justice of the Minnesota Supreme Court in 1979 and 1992. In 1966, he ran for the U.S. House of Representatives from the Fourth District as a Republican candidate. He retired from the bench in 1987.

Stephen Maxwell has been actively involved in the community. Over the years, he has served on numerous boards, such as the Minnesota State Colleges and Universities; Greater St. Paul United Way; St. Paul Chapter of the American Red Cross (Chairman 1971-1974); Minnesota Community College; Urban League; YMCA; Winter Carnival; NAACP; Minnesota Medical Foundation; St. John's University, Collegeville, MN; Indianhead Council Boy Scouts; Service Savings and Loan Association; Vestry of St. Philip's Episcopal Church and the Judicial Council of the National Bar Association.

Judge Stephen L. Maxwell, Jr. married Betty Virginia Rodney, a Duluth native, on 28 March 1944, in Brooklyn, New York, while serving in the United States Coast Guard, during his World War II service. They had two sons: Stephen Lloyd., III, (1946 -1986), and Rodney D. Maxwell (1950-1977).

Andrew Dibble Maxwell, Jr., D.D.S.
1921-1992

ANDREW DIBBLE MAXWELL, JR., D.D.S.

1921-1992

Great-Grandson of Andrew Henry Dibble, Sr.

ANDREW DIBBLE MAXWELL, JR. (1921-1990) *(Andrew, Martha Dibble, Andrew H., Andrew C., Samuel, Samuel, John, Wakefield, Ebenezer, Thomas, Robert)* was born on 5 April 1920, the son of Andrew Dibble Maxwell, Sr., D.D.S. (1888-1958), and his wife the former Florence "Flossie" Parnell (1894-1928). He had one sibling, Henry Johnson Maxwell, III (1918-1919), who is buried in the Walker Cemetery, in Sumter, South Carolina.

Andrew graduated from the Howard University College of Dentistry, in 1946, with his Doctor of Dental Surgery Degree (D.D.S.). He completed an internship emphasizing in Oral and Pedodontics, at Jersey City Medical Center, in New Jersey, after which he received a Fellowship in Pedodontics, in 1947 at Guggenhelm Clinic for Children, in New York City. Andrew served as a Captain in the United States Army Dental Corps, from 1951-1952, in Munich, Germany.

Andrew returned to Patterson, New Jersey, and practiced Dentistry with his father from 1959-1962. He closed his father's office after nearly forty years, with him dying in June 1965. From 1962 to 1965, Andrew worked for the Public Health in Stockholm Sweden and Zurich, Switzerland, after which he worked for the Public Health Service in the Virgin Islands, where he served as a member of the Board of Examiners. From 1972 to 1979, Andrew was affiliated with the Veterans Hospital in Martinez, California, which included teaching at the University of California, at Davis, and the Veterans Hospital in Bedford, Massachusetts, which included teaching at Harvard Dental School. He later was affiliated with the Veterans Medical Center, in Vancouver, Washington and La Jolla, California. Andrew retired from the Veterans Administration in 1988, after many years of service.

Andrew married first, Zoe Jean Crumpler, (2) Lois J. Swan and (3) Diane L. Carmichael. Andrew Dibble Maxwell, Jr., is the father of seven children: Andrew, Zoe, Margot, Bruce (1962-1985), Ian, Soleil, Alma.

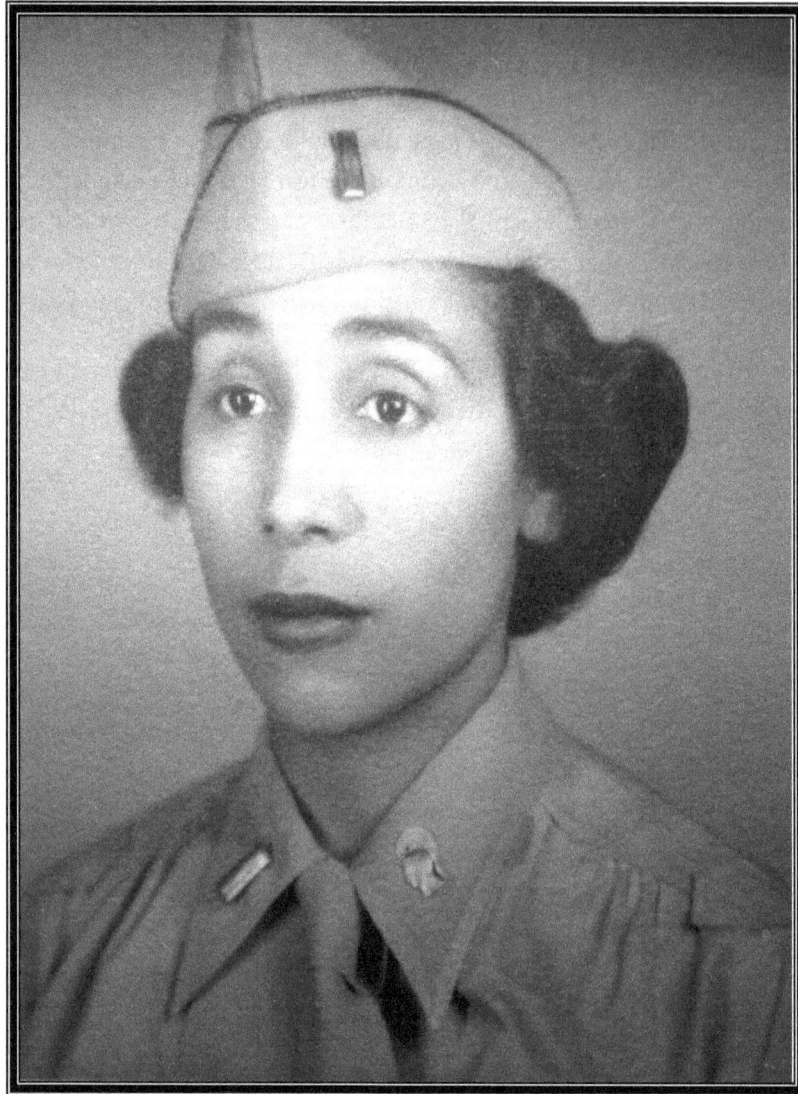

Sarah Elizabeth Murphy
1916-2015

SARAH ELIZABETH MURPHY LEMON PALMORE

1916-2015

Great-Granddaughter of Andrew Henry Dibble, Sr.

SARAH ELIZABETH MURPHY (1916-2015) *(Josephine, Eugene, Andrew H., Andrew C., Samuel, Samuel, John, Wakefield, Ebenezer, Thomas, Robert)* was born on 19 September 1916, in Langston, Oklahoma, and died on 20 May 2015, in the Atlanta area. She was the second daughter of Josephine Dibble Murphy and her husband Harry Saunders Murphy, Sr., formerly of Camden, South Carolina and later, of Atlanta, Georgia.

Sarah spent her early years in Atlanta, where she graduated from the Atlanta University Laboratory High School, in 1933. She received her college work at Spelman College, graduating with her Bachelor of Arts Degree, in 1937. She attended Grinnell College, in Iowa, for graduate work. She received her Master of Arts Degree from New York University, in 1947. Sarah taught at David T. Howard School in Atlanta before joining the first group of women to join the Women's Army Corps, on July 15, 1942, at De Moines, Iowa, therefore, among the first group of women to receive a commission. She was promoted to Captain, before the end of World War II.

In 1950, Sarah married Attorney James Garfield Lemon, Jr., (1910-1982), of Savannah, Georgia, the son of Attorney James G. Lemon, Sr. They became the parents of two children: Ann Josephine and James G. Lemon, III (1952-1972). Sarah and James made their home in Chicago, where she was an Administrator for the Chicago Head Start Program.

Sarah later married Ernest Palmore (1917-2010), of Tuscaloosa, Alabama, where she spent the remainder of her life. She is interned in the Georgia National Cemetery, Canton, Cherokee County, Georgia.

The Honorable Mabel H. Murphy
1918-2006

THE HONORABLE MABEL H. MURPHY SMYTHE-HAITH

1918-2006

Great-Granddaughter of Andrew Henry Dibble, Sr.

MABEL HANCOCK MURPHY SMYTHE-HAITH, Ph.D. (1918-2006) *(Josephine, Eugene, Andrew H., Andrew C., Samuel, Jr., Samuel, Sr., John, Wakefield, Ebenezer, Thomas, Sr., Robert).* Mabel was born on 3 April 1918 in Montgomery, Alabama, the third of four children born to Harry Saunders Murphy and his wife the former Josephine Heriot Dibble, both of Camden, South Carolina, and later Atlanta, Georgia. Mabel died on 7 February 2006, in Tuscaloosa, Alabama.

Mabel graduated from the Atlanta University Laboratory School, after which she attended Spelman College for three years, and then transferred to Mount Holyoke College in Massachusetts where she received her Bachelor of Arts Degree (B.A.), in 1937. She received her Master of Arts (M.A.) Degree from Northwestern University, Evanston, Illinois (economics), in 1940; Doctor of Philosophy (Ph.D.) Degree from University of Wisconsin, Madison, Wisconsin (economics and law), in 1942, and engaged in post-graduate work at NYU in 1949.

Mabel Smythe Haith, educator, humanitarian, former United States Ambassador to the Republic of Equatorial Guinea and to the Republic of the Cameroon, from 1977 to 1980 and Deputy Assistant Secretary of State for African Affairs, 1980-1981. She was Professor of African Studies and Associate Director and Co-director, International Internship Program at Northwestern University in Evanston, Illinois from 1981-1985. She served as United States delegate to the International Conference to Assist Refugees in Africa, held in 1981 at Geneva, Switzerland and was a member of the Refugee Policy Group of the Cosmopolitan Club and was a member of the Council of Foreign Relations.

Mabel Hancock Murphy married Hugh H. Smythe (1913-1977) on July 26, 1939. Hugh received his B.A. Degree from Virginia State University and his M.A. Degree from Atlanta University. In 1946, Hugh received his Ph.D. Degree from Northwestern University. In 1965, President Lyndon B. Johnson appointed Hugh H. Smythe as United States Ambassador to Syrian Arab Republic from 1965- 1967. In December 1967, President Johnson appointed Hugh as United States Ambassador to Malta, Grand Canary. After 38 years of marriage, Ambassador Hugh H. Smyth died in New York City in 1977.

Mabel's teaching career began in 1937 at Fort Valley Normal and Industrial Institute, in Georgia. Other educational positions included assistant and associate professor, acting head of the Economics Department at Lincoln University in Missouri; professor of economics at Tennessee Agricultural and Industrial Institution; lecturer in economics at Brooklyn College (NY); first female professor at Shiga University, Japan; principal at New Lincoln School in NYC; lecturer in economics at City College, NYC., to name a few. She has published numerous articles and publications.

In October 1985, Mabel married Robert Haith, Jr. who was the Director of Veterans Administration Hospital at Fort Howard, Maryland, from which he retired in 1986. They lived in Washington, D. C., until his death in August 1998. Mabel was a kind and caring person who loved her family. She supported the complicated and comprehensive research on her family that has been well-documented.

Mabel and Hugh are the parents of one daughter: Karen Pamela Smythe (1947-2018).

MABEL M. SMYTHE-HAITH, 87

Former envoy to Africa, academic

Harry Saunders Murphy, Jr.
1927-1991

HARRY SAUNDERS MURPHY, JR.

1927-1991

Great-Grandson of Andrew Henry Dibble, Sr.

HARRY SAUNDERS MURPHY, JR. (1927-1991) *(Josephine, Eugene, Andrew H., Andrew C., Samuel, Samuel, John, Wakefield, Ebenezer, Thomas, Robert)* was born on 26 May 1927, in Atlanta, Georgia, the only son of Josephine Dibble Murphy and her husband Harry Sunders Murphy, Sr., formerly of Camden, South Carolina. Harry died on 3 May 1991, in Atlanta.

Harry's early education was at the Atlanta University Laboratory School. His secondary education was at the Boston English School, in Massachusetts, and he received his Bachelor of Arts Degree from Morehouse College, in Atlanta, in 1951.

Harry served in the United States Navy during World War II, at which time, he was enrolled in the V-12 Program at the University of Mississippi, thus becoming the first person of color to integrate the University of Mississippi, in 1945. This was seventeen years before Civil Rights activist James Meredith drew national attention as the first Black student enrolled there.

After the war, Harry worked with his father at the family business "The House of Murphy", in Atlanta. He later moved to New York City where he worked as a graphic designer for printing and advertising companies, the last of which was McCann Erikson, a nationally known advertising agency.

Harry was supportive of the history and genealogy of Naudin-Dibble Family and attended most of the reunions. The family is indebted to Harry for the beautiful graphics of the family logo, in 1981, which he developed from the original drawing by his cousin, William Moreau Goins.

MURPHY

Memorial services for Mr. Harry S. Murphy, Jr., will be held Friday, May 10, 1991 at 1 p.m. at our chapel, with Rev. Joan H. Armstrong officiating. Immediate survivors are three sisters, Mr. and Mrs. Robert Haith (Mable), Mr. and Mrs. Ernest Palmore (Sarah) and Mrs. Doris M. Coates; Miss Ann Lemon, Miss Karen Pamela Smythe and Dr. and Mrs. James D. Palmer. In lieu of flowers contributions may be made to the Morehouse School of Medicine. Ivey Bros. Morticians.

Edmund Perry Palmer, II
1935-2010

EDMUND PERRY PALMER, II

1935-2010

Great-Grandson of Andrew Henry Dibble, Sr.

EDMUND PERRY PALMER, II (1935-2010) *(Ellie Dibble, Eugene, Andrew H., Andrew C., Samuel, Samuel, John, Wakefield, Ebenezer, Thomas, Robert)* was born in Sumter, South Carolina on 9 August 1935, the third of four sons born to Edmund Perry and Ellie Naudin Dibble Palmer. Perry died on 3 February 2010.

According to Perry, *"... his parents instilled in him and his three brothers, (Robert John, James Dibble, and Andrew Dibble Palmer), the ethic that, if you are blessed, you must serve your fellow man."* With his quiet demeanor, always shunning the limelight, Perry Palmer has done just that. He was the President and Director of Palmer Memorial Chaple of Columbia. His successes as a businessman, philanthropist and humanitarian were intertwined with his devotion to mankind. His root in his native state were deep and pervasive. His paternal grandfather, Robert John Palmer and maternal grandfather, Eugene Heriot Dibble served in the South Carolina Legislature during Reconstruction.

His father, Edmund Perry Palmer, was a funeral director and embalmer, so young Perry was born into the funeral profession. He prepared himself early for his life's work by shadowing in the footsteps of his late father, who was the first person of color Funeral Director and Embalmer in Sumter County. Perry is a graduate of Mather Academy in Camden, South Carolina, Moson Academy in Massachusetts, and North Carolina A&T State University in Greensboro, North Carolina. He completed is professional training at the American Academy of Funeral Service in New York.

Active in his church, he was a member of Wesley United Methodist Church where he served in numerous capacities throughout his years in Columbia. As a community servant, he personally sponsored Adopt-A-School programs, Youth at Risk, "Just Say No" and other youth and adult recreation programs. He provided scholarships for students, including the Benjamin E. Mays Academy for Leadership Development and the South Carolina Small Business Minority Business Development Corporation.

E. Perry Palmer touched the lives of many as a philanthropist and humanitarian. In 1998, he received the United Way of the Midlands Humanitarian Award, the first African American to receive the award, since is inception in 1984. On July 7, 1999, the State of South Carolina presented the *"Order of the Silver Crescent."* He received numerous other awards: Joint Concurrent Resolution from the South Carolina Senate and House of Representatives for his humanitarian efforts, induction in the South Carolina Black Hall of Fame, Lifetime Service Award from the Carolina Scholarship, Inc., and many, many more. Throughout the years, Perry served on numerous boards, including the Columbia Urban League, the Indian Waters Council of the Boy Scouts of America, the Palmetto Health Foundation, State Chamber of Commerce, United Way of the Midlands, and numerous others. He was Past President of the South Carolina Morticians Association, Secretary of the Board, Chairman of the Board of Directors, District Governor of the National Funeral Directors, and Morticians Association, as well as President.

Perry married Grace Justine Brooks (1934-1984), formerly of Aiken, South Carolina. Perry and Grace became the parents of two children: Brooks and Ema. Perry and his wife Grace are interred in the Palmetto Cemetery, Columbia, South Carolina.

In 2017, as the results of a DNA test, Genela Altric Curry (1966-2020), who was born on Shaw AF Base in Sumter, South Carolina, was found to be the biological daughter of Edmund Perry Palmer.

James Laurence Dibble Palmer, M. D.
1928-2009

JAMES LAURENCE DIBBLE PALMER, MD

1928-2009.

Great-Grandson of Andrew Henry Dibble, Sr

JAMES LAURENCE DIBBLE PALMER, MD (1928-2009), (*Ellie Dibble, Eugene, Andrew H., Andrew C., Samuel, Samuel, John, Wakefield, Ebenezer, Thomas, Robert*) was born 10 October 1928 in Sumter, South Carolina. The son of Ellie Naudin Dibble (1898-1973), of Camden and her husband, Edmund P. Palmer, Sr. (1896-1949), of Columbia and Sumter, South Carolina. Jim died on 6 February 2009, in Atlanta, Georgia.

Jim graduated from the Mather Academy, Camden, South Carolina in 1945 and Fisk University, Nashville, Tennessee in 1949 with a Bachelor of Arts Degree. Due to the sudden death of his father, he helped his brother, Bob at the Palmer Funeral Home for one year and then entered Meharry Medical School, graduating in the class of 1954. From 1954-1956 and 1958-1960, he completed his Internship and Residency at Jersey City Medical Center in New Jersey. His medical training was interrupted 1956- 1957 when he entered the U. S. Air Force stationed in Tachikawa, Japan, and was honorably discharged at the rank of Major.

From 1960-1961, Jim taught at Seton Hall College in Jersey City. His uncle, Dr. Eugene Dibble, influenced him to come to Tuskegee, Alabama where he served at the VA Hospital for one year. In the early 1960s, he decided to move to Atlanta to open his medical practice. In 1968, he took on an added role as Medical Director of the Atlanta Life Insurance Company. He joined the Board of Trustees and later became a Trustee of the Herndon Foundation. In 1970, he opened a professional office building at 970 Martin Luther King Drive in partnership with Dr's. Howard Golden, John Hall, Robert Jordan and Mrs. Johnnie Clark, CPA.

Jim became the personal physician to most of the Civil Rights leaders from Martin Luther King, Jr. to Daddy King, John Lewis, Julian Bond, H. Rap Brown, and numerous freedom riders. He also helped integrate the staffs of all the major hospitals because Medicare would not pay if African Americans were not on staff. He later saw his dream come to reality when he joined the Board of Overseers in the formation of the Morehouse School of Medicine. Because of his visionary direction and his jovial outgoing personality, Jim at one time held leadership positions in most of the religious, professional, and social organizations he joined. In addition to those already mentioned, others included Warren Memorial United Methodist Church, Association of Life Insurance Medical Directors, Hughes Spalding and Southwest Hospitals, Sadie Mays Nursing Home, Visiting Nurses Association, Sigma Pi Phi Fraternity (Kappa Boule), Omega Psi Phi Fraternity, Inc. Guardsmen and the Atlanta, Georgia State, and National Medical Associations.

Jim married Madelyn Rose Martin, the daughter of Helen Madelyn Harrison (1899-1984) and her husband Eugene Marcus Martin, Jr. (1888-1969), of Atlanta, Georgia. They are the parents of one son: James. According to his son, *"Jim was an outgoing, fun-loving person who loved people and especially those in his practice. He knew the therapeutic value of laughter and gave credence to the adage that "Laughter is the best medicine."* Dr. Palmer spent over 40 years prescribing this remedy.

Robert John Palmer, III
1926-1995

ROBERT JOHN PALMER

1926-1995

Great-Grandson of Andrew Henry Dibble, Sr.

ROBERT JOHN PALMER (1926-1995) *(Ellie Dibble, Eugene, Andrew H., Andrew C., Samuel, Samuel, John, Wakefield, Ebenezer, Thomas, Robert)* was born on 18 June 1926, in Sumter, South Carolina, the son of Edmund Perry Palmer and his wife, Ellie Naudin Dibble. He died on 14 June 1995, in Columbia, South Carolina.

Robert John was a graduate of Mather Academy, West Virginia State College, and Renouard School of Mortuary Science in New York City. At 23, because of the death of his father, he, along with his mother assumed the responsibility of the family funeral business, and the maintenance of the home.

In August 1954, he met the former Theodis Parsons in Washington, D. C. On July 3, 1955, they were united in marriage and became life-long partners working side-by-side in the family business. In 1958, together, they founded the Guaranty Insurance Agency which was later sold.

During the 1960s, 70s, and 80s, Robert led an active church, civic and political life. His church activities included: Chairman of the Board of Directors of Mather Academy, Treasurer of the Southern Association of United Methodist Church Mission Schools, Chairman of the Board of Trustees Emmanuel United Methodist Church, Steward, former member of the Executive Committee of Black Methodist for Church Renewal, former member of the National Division Board of Global Ministries; Delegate to three General Conferences and four Jurisdictional Conferences of the United Methodist Church, member of the Black Economic Developers, UMC, member of the Executive Committee of Black Community Developers, UMC, and a life-long member of Emanuel United Methodist Church.

Civic and Political Sketches: "Bob" will be long remembered for his distinguished involvements in the community, helping people economically, civically, and politically, often behind the scene, investing money and talent in helping to break barriers and helping other minorities take advantage of opportunities resulting from hard eared Civil and Political Rights accomplishments. Some of the organizations to which he gave his talent and time were: the Executive Committee, Southern Regional Council, Executive Committee Voter Education Project, Economic Development Commission of Sumter County, Life member of the NAAACP, Sumter County Economic Development Advisory Committee, Santee-Wateree Regional Planning Council, Sumter County Vocational Rehabilitation Center Advisory Board, Charter member and Board of Directors of the Alston Wilks Society. A sketch of Fraternal and Social organizations include: Omega Psi Phi Fraternity, Epsilon Mu Delta Chapter, 32nd degree Mason and Shriner, Past Master of St. Paul Lodge #8, The Goodfellows Club, YMCA, and the Savannah Chapter of the National Guardsman.

Bob and Theodis are interred in the Hillside Memorial Park, Sumter, South Carolina.

Robert (Bob) and Theodis are the parents of Lorin and Vikki.

Eugene Heriot Dibble, III
1929-2014

EUGENE HERIOT DIBBLE, III

1929-2014

Great-Grandson of Andrew Henry Dibble, Sr.

EUGENE HERIOT DIBBLE, III (1929-2014) *(Eugene, Eugene, Andrew H. Andrew C., Samuel, Samuel, John, Wakefield, Ebenezer, Thomas, Robert)* was born on 22 July 1929 in Tuskegee, Alabama, and died on 6 June 2014, in Montgomery County, Maryland, at age 84. He was the second child of Dr. Eugene Heriot Dibble, Jr. (1893-1969) and his wife the former Helen Taylor (1900-1980), of Tuskegee.

Eugene grew up in Tuskegee along with his four siblings: Helen, Robert, Ann and Clarice. He married Jeanette Campbell. His father was the Medical Director of the John Andrew Memorial Hospital and served as a Colonel in the Medical Corps in charge of the Veterans Hospital during World War II. Eugene's mother was the daughter of Robert Robinson Taylor, the prominent architect to design many of the buildings at Tuskegee.

According to:
The History Makers
Interview: June 6, 2008

Dibble graduated from the Monson Academy preparatory school in Massachusetts and then received his B.S. degree in chemistry from the Tuskegee Institute in 1952. During his undergraduate career, Dibble also worked in the chemistry laboratory at John A. Andrew Memorial Hospital under the tutelage of famed immunologist Dr. Reuben Kahn at the University of Michigan. Following college graduation, Dibble was called to active duty in the United States Air Force and served as a munitions and demolition officer. He was discharged at the rank of second lieutenant.

Following his tenure in the U.S. Air Force, Dibble attended the New York Institute of Finance and completed the broker's trainee program in 1954. Dibble worked as a stockbroker for the investment firm of Strauss, Blosser and MacDowell from 1956 until 1962. Dibble was one of only three African American stockbrokers working in Chicago investment firms. In 1965, Dibble and Rufus Cook began the Astro Investment Company. The goal of this business was to expand African American influence within the economy through direct investment. Muhammad Ali was one of his clients. In 1966, Dibble ran as the Republican candidate for Water Commissioner for the City of Chicago and was elected to a six-year term. He also served as trustee and chairman of the Metropolitan Sanitary District's Committee on Maintenance and Operation in 1972. Following his tenure in this position, he owned numerous businesses. He married Jeanette Campbell on August 6, 1955. She is a graduate of Wellesley College and the Yale University School of Nursing.

They had five children: Rochon, Chyla, Eugene, IV, Andrew E., and Hillary

Eugene H. Dibble, III is interred at Tuskegee, Alabama.

Elizabeth McLain Levy
1915-2004

ELIZABETH McLAIN LEVY PORTER

1915-2004

Great-Granddaughter of Andrew Henry Dibble, Sr.

ELIZABETH McLAIN LEVY PORTER (1915-2004) *(Eugene Levy, Ella Dibble, Andrew H Andrew C., Samuel, Samuel, John, Wakefield, Ebenezer, Thomas, Robert)* was born on 25 September 1915, in Camden, Kershaw County, South Carolina, the daughter of Eugene Dibble Levy (1890-1958) and his wife the former Idalean Elizabeth McLain (1894–1982), of Camden, South Carolina. Elizabeth has three siblings, Theodore John, Dennis Dibble, and Idalean Helen Levy. Elizabeth died on 22 September 2004, in Prince George County, Maryland.

Elizabeth's father, Eugene Dibble Levy is the son of Ella Naudin Dibble (1865-1913) and Theodore John Levy, Jr. (1862-1917), of Camden and Orangeburg, South Carolina. Theodore was a successful businessman, where he owned and operated two barber shops in downtown Orangeburg, at the turn of the twentieth century. The Levy home was at 114 Amelia Street, at the corner of Treadwell, in Orangeburg. The home was sold to Dr. Daniel Moorer, after the death of both parents, and was later destroyed by fire in the later 1960s.

Elizabeth is seen in the 1930 Census, as a 15-year-old, at home with her parents and siblings. Elizabeth married Lester Nathaniel Porter, Sr., (1906-2004), whose World War II Registration tells us he was working for the United States Government at the Government Printing Office, in Washington, D. C. Lester is later seen as a building contractor.

Elizabeth and Lester became the parents of three sons: Lester Nathaniel Porter, Jr. (1935-1995) , Norman Eugene, and Glen Maurice

Elizabeth and Lester are interned at the National Harmony Memorial Park Cemetery, in Prince George County, Maryland.

Ella Naomi Davis
1922-2002

ELLA NAOMI DAVIS JORDAN

1922-2002

Great-Granddaughter of Andrew Henry Dibble, Sr.

ELLA NAOMI DAVIS JORDAN (1922-2002) *(Elizabeth Levy, Ella Dibble, Andrew H., Andrew C., Samuel, Samuel, John, Wakefield, Ebenezer, Thomas, Robert),* was born on 19 December 1922, in Washington, D. C., the daughter of Elizabeth Catherine Levy (1889-1954) and Harry Winfred Davis. She is the granddaughter of Ella Naudin Dibble (1865-1913) and Theodore John Levy, Jr. (1862-1917), of Camden and later Orangeburg. Ella Naomi died on 27 October 2002, in Washington, D.C.

Ella graduated from Dunbar High School in 1940, after which she attended Howard University, majoring in Fine Arts, excelling in piano studies.

On 21 February 1946, Ella married Thomas Augustus "Gus" Jordan. It was a match most of their friends had expected since junior high school. Gus Jordan had been a close friend of Ella's brother John Dibble Davis. She

186

became a military wife and after two years, fulfilled one of her dearest wishes by becoming a mother. With a growing family in tow, she traveled with her husband to Fort Campbell, Kentucky. They later returned to Washington and eventually settled into civilian life.

Ella and Gus had six children who were her greatest joy. She cried on their first day of school and she attended their school events and her children's sports events, as well. She was their fiercest defender if they were wronged and became a seasoned veteran when it came to interceding on their behalf with their father. Her talent and skill gave life to a piano. Beethoven or Mancini, it did not matter, Ella on the keyboard was a source of utter enjoyment to her husband and later to her children, as they began to appreciate her gift.

As the young ones grew older and moved out, Ella moved into the work force. She became a receptionist and clerk at Howard University Hospital where she saw Wendell regularly. This work environment gave her a sense of independence and another kind of accomplishment. When she retired, she spent time with friends and family.

Since my son Wendell and Ella's son Mark were the same age, they spent time together and both enjoyed the time they spent together in the same Boy Scout troop. They also spent time socially through high school, college, and graduate school. Wendell often visited Cousin Ella, where she would often have a large pot of spaghetti, awaiting on the stove.

Ella and Gus are the parents of six children: Gregory, Cassandra, Mark Winfred (1954-2016), Victor, Rebecca, Susan.

Wilhelmina Dibble Warfield
1932-2004

WILHELMINIA DIBBLE WARFIELD MCCLELLAN

1932-2004

Great-Granddaughter of Andrew Henry Dibble, Sr.

WILHELMINA DIBBLE WARFIELD McCLELLAN (1932-2004) (*Wilhelmina Dibble, Dennis, Andrew H. Andrew C., Samuel, Samuel, John, Wakefield, Ebenezer, Thomas, Robert*) was born on 13 June 1932, in Camden, South Carolina, the daughter of Wilhelmina Lee Dibble Warfield and her husband Dr. William Alonzo Warfield, of Washington, D.C. She died on 9 September 2004, in Dallas, Texas. She had one brother, E. Von Rettig, Jr.

Wilhelmina spent much of her youth, visiting Camden in the summers, where her grandparents, "Bubba Den and Aunt Bessie" lived. She spent time with her many cousins, the grandchildren of her Uncle Eugene, who also visited Camden in the summers.

Her early education was in the Dallas school system; she later attended Fisk University in Nashville, Tennessee, for her undergraduate work, receiving her Bachelor of Arts Degree (B.A.). She received her Master's Degree in Education from Bishop College, in Marshall, Texas.

Wilhelmina married Van Buren McClellan, Jr., (1930-1962) on June 13, 1952, in Dallas, Texas. Wilhelmina taught school for many years in the Dallas Independent School District, before her retirement.

They became the parents to three children: Leslie, Dawn, Van Buren, III.

Catherine Allen Taylor
1929-1996

CATHERINE ALLEN TAYLOR HOWARD MCCONNELL

1929-1996

Great-Granddaughter of Andrew Henry Dibble, Sr.

CATHERINE ALLEN TAYLOR (1929-1996) *(John Taylor, Harriet Dibble, Andrew H., Andrew C., Samuel, Samuel, John, Wakefield, Ebenezer, Thomas, Robert).* Catherine was born on 31 August 1929, in Asheville, North Carolina, the daughter of John Benjamin Taylor, Jr. (1903-1980), and his wife Amanda Felicia Allen Taylor (1907-2004), the eldest of five children born to this union. She was baptized at Trinity Methodist Episcopal Church in Orangeburg, South Carolina, by her grandfather, the Reverend Dr. John B. Taylor, Sr. (1867-1936), who had pastored there at the turn of the Century. Catherine died on 16 May 1996, in Baltimore, Maryland.

Catherine's early education was in Asheville, North Carolina, graduating from Dunbar High School in Washington, D.C. In 1950, she graduated with her Bachelor of Arts Degree (BA) from Howard University with a major in History. She did graduate work in history and Library Science. She began her professional career teaching history at Lincoln Junior High in Montgomery County, Maryland, in the early 1950s. She was among the early teachers who integrated the Montgomery County schools. Catherine moved to Baltimore in 1964, where her career included teaching history, high school librarian, Media Department Chairman and Assistant Principal, in the public school system of Baltimore, Maryland, retiring in 1983.

Catherine married Attorney Charles P. Howard, Jr. in 1962 and subsequently had two children: Catherine, and Charles.

In 1979, Catherine co-founded with her sister Elsie, the first *Naudin-Dibble Family Reunion*, held in Washington, D.C. area with five generations present. This reunion brought together members of the family from three Continents, among the more than one hundred members present. One of Catherine's earliest ancestors in this country was Catherine Cleveland who arrived in the South Carolina British Colony, in 1764. She was the great-grandmother of Andrew Henry Dibble, Sr. The name "Catherine" has been passed down in every generation for over two hundred years, and continues to honor those who came before, and especially the original Catherine who came into this British Colony prior to the American Revolution.

In 1983, she married Dr. Roland C. McConnell (1909-2007), Professor Emeritus, at Morgan State University. Roland, was a native of Nova Scotia. Catherine and Roland continued their interest in history, family research and genealogy. Catherine enjoyed traveling, and playing bridge, and a supporter of the Fine Arts. She loved to be in the company of people, and was a member of several educational, historical, and genealogical organizations. Catherine was studious and scholarly, researching and presenting papers at annual historical conferences and meetings. She gave numerous presentations at the *Naudin-Dibble Family Reunions*, regarding the research and documentation of the family history. In 1995, Catherine co-authored, with her sister Elsie the, *Naudin-Dibble Family Selected South Carolina Historic Sites*. Catherine and her husband, Roland C. McConnell, Ph.D. (1910-200) were Guest-Editors for the *Journal of the Afro-American Historical and Genealogical Society,* Vol. 12, Numbers 1 & 2, Spring/Summer 1991, *Special Issue*, titled, "*African Americans in the Military.*"

Taylor Family Plot
Orangeburg Cemetery
Orangeburg, Sout Carolina

Emma Hattie Humphrey
1928-2022

EMMA HATTIE HUMPHREY PENDERGRASS

1928-2022

Great-Granddaughter of Andrew Henry Dibble, Sr.

EMMA HATTIE HUMPHREY (1928-2022) *(Catherine Taylor, Harriet Dibble, Andrew H. Andrew C., Samuel, Samuel, John, Wakefield, Ebenezer, Thomas, Robert)* was born on 1 June 1928, in Orangeburg, South, daughter of Catherine Springs Taylor and her husband William Walter Humphrey. She died in Oakland, California on 17 August 2022. She is the granddaughter of Harriet Catherine Dibble (1873-1918), and the Reverend Dr. John B. Taylor, Sr.

She was a devoted mother and sister, an outstanding attorney, an inspirational educator, a consummate travel agent, a true leader, and a wonderful friend. Emma spent her early years at Mather Academy in Camden where she and her cousin James Dibble Palmer were classmates. Later she graduated from Paul Laurence Dunbar High School in 1945 in Washington DC and where she attended Howard University, earning a Bachelor of Science Degree in Chemistry, in 1949. She also earned both a Master's Degree and a Ph.D. in Education.

Emma's early career was spent as a high school chemistry teacher and counselor. It was during this period that her desire to become an attorney was piqued. To that end, Emma continued working in the field of education while simultaneously attending night law school, graduating, and passing the ever- difficult California Bar Examination on her first attempt. Thereafter, for the next 4 decades, Emma established a very successful private law practice in Oakland, California, specializing and becoming an expert in the areas of Family and Probate Law. Commensurate with her desire to travel the world and broaden her horizons, Emma opened the Emma H. Pendergrass Travel Agency in 2009, where she organized numerous cruises and trips to worldwide destinations through 2020.

Emma was a role model of excellence, determination, and unrivaled talent who exhibited elegance, style, and grace in all aspects of her life. She possessed a spirit of kindness that touched all who knew her.

Emma was always willing to lend her legal knowledge and assistance to her colleagues and to young members of the legal profession. True to her fun-loving nature, Emma lived life to the fullest, traveling to all parts of the world, and never forgoing an opportunity to dance, laugh, and eat a bowl of vanilla ice cream. Emma was a loving and unyieldingly supportive mother to her two sons, Bailey Ill and Gary, whom she shared with her former husband of over 40 years, Bailey Pendergrass II. She cherished the relationships

Emma lived a life of service and was a stalwart, Christian woman. She was a dutiful and faithful member of Allen Temple Baptist Church for 47 years. She was a conscientious and dedicated member of the legal profession who inspired and motivated others through her tireless labor in a myriad of leadership positions. Emma was a lifetime member of the National Bar Association and served as its Region IX Director and member of the Board; the President, Vice-President, Treasurer, and member of the Board of the Charles Houston Bar Association; the President, Vice-President, and member of the Board of the California Association of Black Lawyers. Emma received numerous awards, honors, and recognition for her outstanding service in the law.

Attorney Emma Humphrey Pendergrass is interred in the Orangeburg Cemetery, Orangeburg, South Carolina.

ANDREW HENRY DIBBLE FAMILY HOMES
IN SOUTH CAROLINA

Andrew Henry and Ellie Naomi Naudin Dibble purchased this lot at 1216 Campbell Street (earlier known as 8th Avenue) on June 18, 1863. The home was probably built at this time. The home sat high on brick pillars to allow cool air to circulate during the hot summers. It was a sizeable home for this period with numerous windows for good ventilation and a nice rambling front porch. The lot was one hundred feet (100) across, fronting on Campbell Street, with a depth of five hundred seventy-three feet (573). This is the home where the younger Dibble children were born and where the family lived for more than sixty years. The back yard abutted the home of Dr. Simon Baruch, who was born in Prussia of Jewish heritage, and a surgeon in the Confederate Army, who lived 1201 Broad Street. His son Bernard Baruch was a world known financier and philanthropist, who was advisor to Presidents Woodrow Wilson and Harry S. Truman. Family lore tells of Dr. Baruch helping with the delivery of some of the younger Dibble children. The home was sold in 1923, after Ellie's death, as a part of her estate.

Of the six children who had families, only photographs of homes of three of the Dibble siblings have survived: Their oldest daughter Martha, their son Eugene and their youngest daughter, Harriet.

c.1890: Home of Andrew Henry and Ellie Naudin Dibble 1216 Campbell Street
Camden, South Carolina
Home built about 1863 when lot was purchased
Bubba Will, Hattie, Grandma Ellie on steps, and Bubba Gene

HOMES OF
MARTHA LOUISA DIBBLE & SENATOR HENRY JOHNSON MAXWELL, SR.

c. 1885: Maxwell 44-acre farm with Home, Sumter County, S. C.
Ella, Naomi, Henry J. and Martha (parents), C. Wendell and Andrew

c.1910: Maxwell Home
10 Council Street, Sumter, SC
Martha Louise Dibble Maxwell (on porch), C. Wendell and wife Pansy

195

HOME OF
EUGENE HERIOT DIBBLE, SR. & SARAH REBECCA LEE DIBBLE

c.1921: 808 Lafayette Avenue
Camden, South Carolina

HOME OF

HARRIET CATHERINE DIBBLE & REV. DR. JOHN BENJAMIN TAYLOR, SR.

c.1900/1902: 385 North Boulevard
Orangeburg, South Carolina
Lot purchased in 1900

PART IV

Philander Virgil Dibble

_____

Books constitute capital.
A library book lasts as long as a house,
for hundreds of years.
It is not an article of mere consumption
but fairly of capital,
and often in the case of professional men,
setting out in life,
it is their only capital.

Thomas Jefferson, 1821

Philander Virgil and Frances Ann Evans Dibble

PHILANDER VIRGIL DIBBLE (P.V.) (1808-1883) *(Samuel, Samuel, John, Wakefield, Ebenezer, Thomas, Robert),* was born 30 November 1808 in Danbury, Connecticut, the son of Samuel Dibble and his wife Mary "Polly" Comstock. He died on 10 March 1883, in Orangeburg, South Carolina.

Philander Virgil is first seen arriving in Charleston according to the *Charleston Courier Newspaper*, which states he arrived on Thursday, 16 August 1827, as a passenger on a ship, from New York. He came to Charleston, at age 18 years, nine months, to work with Z. Wildman and later worked alongside his brother, Andrew Comstock Dibble. He is seen in *1829 Charleston City Directory* working in the Wildman Hat Shop. The Wildman Hat shop was started by Zalmon Wildman of Danbury, Connecticut, who was the first person to establish a hat shop in Charleston and Savannah, in 1804. Both Dibble brothers worked for the Wildman Hat Shop prior to the opening of their "Dibble Hat Shop."

From August 1827 through the 1860s, there are numerous notices seen in the Charleston newspapers of P.V. arriving as a passenger on a ship or his receiving merchandize in Charleston, for the Dibble Hat Shop, that he operated in the 1850s and 1860s, after his brother Andrew Comstock's death in September 1846.

Philander Virgil Dibble, often referred to and seen in many documents as "P.V." He married Frances Ann Evans (1815-1891) on 25 May 1836. She was the daughter of Williams Evans and Susannah Gabeau. Philander and his wife Frances had a large family of about nine (9) children, including seven sons and two daughters born between 1837 and 1859. P.V. had one son named Andrew Comstock Dibble, Sr. (1849-1924), and his grandson, Andrew Comstock Dibble, Jr. (1895-1982), and a great- grandson, Andrew Comstock Dibble, III (1922-2006) (All having the same name as his brother, who was named for their maternal grandfather Andrew Comstock.). P. V.'s two daughters never married. Philander Virgil Dibble lived in Charleston with his wife and family until about 1862 when they relocated to Orangeburg, at the onset of the Civil War. He and his family remained in Orangeburg for the remainder of his life and most of his children made Orangeburg their home for several generations thereafter.

As the years passed and in the latter part of the 1800s, and 1900s, more and more persons appeared with the surname of "Dibble," because there were many sons: P.V. Dibble had six sons who grew to adulthood, and all had descendants and his brother Andrew Comstock Dibble had three sons who grew to adulthood. Whereas, initially (in the 1820s), there were only the two brothers in South Carolina with the surname of "Dibble."

According to the and *Times and Democrat Newspaper,* of 15 March 1883:

> *"P. V. DIBBLE: After an illness of several weeks, in which he was called upon to endure the most intense suffering, he passed away about 8 O'clock on Saturday night. He was born in Danbury, Conn., in 1808, and at the age of nineteen moved to Charleston, where he engaged in mercantile pursuits, and continued until the breaking out of the Confederate War. In 1862 he came to Orangeburg, where he has resided until his death, living a life of uniform religious consistency which stands forth as an example to all. In deportment, he was quiet and, unobtrusive, and on this account, his true worth was known only to those with whom he was most intimately acquainted. He has left a large family of children. He was in every way a most conscientious and consistent Christian. The church has lost in him a strong pillar, and the community a valued citizen. He has been an officer in the Methodist Church for many years. The body of the deceased was taken to the Episcopal burying ground."*

Philander Virgil and Frances Ann Evans Dibble Sunnyside Cemetery, Orangeburg, South Carolina

Philander Virgil DIBBLE and his wife Frances Ann Evans are the parents of seven sons and two daughters:

> Samuel Dibble (1837-1913) (Civil War, Confederate) Congressman), mar. Mary Christina Louis
>   (1844-1922)
> William Henley Dibble (1840-1840)
> Virgil Cornelius Dibble, (Reverend), (1841-1918), (Sgt.Maj., Civil War, Confederate)
>   mar. Elizabeth Evans Bates (1844-1882)
> Frederick Seeley Dibble, (1844-1917) (Civil War, Confederate),
>   mar. Mary Elizabeth Albergetti (1852-1941)
> Frances "Fannie" Anna Dibble (1846-1875) (never married)
> Andrew Comstock Dibble, Sr. (1849-1924) (Major, Civil War, Confederate), mar.
>   (1) Mary Jane Clark (1851-1880);
>   (2) Rachel Agnes Clark
> Susan Elizabeth Dibble (1852-1884) (never married)
> Edward Courtenay Dibble (1855-1899),
>   mar. Mary Elizabeth Patton Smith (1862-1937)
> Thomas Osmond Summers Dibble (1859-1935),
>   mar. Mary "Minnie" Porcher Wightman (1858-1928)

In this collection, I will only include some of Philander Virgil Dibble descendants, up to the second generation. Although I have concentrated mainly on Andrew Comstock Dibble (1800-1846) and his son Andrew Henry Dibble (1825-1873), I have included P. V., because he also came to Charleston during the 1820s, joining his brother in the hat business, and had a large family, which produced many Dibble descendants, who lived in South Carolina.

DESCENDANTS OF PHILANDER VIRGIL DIBBLE
1808-1883
Charleston and Orangeburg, South Carolina

I. **PHILANDER VIRGIL**[1] **DIBBLE** (Hat Store in Charleston) was born on 30 Nov 1808 in Danbury, Connecticut, USA He died on 10 Mar 1883 in Orangeburg, South Carolina, USA (Age: 74). He married (1) **FRANCES ANN EVANS** (daughter of William EVANS and Susannah Gabeau). She was born on 30 Jul 1815 in Charleston, South Carolina, USA (Born in Charleston, SC.). She died on 22 Oct 1891 in Orangeburg, South Carolina, USA (Buried Sunnyside Cemetery, Orangeburg, SC).

Philander Virgil DIBBLE (Hat Store Charleston) and Frances Ann EVANS had the following children:

CHILDREN

1. **SAMUEL DIBBLE (1837-1913)** *(Philander, Samuel, Samuel, John, Wakefield, Ebenezer, Thomas, Robert)* was born in Charleston of 16 September 1837 and died in Orangeburg on 16 September 1913. He is buried in Sunny Side Cemetery, in Orangeburg, South Carolina. The eldest child of P. V. Dibble and his wife Frances Ann Evans (1815- 1891), had a full and dedicated military and life of public service. In 1853, he enrolled in the College of Charleston, transferring to Wofford College, in Spartanburg, in 1855 and graduating in 1856. He was admitted to the South Carolina Bar in 1859. He enlisted and served as a Sergeant and Lieutenant in the 25th South Carolina Volunteers (Edisto Rifles, Eutaw Regiment), during the Civil War. During his military career, he participated in the Battle of First Manassas in July 21, 1861 and the Battle of Secession Ville, on James Island on June 16, 1862. He was captured by the Union Army on Long Island, South Carolina, on July 8, 1863 and imprisoned at Hilton Head and later to Johnson's Island as POW. He was released from Johnson's Island in later October, 1864. He resumed service in the 25th South Carolina Volunteer in January 1865 and was captured by the Union Troops at Town Creek, North Carolina in February 1865 and imprisoned at Old Capitol Prison in Washington, DC and at Fort Delaware, before he was released.

    He served in the South Carolina House of Representatives, 1877-1888, and the United States Congress representing South Caroline from 1881-1882 and 1883 to 1891. He served as a Trustee for the University of South Carolina, 1878. Samuel Dibble married Mary Christina Louis, daughter of Deopold Louis and Anna Hall on November 10, 1864. She was born on 22 Jun 1844 in Orangeburg, South Carolina. She died on 25 Oct 1922 in Orangeburg, South Carolina (Age 78). They became the parents of two daughters and two sons

2. WILLIAM HENLEY DIBBLE (son of Philander Virgil DIBBLE and Frances Ann EVANS) was born in 1840 in Charleston, South Carolina. He died in 1840 in Charleston, South Carolina, USA

3. VIRGIL CORNELIUS DIBBLE (Rev.) (LT., Civil War, Confederate) (son of Philander Virgil DIBBLE and Frances Ann EVANS, was born on 08 Sep 1841, in Charleston, South Carolina, USA. He died on 14 Aug 1918, In Marion County, USA (Age at Death 76; Buried at Magnolia Cemetery in Charleston). He married (1) Elizabeth Evans Bates (daughter of Rezin Westley Bates and Mary Elizabeth Evans). She was born on 27 Apr 1844 in Saint Mathew's Pariah. She died on 23 Dec 1882, in Charleston, South Carolina, USA (Age 38). He married (W#2) Louise Pemberton (daughter of William F. Pemberton and Mary H Whitman), in 1890, in Charleston, South Carolina, USA. She was born on 30 Dec 1855 in Augusta, Georgia. She died on 03 Dec 1912, in Charleston, Berkeley, South Carolina, USA.

4. FREDERICK SEELEY DIBBLE (Civil War Confederate) (son of Philander Virgil DIBBLE and Frances Ann EVANS) was born on 26 Apr 1844 in Charleston, South Carolina, USA He died on 11 Jul 1917 in Orangeburg, South Carolina, USA He married Mary Elizabeth "Mamie" ALBERGETTI on 24 Mar 1883 in Charleston, SC. She was born on 24 Mar 1852 in South Carolina. She died on 30 Apr 1941 in Orangeburg, South Carolina (Age: 89).

5. FRANCES ANNA (FANNIE) DIBBLE (Daughter of Philander Virgil DIBBLE and Frances Ann EVANS) was born on 01 Jul 1846 in Charleston, South Carolina. She died on 20 Aug 1875 in Sullivan's Island, South Carolina, USA (Buried: Orangeburg, SC).

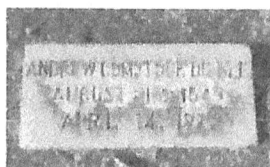

6. ANDREW COMSTOCK DIBBLE SR. (Major) (Civil War, Confederate) (son of Philander Virgil DIBBLE and Frances Ann EVANS) was born on 13 Aug 1849 in Charleston, South Carolina, USA. He died on 14 Apr 1924 in Orangeburg, South Carolina, USA (Age: 74). He married (1) MARY JANE CLARK (First wife) (daughter of CLARK). She was born on 01 Apr 1851 in Orangeburg, Orangeburg, South Carolina. She died on 04 Oct 1880 in Orangeburg, South Carolina. He married (2) RACHEL AGNES CLARK (daughter of CLARK) in 1890. She was born on 18 Feb 1859 in South Carolina, USA. She died on 20 Sep 1944 in Orangeburg, South Carolina.

7. SUSAN ELIZABETH DIBBLE {Never married) (daughter of Philander Virgil DIBBLE and Frances Ann EVANS) was born on 03 Feb 1852 in Charleston, South Carolina. She died on 03 Aug 1934 in Richland, South Carolina, USA (Buried: Orangeburg, SC)

8. EDWARD COURTENAY DIBBLE (son of Philander Virgil DIBBLE and Frances Ann EVANS) was born on 22 Jul 1855 in Charleston, South Carolina, USA. He died on 13 Mar 1899 in South Carolina (Buried in Sunnyside Cemetery, Orangeburg, SC). He married Mary "Mamie" Elizabeth Patton SMITH (daughter of William Walton SMITH Sr. and Julia Henrietta DIBBLE) on 08 Apr 1884 in Charleston, South Carolina. She was born on 24 Oct 1863 in Charleston County, South Carolina, USA. She died on 12 Feb 1937 in Columbia, Richland, South Carolina, United States (Buried at Sunnyside Cemetery, Orangeburg, SC at age 73).

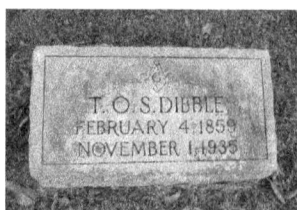

9. THOMAS OSMOND SUMMERS DIBBLE (T.O.S.) son of Philander Virgil Dibble and Frances Ann EVANS) was born on 04 Feb 1859, in Charleston, South Carolina. He died on 01 Nov 1935 in Orangeburg,

South Carolina, USA. (Age at death, 76). He married Mary "Minnie" Porcher Wightman in 1884. Se was born on 15 Nov 1858 in Charleston County, South Carolina, USA. She died on 03 Dec 1928 in Orangeburg, South Carolina, USA (Age 70).

GRANDCHILDREN

1. **SAMUEL DIBBLE (U.S. Congress) (Civil War),** (son of Philander Virgil) was born on 16 Sep 1837 in Charleston, South Carolina, USA. He died on 16 Sep 1913 in Orangeburg, South Carolina, USA (Age: 76). He married Mary Christina LOUIS (daughter of Deopold LEWIS and Ann Agnes Louis). She was born on 22 Jun 1844 in Orangeburg, South Carolina, USA. She died on 25 Oct 1922 in Orangeburg, South Carolina (Age: 78). Samuel DIBBLE (U.S. Congress) (Civil War) and Mary Christina LOUIS had the following children:

   i. **FRANCES AGNES DIBBLE**, (daughter of Samuel DIBBLE and Mary Christina LOUIS) was born on 03 Dec 1866 in Orangeburg, South Carolina, USA. She died on 23 Jun 1941 in South Carolina. She married BENJAMIN HART Moss (JUDGE) (son of William Crawford Moss and Rebecca Carolina Moss). He was born on 17 Jan 1862 in South Carolina. He died on 22 Apr 1939 in Orangeburg, South Carolina, USA.

   ii. **SAMUEL DIBBLE II**, (son of Samuel DIBBLE and Mary Christina LOUIS) was born on 25 Nov 1869 in Charleston County, South Carolina, USA He died on 28 Apr 1952 in Orangeburg County, South Carolina, USA (Age: 83). He married Annie Wyatt.

iii. **LOUIS VIRGIL DIBBLE** (son of Samuel DIBBLE and Mary Christina LOUIS) was born on 26 Feb 1873 in Orangeburg, Orangeburg County, South Carolina, USA He died on 19 Jun 1917 in Orangeburg, Orangeburg County, South Carolina, USA He married Annie Elizabeth Leak WYATT (daughter of Thomas Barton WYATT and Ann E. LEAK) on 15 Jan 1902 in Anson, North Carolina, USA She was born on 1O Aug 1879 in Wadesboro, North Carolina, USA She died on 20 June 1959, Sanitarium, in Orangeburg, South Carolina, USA (Age: 79).

iv. **MARY HENLEY DIBBLE** (daughter of Samuel DIBBLE and Mary Christina LOUIS) was born on 09 Dec 1874 in Orangeburg, South Carolina. She died on 07 Jan 1934 in Orangeburg County, South Carolina, USA She married WHITEFIELD WILLIAM WATSON (son of Artemas Briggs Watson and Angelina Watson). He was born on 15 Jan 1872 in Orangeburg County, South Carolina, USA He died in 1941 in Orangeburg County, South Carolina, USA

2. **VIRGIL CORNELIUS DIBBLE (Minister) (Lt. Civil War)** (Confederate) was born on 08 Sep 1841 in Charleston, South Carolina, USA. He died on14 Aug. 1918, is Buried at Magnolia Cemetery in Charleston). He married ELIZABETH **EVANS BATES {W.#1)** {daughter of Rezin Wesley Bates and Mary Elizabeth EVANS). She was born on 27 Apr 1844 in Saint Mathew's Parish. She died on 23 Dec 1882 in Charleston, South Carolina, USA (Age: 38). He married (2) LOUISE **PEMBERTON** (daughter of William F. Pemberton and Mary H. Whitman) in 1890 in Charleston, South Carolina, USA. She was born on 30 Dec 1855 in Augusta, Georgia. She died on 03 Dec 1912 in Charleston Berkeley, Carolina, USA

Virgil Cornelius DIBBLE (Rev.) (LT. Civil War Confederate) and Elizabeth Evans BATES (W.#1) had the following children:

i.   **VIRGIL CORNELIUS DIBBLE JR.**, (son of Virgil Cornelius DIBBLE (Rev.) and Elizabeth Evans BATES (W.#1)) was born in Aug 1876 in Charleston County, South Carolina, USA He died on 25 Jan 1947 in Greenville County, (Age: Age 70). He married AMELIA CLAASEN DIXON (daughter of August F Claasen and Dora Mensch). She was born in May 1881 in Kentucky. She died on 03 Jul 1930 in Richland, South Carolina, USA.

ii.   **ENOCH MARVIN DIBBLE DR.** (CAPT. MC). (son of Virgil Cornelius DIBBLE (Rev.) and Elizabeth Evans BATES (W.#1)) was born on 09 Apr 1878 in Charleston, South Carolina, United States. He died on 18 Feb 1962 in Marion County, South Carolina, USA. He married H. Alison WEBB (daughter of Hyleman Alison Webb and Martha Ann Webb). She was born on 13 Feb 1875 in Hampton County, South Carolina, United States of America. She died on 24 Jun 1962 in Marion, Marion County, South Carolina.

iii. **EDITH MAE DIBBLE**, (daughter of Virgil Cornelius DIBBLE **(Rev.)** and Elizabeth Evans BATES (W.#1)) was born on 06 May 1881 in Charleston, Berkeley County, SC. She died on 02 Jun 1965 in Greenville County, South Carolina, USA She married JAMES ERNEST DANIEL (MD) (COL. MEDICAL CORPS) (son of James Walter Daniel and Emma Nancy). He was born on 05 Jun 1883 in Greenville, South Carolina, USA He died on 24 Sep 1938

iv.   **EVANS BATES DIBBLE** (WW I, Sgt.), (son of Virgil Cornelius Dibble and Elizabeth Evans BATES) was born on 22 Dec. 1882, in Charleston, Berkeley County, South Carolina., USA. He died on 14 Oct. 11951, in Orangeburg.

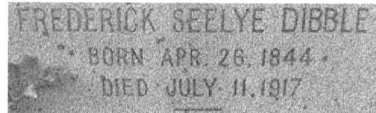

4. **FREDERICK SEELEY DIBBLE (Civil War, Confederate)** was born on 26 Apr 1844 in Charleston, South Carolina, USA. He died on 11 Jul 1917, in Orangeburg, South Carolina, USA. He married Mary Elizabeth "Mamie" Albergetti on 24 Mar 1883 in Charleston, SC. She was born on 24 Mar 1852 in South Carolina. She died on 30 Apr 1941 in Orangeburg, South Carolina (Age 89.)

Frederick Seeley DIBBLE (Civil War Confederate) and Mary Elizabeth "Mamie" ALBERGETTI had the following children:

i.   **FRANCES EVANS FANNY DIBBLE** (daughter of Frederick Seeley DIBBLE and Mary Elizabeth "Mamie" ALBERGETTI) was born in Jan 1886 in Orangeburg, SC and died 7 Feb 1972. She married Rozier Guillard Smith, Sr., (1884-1947).

ii.   **MARGARET ALDRET DIBBLE** (daughter of Frederick Seeley DIBBLE and Mary Elizabeth "Mamie" ALBERGETTI) was born in Jan 1886. She died in 1887.

iii.   **FEDERICK WARREN DIBBLE Rev**(son of Frederick Seeley DIBBLE and Mary Elizabeth "Mamie" ALBERGETTI was born on 02 Apr 1889 in Orangeburg, South Carolina, USA He died on 10 Dec 1966 in Marlin, Falls, Texas, USA He married (1) May DOSHER. She was born on 09 May 1890 in Louisiana, USA She died on 25 Jul 1975 in Houston, Harris County, Texas, USA He married (2) Ava Lee TAPP, daughter of James Lee TAPP and Ava Len. She was born on 20 Jan 1894 in Charlotte, Mecklenburg County, North Carolina, USA She died Dec 1989 in Columbia, Richland County, South Carolina.

5. **ANDREW COMSTOCK DIBBLE SR. (Major) (Civil War Confederate))** was born on 13 Aug 1849 in Charleston, South Carolina, USA. He died on 14 Apr 1924 in Orangeburg, South Carolina, USA (Age: 74). He married (1) Mary Jane Clark (daughter of Samuel Hill CLARK). She was born on 01 Apr 1851 in Orangeburg, Orangeburg, South Carolina. She died on 04 Oct 1880 in Orangeburg, South Carolina. He married (2) Rachel Agnes Clark (daughter of Samuel Hill CLARK), in 1890. She was born on 18 Feb 1859 in South Carolina, USA. She died on 20 Sep 1944 in Orangeburg, South Carolina. He married two sisters.

Andrew Comstock DIBBLE Sr. (Major) (Civil War Confederate) and Mary Jane CLARK had the following children:

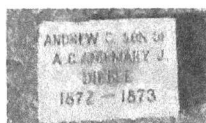

   i.   **ANDREW COMSTOCK DIBBLE (Died as infant))**
        and Mary Jane CLARK was born on 03 Sep 1872 in Orangeburg County, South Carolina, USA. He died on 17 Jul 1873 in Orangeburg County, South Carolina, USA ((Sunnyside Cemetery)).

   ii. **FRANCIS ELDON DIBBLE (Minister, Methodist Episcopal Church),** son of Andrew Comstock Dibble and Mary Jane CLARK was born on 23 Nov 1875 in Bamburgh, South Carolina, USA. He died on 20 Jun 1952 in Richland, South Carolina, USA. He married Nivea Blanche. She was born on 26 May 1867 in Gray Court, Laurens County, South Carolina, USA. She died on 21 Jun 1952 in Orangeburg, South Carolina, USA.

   iii. **EMMET CLARK DIBBLE,** (son of Andrew Comstock Dibble and Mary Jane CLARK) was born on 06 Feb 1878 in Bamberg County, South Carolina, USA. He died on 12 May 1952 in Baymo, Cuba (Orangeburg Native).

        Andrew Comstock DIBBLE Sr. (Major)(Civil War Confederate) and Rachel Agnes CLARK had the following children:

iv. **RUTH ANN DIBBLE,** (daughter of Andrew Comstock DIBBLE Sr. and Rachel Agnes CLARK) was born on 19 Oct 1890 in Orangeburg County, South Carolina, USA. She died on 02 Jul 1986 in Orange, Orangeburg, South Carolina.

v. **INFANT DIBBLE,** (daughter of Andrew Comstock DIBBLE Sr. daughter of Rachel Agnes CLARK) was born in 1891 in Orangeburg, South Carolina. She died in 1891 in Orangeburg, Orangeburg, South Carolina.

vi. **MARY LOU DIBBLE,** (daughter of Andrew Comstock and Rachel Agnes CLARK) was born on 28 Nov 1893 in Orangeburg County, South Carolina, USA. She died on 02 Jun 1983 in Orangeburg, South Carolina, USA.

vii. **ANDREW COMSTOCK DIBBLE JR.,** (son of Andrew Comstock DIBBLE Sr. and Rachel Agnes CLARK) was born on 13 Feb 1895 in Orangeburg County, South Carolina, USA. He died on 18 May 1982 in Orangeburg, Orangeburg, South Carolina, United States of America. He married Lucille Murchison Jackson daughter of Alex Jackson). She was born on 11 Feb 1899 in South Carolina; South Carolina. She died on 09 Aug 1986 in Orangeburg, South Carolina, United States of America.

6. **EDWARD COURTENAY[2] DIBBLE,** (son of Philander Virgil Dibble) was born on 22 Jul 1855 in Charleston, South Carolina, USA. He died on 13 Mar 1899 in South Carolina (Buried in Sunnyside Cemetery, Orangeburg, SC). He married Mary "Mamie" Elizabeth Patton Smith (daughter of William Walton Smith, Sr. and Julia Henrietta Dibble) on 08 Apr 1884 in Charleston, South Carolina. She was born on 24 Oct 1863 in Charleston County, South Carolina, USA. She died on 12 Feb 1937 in Columbia, Richland, South Carolina, United States (Buried at Sunnyside Cemetery, Orangeburg, SC at age 73). Edward Courtenay DIBBLE and Mary "Mamie" Elizabeth Patton SMITH had the following children:

i. **COURTENAY DIBBLE, SR.,** (son of Edward Courtenay DIBBLE and Mary "Mamie" Elizabeth Patton SMITH), was born on 06 Nov 1887 in Orangeburg County, South Carolina, USA. He died on 13 May 1888 in Orangeburg, South Carolina, United States.

ii. **JULIA GERTRUDE DIBBLE,** (daughter of Edward Courtenay DIBBLE and Mary "Mamie" Elizabeth Patton SMITH) was born on 30 Nov 1888 in Orangeburg, South Carolina, United States. She died on 04 Feb 1956 in Columbia Ward 1, Richland, South Carolin

iii. **WILLIAM VIRGIL DIBBLE** {Methodist Minister) (son of Edward Courtenay DIBBLE and Mary "Mamie" Patton SMITH) was born on 25 May 1890 in Orangeburg, South Carolina. He died on 1O Apr 1970 in Chatham, Georgia. He married AUGUSTUS "GUSSIE" MUCKENFUSS (daughter of Charles Henry Muckenfuss and Augusta E. Hicklin). She was born on 30 Jul 1887 in Charleston Berkeley, South Carolina, USA. She died on 14 Jan 1976.

iv. **FRANCES DIBBLE,** (daughter of Edward Courtenay DIBBLE and Mary "Mamie" Elizabeth Patton SMITH) was born on 11 Nov 1891 in Orangeburg, Orangeburg, South Carolina, United States. She died on 22 May 1892 in Orangeburg, County, South Carolina, USA

211

v.   **MARY COURTENAY DIBBLE,** (daughter of Edward Courtenay DIBBLE and Mary "Mamie" Elizabeth Patton SMITH) was born on 01 Jul 1893 in Orangeburg, South Carolina, USA She died on 10 Nov 1998 in Orangeburg, South Carolina, USA.

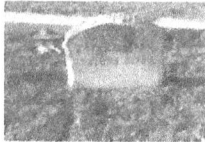

vi. **BESSIE DIBBLE**, (daughter of Edward Courtenay DIBBLE and Mary "Mamie" Elizabeth Patton SMITH) was born on 09 May 1896 in Orangeburg, South Carolina, USA She died on 22 May 1896, Orangeburg County, SC.

7.   **THOMAS OSMOND SUMMERS DIBBLE** (T.O.S.) (son of Philander Virgil) was born on 04 Feb 1859 in Orangeburg, South Carolina, USA He died on 01 Nov 1935 in Orangeburg, South Carolina, USA (Age at Death: 76). He married Mary "Minnie" Porcher Wightman in 1884. She was born on 15 Nov 1858 in Charleston County, South Carolina, USA. She died on 03 Dec 1928 in Orangeburg, South Carolina, USA (Age: 70).

Thomas Osmond Summers DIBBLE (T.O.S.) and Mary "Minnie" Porcher Wightman had the following children:

i.   **SUMMERS WIGHTMAN DIBBLE,** (son of Thomas Osmond Summers DIBBLE (T.O.S.) and Mary "Minnie" Porcher Wightman) was born on 22 Apr 1886 in Orangeburg, South Carolina, USA He died on 17 Nov 1959 in Orangeburg, South Carolina, USA (Age: 73). He married Margaret Annie TARRANT daughter of Robert Benson Tarrant and Margaret Anne Argoe. She was born on 02 Apr 1885 in South Carolina. She died on 16 Oct 1958 in Orangeburg, South Carolina, USA.

ii. **SUSAN VICTORIA DIBBLE,** (daughter of Thomas Osmond Summers DIBBLE (T.O.S.) and Mary "Minnie" Porcher Wightman) was born on 01 Nov 1889 Orangeburg, South Carolina. She died on 15 Dec 1984.

iii. **MINNIE MELLICHAMP MOWRY,** (daughter of Thomas Osmond Summers DIBBLE (T.O.S.) and Mary "Minnie" Porcher Wightman) was born on 28 Apr 1891 in Orangeburg, South Carolina, USA She died on 01 Feb 1961 in Orangeburg, Orangeburg County, South Carolina, USA She married Edward Manigault MOWRY SR. He was born on 06 Dec 1892. He died on 16 Jan 1965.

iv. **LUCILE HENLEY DIBBLE,** (daughter of Thomas Osmond Summers DIBBLE (T.O.S.) and Mary "Minnie" Porcher Wightman) was born on 07 Aug 1900 in Georgia, USA. She died on 27 Feb 1988 in Spartanburg, South Carolina, USA. She married William Oliver YOUNG SR. He was born on 05 Mar 1897 in Gainesville, Hall County, Georgia, USA. He died on 10 Mar 1973 in Columbia, Richland County, South Carolina.

v.   **WIGHTMAN DIBBLE,** (son of Thomas Osmond Summers DIBBLE (T.O.S.) and Mary "Minnie" Porcher Wightman) was born on 22 Oct 1901. He died on 02 Jun 1902.

vi. **OLA REGARD DIBBLE,** (daughter of Thomas Osmond Summers DIBBLE (T.O.S.) and Mary "Minnie" Porcher Wightman) was born on 14 Oct 1904. She died on 04 Jun 1905.

APPENDICES

"We hold these Truths to be self-evident,
that all men are created equal,
that they are endowed by their Creator
with certain unalienable Rights,
that among these are
Life, Liberty, and the Pursuit of Happiness…"

The Declaration of
Independence, July 4, 1776

The appendices included in this section are important for the many of the Dibble descendants to be aware of, since these early ancestors married women who also came from families which have a heritage that has been documented in many instances. Naturally, I have not included all the female lines. I have selected the Trowbridge and Comstock Families because they are closer related to me since these two ladies, Sarah Trowbridge (1743-1772) and Mary "Polly" Comstock (1778-1866) married Samuel Dibble, Sr., and Samuel Dibble, Jr., who are the Great-Grandfather and Grandfather of Andrew Henry Dibble, Sr.

SARAH TROWBRIDGE (1743-1772), can trace her heritage through several generations of the Prowse line from John Prowse II (Gentleman) (-1598) to John Prowse (1377-) and Agnes Bamfield (1386) to thirty-two more generations to Pepin of Lombardy (0775-0810) and then **CHARLES I, (CHARLEMANGE, 0742-0814)).**

The **STARR FAMILY** was selected since Andrew Comstock (1752-1789) married Mercy H. Starr (1750-1841). The Starr family can trace its heritage in America back to Thomas Starr, I (1567-1640) and Dr. Comfort Starr (1589- 1659), and Dr. Thomas Star, II (1615-1658) (who are father, son, grandson), these three generations all arrived in the Massachusetts Bay Colony, in 1635.

The Appendix on The **FYLER FAMIY** is important also, since the name of Lt. Walter Fyler (1613- 1683) is included among the one hundred and forty names on the Founder's Monument in Windsor, Connecticut. He arrived in the Massachusetts Bay Colony, in 1630, before settling in Windsor. Other names of our ancestors, who are included on the Founder's Monument are: Robert and Thomas Dibble, Thomas Ford, and Simon Hoyt.

I have only included four of these ancestral lines through a female. Of course, there are many, many more that have not been included, although they are equally as important.

215

APPENDIX I

The Trowbridge Family

England to Massachusetts and Connecticut

SAMUEL DIBBLE, SR. (1742-1821) married SARAH TROWBRIDGE (1743-1772), who descends from the well-known family of **CAPTAIN THOMAS TROWBRIDGE (c.1598-1672),** the first Trowbridge to come to Dorchester, Massachusetts from England in 1636, and **ELIZABETH MARSHALL** (1603-1641).

There is a town called Trowbridge in Wiltshire, England, which had its own castle and village as early as the middle of the Twelfth Century. There is mention of one John Troubrige (or Trowbridge) in the early records there. It is supposed that a member of the family moved to Devonshire, England in the thirteenth Century. Chapman is his genealogy of the Trowbridge Family says, *"The very ancient name of Trowbridge drives its name from its inheritance in the Parish of Crittendon, Devon, where it has resided for many centuries and was the property of Peter de Trowbridge in the reign of Edward I."* Edward I, reined in the thirteenth century (1272-1307). A younger branch of the family moved to Taunton, Somersetshire, a neighboring shire, about 1550. Taunton lies between Exeter and Bridgewater Exeter and Plymouth. The town of Taunton was a center for the woolen trade.

The earliest known Trowbridge is **THOMAS**, born about 1482 in Brushford, Somersetshire, England. He married a lady named "Ann" about 1510. Thomas died in 1525, in Taunton, Somersetshire. This union had one known son named JOHN, born about 1512, in Taunton.

JOHN TROWBRIDGE, born about 1512 in Shaford, Essex, England, married ALICE about 1537, in Bushford, Somersetshire. He died about 1545 in Taunton, Somersetshire. John and Alice had one known child, THOMAS, born in 1542, in Taunton.

This **THOMAS TROWBRIDGE**, born about 1542, in Taunton, married JOAN HUTCHINS LAURENCE, about 1569, in Somersetshire, England. Joan, born about 1546, was the daughter of John Laurence and Alice Hitchins. Thomas was a prominent merchant in Taunton and operated a store, were he sold woolen cloth and other goods at No. 15 Fore Street, Taunton. He leased the store for 99 years from the Portman family and was responsible for the maintenance of the building. He remodeled it in about 1578 and carved the date, "1578," on the board, together with his initials, "TT", on one side and the initials of his wife "JT" on the other side. This sign (or a replica) is still hanging over the second story window in the front of the store. Thomas operated the store until about 1606, stating at this time that he had operated it for 30 years. The store is currently operated as a Pub, known as the "Tudor Tavern." There is a very nice plaque hanging in the vestibule of St. Mary Magdalene Church, which briefly describes this Charitable Gift that Thomas created back in December 1614, of giving eight acres of land in West Monkton to God, for "the residue of 1,000 years." Thomas died 20 February 1619, in Taunton, and his wife died the same day. They had three children: Alice, Dorothy and JOHN, born 1570.

JOHN TROWBRIDGE, born 25 March 1570, in Taunton, Somersetshire, England and died on 5 July 1649, at age 79 years. He married AGNES PROWSE on 31 July 1597 in St. Peter's, Tiverton,

Devonshire, England. Agnes was born in Tiverton on 15 April 1575 and was buried on 6 June 1622. John was the sole son and heir at his father's death in 1619, and served Taunton as Mayor 1629-30 and 1637-38 and was also magistrate, and served as Warden of St. Mary Magdalen, constable & portreve of Taunton Castle manor. John was even more prominent than his father. He was a wool merchant and had a shop next to his father's on Fore Street. He also held property in Strogursey and Cannington and trade with Bristol and London. John's wife Agnes Prowse was also from well to do merchants and through the Prouse Family it is possible to trace my ancestry back to Alfred the Great, Cerdic the Saxon, Rollo the Viking and Charlemagne the Holy Roman Emperor. JOHN TROWBRIDGE and AGNES PROWSE TROWBRIDGE had nine children. **THOMAS**, Elizabeth, John, Prudence, Agnes, William, James, Joan and Tracy. John married a second time to Alice Reed of Tiverton, on 11 March 1623/4, of Tiverton. I descend from this THOMAS TROWBRIDGE, born 1598, who migrated to New England in 1636 and who is my 8th Great- Grandfather.

As a young man, **THOMAS TROWBRIDGE, (Capt.) (c.1598-1672), (John, Thomas, John, Thomas)** the son of **JOHN (1570-1649)**, settled in Exeter where he became a member of the powerful Merchants and Adventurer's Guild. He married **ELIZABETH MARSHALL (1603-1641),** daughter of **John MARSHALL,** on 20 December 1624, in St. Mary's Arches, Exeter, Devonshire, England. Elizabeth's father John was Sheriff, Alderman and Mayor of Exeter and Elizabeth's grandfather, Richard Bevys (Beavis) (BEAVIS), was Mayor of Exeter from1600-1603 when he died in office. John Marshall, in addition to his political offices, was a successful merchant. It was probably through his connections that Thomas was able to gain entrance to this Guild. Thomas was named in his father's Will of 1 July 1649, as "eldest son."

THOMAS TROWBRIDGE was the *First Trowbridge* to come to Dorchester, Massachusetts from England, in 1636. When Thomas immigrated to America, he was working as a merchant engaged in wool and was therefore not one of the Puritans in the settlement at Dorchester, Massachusetts. He sided with those who were dissatisfied with conditions at Dorchester and moved with them in 1639 to the New Haven Colony. He appeared to have spent very little time in New Haven, making several voyages to Barbados and England in pursuit of his business. His wife, Elizabeth, died in about 1641, in New Haven, possibly while he was away. He never returned to New Haven but returned to Taunton, England where he got caught up in the English Civil War of 1645. Thomas served as a Captain in the Parliamentary Troops, serving under Colonel Blake in the defense of Taunton. He later married his first cousin, widow, Frances Shattuck, daughter of his aunt Dorothy Trowbridge.

During his many absences in the Colony, he left his family under the care of his steward, Henry Gibbons, who appeared to be an unfaithful servant who seized Thomas' property and deserted the three boys, **Thomas**, William, and James. Town records show where the boys were declared wards of the Colony and Sergeant Thomas Jeffries who took them into his home to rear and educate. **Thomas** corresponded with his sons and when they became of age, he gave them power of attorney to regain his property from Gibbons, on 14 January 1664. The sons (Thomas II, William, and James Trowbridge) were successful in reclaiming their father's estate, which he gave them on a share and share alike basis. Thomas left his older son John (1629-1653) in Taunton, England when he came to America, with his wife and young sons, Thomas, II (1631-1702), **William (1633-1688).** His youngest son James (1636-1717) was born and baptized in Dorchester Massachusetts in 1637/38. These three sons of Thomas are the ancestors of the Trowbridge Family in America. I descend from Thomas' son WILLIAM TROWBRIDGE. His signature:

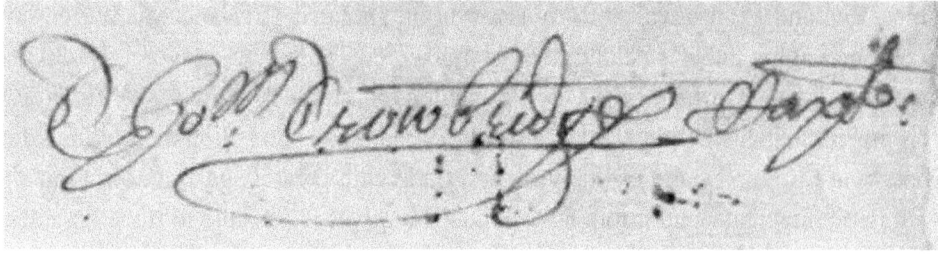

WILLIAM TROWBRIDGE (CAPTAIN) (1633-1688) (Thomas (1598), John (1570), Thomas

(1542), John (1512), Thomas (c.1482)) was baptized on 3 September 1633, in Exeter, Devonshire, England and died November, 1688 in West Haven, Connecticut. He came to the Massachusetts Bay Colony with his parents and brothers while still a youngster, and then to the plantation in New Haven. When his father was called back to England, he and his brothers were left here in America. On 9 March 1656, **WILLIAM** married **ELIZAETH LAMBERTON (1632-1710)**, daughter of **CAPTAIN GEORGE LAMBERTON**

(1604-1646), who was born in England and vanished at sea in 1646. William was Master of sloop ship *"Cocke"*, making a number of trips out of New Haven. I descend from **WILLIAM**'s son, **SAMUEL TROWBRIDGE, Sr.**

CAPT. WILLIAM TROWBRIDGE and ELIZABETH LAMBERTON are the parents of:

> William Trowbridge (1657-1703)
> Thomas Trowbridge (1659-)
> Elizabeth Trowbridge (1602-1732)
> James Trowbridge (1664-1732)
> Margaret Trowbridge (1666-)
> Hannah Trowbridge (1668-)
> Abigail Trowbridge (1670-1670) (twin)
> SAMUEL TROWBRIDGE, SR. (1670-1741) (twin)
> **married Sarah Lacy (1674-1753)**
> Mary Trowbridge (1672-
> Joseph Trowbridge (1676-1715)

SAMUEL TROWBRIDGE, SR. (William (1633), Thomas (1598), John (1570), Thomas **(1542), John (1512), Thomas (1482)** was born on 7 October 1670 in New Haven, Connecticut and died in 1741. He married **Sarah Lacy (1674-1753).** I descend from **SAMUEL, SR.**'s son, **SAMUEL TROWBRIDGE, JR. (1700-1780).**

SAMUEL TROWBRIDGE, SR. and SARAH LACY are the parents of:

> Sarah Trowbridge (1699-)
> **SAMUEL TROWBRIDGE, JR., (1700-1782)**
> John Trowbridge (1705-)
> Elizabeth Trowbridge (1710-1780)
> Hannah Trowbridge (1712-

SAMUEL TROWBIDGE, JR. (Samuel, William, Thomas, John (1570-), Thomas, John, Thomas (1482)) was born on 26 August 1700 in Stafford, Connecticut, and died in 1782. He married **Sarah Seeley (1698-1751).**

SAMUEL TROWBRIDGE, JR., and SARAH SEELEY, of New Fairfield Congregational Church, became the parents of about nine children:

> Abigail Trowbridge (1724-)
> Stephen Trowbridge (1726-)
> Seth Trowbridge (1729-)
> William Trowbridge (1732-)
> Mehitable Trowbridge (1735-1758)
> Hannah Trowbridge (1740-1713)
> **SARAH TROWBRIDGE (1743-1772),**
>   **mar. SAMUEL DIBBLE, SR.**
> John Trowbridge (1746-1825) (Sergeant, Revolutionary Patriot)
> Billy Trowbridge (1748-)

SARAH TROWBRIDGE (Samuel (1700), Samuel (1670), William (1633), Thomas (1598), John (1570), Thomas (1542), John (1512), Thomas (1482), was born on 27 April 1743 and died 15 July 1772, probably in childbirth of her last child, Sarah. **Sarah TROWBRIDGE** was the first wife of **SAMUEL DIBBLE, SR., (1742-1821)** of Danbury, Connecticut. He was born 8 December 1742 and died 23 October 1821. Sarah had seven children, with only one son, **Samuel**. Samuel Dibble, Sr.'s second wife was Phoebe Benedict (1750-1828), who he had seven children. Samuel's third wife was Ruth Benedict.

SAMUEL DIBBLE, SR. married SARAH TROWBRIDGE who descends from the well-known family of **CAPTAIN THOMAS TROWBRIDGE (c.1598-1672).** He was buried 3 February 1672 in Taunton, England. **Thomas** married on 26 March 1627 to **Elizabeth Marshall**, baptized 24 March 1602/03, in Exeter, England and she died about 1641, probably in New Haven, Connecticut.

I descend from **SARAH TROWBRIDGE's** son, **SAMUEL DIBBLE, JR.**

SARAH TROWBRIDGE and SAMUEL DIBBLE, SR., are the parents of:

> Mabel Dibble (1763-1861
> Rodah Dibble (1765-)
> Sallome Dibble (1767-1807)
> **SAMUEL DIBBLE, JR., (1769-1860)** mar.
>   (1) Rue Marie Benedict (1768-1796);
>   (2) **MARY "POLLY" COMSTOCK (1778-1866)**
> Sarah Dibble (1772-1772)

(SAMUEL DIBBLE, SR. (1742-1821) and SARAH TROWBRIDGE (1743-1772), and SAMUEL DIBBLE, JR. (1769-1860) and MARY "POLLY COMSTOCK (1778-1866) are discussed further in the DIBBLE portion of this document.)

Francis Bacon Trowbridge. *Trowbridge Genealogy, History of the Trowbridge Family*, (1908).

Trowbridge

Trowbridge Castle owned by Thomas Trowbridge, Taunton, Somershire, England

St. Mary Arches Church
Thomas and Elizabeth Marshall Trowbridge were married, 24 March 1627
Exeter, Devon, England

ANDREW HENRY DIBBLE, SR.
TROWBRIDGE GENEALOGY

ANDREW HENRY DIBBLE, SR. (1825-1873)
(m.) Ellie Naomi NAUDIN (1828-1920), of South Carolina

Son of **ANDREW COMSTOCK DIBBLE** (1800-1846)
(m.) Martha Smith (1800-1849), of Connecticut and South Carolina

Grandson of **SAMUEL DIBBLE, JR.** (1769-1860)
(m.) Mary "Polly **COMSTOCK (**1778-1866), of Connecticut

Great-Grandson of **SAMUEL DIBBLE, SR.** (1742-1821)
(m.) **SARAH TROWBRIDGE** (1743-1772), of Connecticut
(Revolutionary War Patriot)

2nd Great-Grandson of **SAMUEL TROWBRIDGE, JR.** (1700-1782)
(m.) Sarah Seeley (1703-1752), of Connecticut

3rd Great-Grandson of **SAMUEL TROWBRIDGE, SR.** (1670-1742)
(m.) Sarah Lacy (1674-1753), of Connecticut

4th Great-Grandson of **WILLIAM TROWBRIDGE, CAPT** (1633-1688)
(m.) Elizabeth Lamberton (1632-1716), of Connecticut

5th Great-Grandson of **THOMAS TROWBRIGE, II, CAPT** (1598-1672)
(m.) Elizabeth Marshall (1603-1641), of England and Connecticut
(First Trowbridge to America, 1636)

6th Great-Grandson of **JOHN TROWBRIDGE** (1570- 1649),
(m.) Agnes Prowse (1575-1622), of England

7th Great-Grandson of **THOMAS TROWBRIDGE** (1542-1619)
(m.) Joan H. Laurence (1546-1570)

8th Great-Grandson of **JOHN TROWBRIDGW** (1512- 1545)
(m. Alice _(1512-1556)

APPENDIX II

The Comstock Family
England to Massachusetts and Connecticut

SAMUEL DIBBLE, JR. (1769-1860) married **MARY "POLLY" COMSTOCK (1778-1866),** the daughter of **ANDREW COMSTOCK (1752-1789),** and **MERCY H. STARR (1750-1841)**

The **COMSTOCK** family/name traces its origins to a village in Devonshire, England called Culmstock, which is located off the River Clum about ten miles east of Tiverton and about ten miles south of Taunton. The named goes back to the Eleventh or Twelfth centuries. There are numerous Comstock generations, such as:

John Comstock I

John II (1528-1584) who married Agnes Bate (1528-1610)

John Comstock III (1546-1619) married Joan Wylde (1546-1610) William Goodman Comstock
          (1569-1595), of Culmstock (Comstock),

England and his wife Abigail Margaret Wethersfield.

William Wethersfield Comstock (1596-1683)

The earliest Comstock to arrive in the American colony was **WILLIAM WETHERSFIELD COMSTOCK (1596-1683), (William, John, John, John).** William was born 4 July 1596 in Comstock, Devonshire, England, and died in 1683 in New London, Connecticut. He arrived in Massachusetts in 1635 with his second wife, the former, Elizabeth Daniel (1608-1665). While attractive because of the freedoms it offered, Connecticut was still a frontier establishment subject to the threat of Indian attack. The Pequot Indians of the Connecticut River Valley were the most feared of all the tribes in the area, and war with the settlers broke out in 1636.

Ninety Connecticut men were mobilized and put under the command of an experienced army officer, Captain John Mason. Twenty-six of the men were from Wethersfield, and William Comstock was among them. The colonists were joined by nearly a hundred Indians of the friendly Mohegan tribe and about five hundred Narragansett warriors. According to the *"History of Wethersfield,"* William Comstock was one of the fifty-six men who under the leadership of Captain John Mason, captured the Pequot Fort at Mystic, Connecticut on 26 May 1637, and killed about 500 Native Americans (Indians).

Around 1650, thirteen years after the battle (or massacre) of the Pequot, William Comstock, now about 55 years of age, received a grant of land near the site of the former action, located at the present-day New London, Connecticut. He moved and made his home there. That same year he agreed to cooperate with a John Winthrop to establish a water powered grist mill. That mill still stands and is a prominent tourist attraction at New London. This William, who is my 8th Great-grandfather, came to this American colony as most of these early puritan settlers because of religious freedoms they hoped to find here.

WILLIAM WETHERSFIELD COMSTOCK married Elizabeth DANIEL (1608-1665) and had several children:

> John Comstock (1624-1680)
> Samuel Comstock (1628-1660)
> Daniel Comstock (1629-1683)
> Elizabeth Comstock (1633-1659)
> William Comstock (1634-)
> **CHRISOPHER COMSTOCK (1635-1702)**

CHRISTOPHER COMSTOCK (1635-1702) (*William, William, John, John, John*) was born on the 7 October 1635 in England and died 28 December 1702, in Milford, Fairfield, Connecticut. Christopher served as a Sergeant in the French and Indian War. Christopher's Will is dated December 22, 1702, in which he mentions his sons Moses and Samuel and daughters Hannah and Mercy.

CHRISTOPHER COMSTOCK and HANNAH PLATT became the parents of:

> Daniel Comstock (1664-1694)
> Hannah Comstock 1666-1701)
> Abigail Comstock (1669-1689)
> Mary Comstock (1671-1749)
> Elizabeth Comstock (1674-1723)
> Mercy Comstock (1676-1752)
> **SAMUEL COMSTOCK (6 Feb. 1680, died 6 Oct 1752)**
> **(Capt.) (French and Indian War);**
> **Marr. (2) Sarah HANFORD (1677-1752)**
> Nathan Comstock (1682-)
> Moses Comstock (1685-1766)

SAMUEL COMSTOCK (1680-1752) (*Christopher, William, William, John, John, John)* and **SARAH HANFORD** became the parents of:

> Sarah Comstock (1707-1781)
> Samuel Comstock (1708-1743)
> Mary Comstock (1710-1777)
> Lydia Comstock (1713-)
> Nathan Comstock (1714-1794)
> Daniel Comstock (1716-1757)
> **DAVID COMSTOCK, Sr. (29 Feb. 1720, died 19 Nov.1782) (Revolutionary Patriot); Mar.**
> **Rebekah GRUMMON (1727-1812)**

DAVID COMSTOCK (1720-1782) *(Samuel, Christopher, William, William, John, John, John)* and **REBEKAH GRUMMON** became the parents of:

> Hannah Comstock 1747-1759)
> William Comstock (1748-1776)
> Rebecca Comstock (1750-1829)
> ANDREW COMSTOCK (8 Mar.1752, died 7 Mar.1789) (Capt.)

(Revolutionary Patriot); Mar. Mercy Hickok STARR (1750-1841)
Mary Comstock (1753-1776)
Sarah Comstock (1755-1838)
Lydia Comstock (1758-1759) David Comstock, II (1760-1846)

ANDREW COMSTOCK (1752-1789) *(David, Samuel, Christopher, William, William, John, John, John)* and MERCY STARR became the parents of:

> Mary "Polly" Comstock ((1774-1775)
> William "Billy" Comstock (1776-1823)
> Betty Comstock (1778-)
> **MARY "POLLY" COMSTOCK (19 Jun 1778, died 14 Apr 1866)**
> > **Mar. SAMUEL DIBBLE, JR. (6 Nov 1769, died 14 Oct 1860) (War of 1812)**
> Rebecca Comstock (1784-1836)
> Mercy Laurana Comstock (1787-1875)
> **SAMUEL DIBBLE, JR. (1769-1860)** and (1) Rue Maria Benedict had one daughter:
> > Sarah Dibble (1793-1816)
> Polly Mariette **DIBBLE (1798-1876**) Married 20 Jan 1819 to Frederick Seeley, of Danbury, Connecticut.

SAMUEL DIBBLE, JR. (1769-1860) and wife (2) MARY "POLLY" COMSTOCK *(Andrew, David, Samuel, Christopher, William, William, John, John, John)* are the parents of six children:

ANDREW COMSTOCK DIBBLE (1800-1846), Born in Danbury, Connecticut, and migrated to Charleston, South Carolina on 10 December 1821, where he lived the remainder of his life. ANDREW COMSTOCK DIBBLE and MARTHA SMITH (1800-1849) became the parents of (1) ANDREW HENRY DIBBLE (1825-1873), born in Charleston; Mar. (2) Henrietta M. Wagner (1812-1882), of Charleston, SC, and with this union, Andrew Comstock and Henrietta Wagner DIBBLE became the parents of ten (10) children, all born in Charleston, SC.

Horace Benedict **DIBBLE** (1803-1819), born in Danbury, Connecticut.

Rue Maria **DIBBLE (1806-1807**), born in Danbury, Connecticut.

Philander Virgil DIBBLE (1808-1883), born in Danbury, migrated to Charleston, SC in August 1828. He married Frances Anna Evans (1815-1891**)**

Samuel Lorenzo **DIBBLE** (1812-1896), born in Danbury, married Sarah Smith (1816-1929) in Danbury, Connecticut and had about twelve children.

Cornelius Augustus **DIBBLE** (1815-1900), married Nancy Jane Delevan (1824-1886), in Danbury, Connecticut and had about seven children with one son named Andrew Comstock Dibble (1845-1936) who was born in Danbury and died in Nevada.

Two of these **DIBBLE** men (sons of Samuel Dibble, **Jr.**, and **Mary "Polly" COMSTOCK**) migrated to Charleston, South Carolina on 10 December 1821 and 16 August 1828, respectively. (These two **DIBBLE** men are discussed further in the **DIBBLE** portion of this document.)

Wm. Comstock, Seedsman

Comstock Coat of Arms

ANDREW HENRY DIBBLE, SR.
COMSTOCK GENEALOGY

ANDREW HENRY DIBBLE, SR.., (1825-1873)
(m.) Ellie Naomi NAUDIN (1828-1920), of South Carolina

Son of **ANDREW COMSTOCK DIBBLE** (1800-1846)
Martha Smith (1800-1849), of Connecticut and South Carolina

Grandson of **SAMUEL DIBBLE, JR.** (1769-1860)
(m.) Mary "Polly" **COMSTOCK (**1778-1866), of Connecticut

Great-Grandson of **ANDREW COMSTOCK** (1752-1789)
(m.) Mercy Hickok STARR (1750-1841), of Connecticut
(Revolutionary War Patriot)

2nd Great-Grandson of **DAVID COMSTOCK** (1720-1782)
(m.) Rebekah G. Grummon (1727-1812), of Connecticut
(Revolutionary War Patriot)

3rd Great-Grandson of **Captain SAMUEL COMSTOCK** (1680-1752) (m.) Sarah Hanford (1678-1752), of Connecticut
(South Company of Norwalk)

4th Great-Grandson of **Sgt. CHRISTOPHER COMSTOCK** (1635-1702)
(m.) Hannah Platt (1643-1702), of Connecticut
(Colonial Militia/King Philip's War) (First Comstock to America, 1635)

5th Great-Grandson of **WILLIAM COMSTOCK** (1596-1683) (m.) Elizabeth Daniel (1608-1665), of England
(First Comstock to America, 1635)

6th Great-Grandson of **WILLIAM COMSTOCK** (1569-1595), England
(m.) Frances A. (1568-), England, United Kingdom

Comstock Coat of Arms

226

APPENDIX III

The Starr Family

England to Massachusetts and Connecticut

ANDREW COMSTOCK (1752-1789) married MERCY HICKOK STARR (1750-1841), who descended from the well-known STARR(E) Family of Devonshire, England.

The First Starr to come to America was **THOMAS STARR (1567-1640).** Thomas sailed from Sandwich, England in March 1635, aboard the ship *"Hercules,"* being the oldest of three generations of Starr's who travelled together to the New England Colony of Massachusetts, bringing three servants. Thomas married Susan Hendrickson (1569-1640). Susan joined the Dorchester Church on November 4, 1639. After their arrival here, they lived at Cambridge, Duxbury and Dodham, Massachusetts.

The Starr Family is seen in Surry, England as early as the 1400s, where Nicholas Starr (Stearre) (Steere) (1427-1507) is seen. He married Elizabeth.

This Thomas who came to the Boston area in 1635 was the son of Thomas Starr, the Mayor (1538- 1594) and Agnes Russell of Kent, New Romney, England.

Before coming to America, Thomas II was a wool merchant. He lived in St. Mary's Parish, Ashford, Kent, England where five of his children were born and baptized, and probably moved to Canterbury for he was listed as from that place when he sailed for Sandwich. He left a son, Johnosophat, at Canterbury, a man of considerable wealth.

Thomas and Susan are the parents to thirteen children:

> Jonosophat Starr m. Mary
> **Dr. COMFORT STARR, born July 6 1589, Baptized in Cranbrook**
> Nostrength Starr, baptized, 10-1-1591
> Norogift Starr, baptized, 10-1-1592
> William Starr, baptized, 2-26-1594
> Mercy Starr, baptized, 2-26-1596
> Surctrust Starr (female) baptized. 12-3-1598
> Judith Starr, baptized, 10-17-1602
> Standfast or Stanwell Starr, baptized, 4-13-1600
> Truth-Shall-Prevail Starr, baptized, 12-19-1604
> Joyful Starr, baptized, 3-6-1607
> Constant Starr, baptized, 12-23-1610
> Beloved Starr, baptized, 3-27-1616

Dr. COMFORT STARR (*Thomas II, Thomas*) married first Hannah, and married (2) Elizabeth Veritas Mitchell (1595-1658) who died in 63 years old. Elizabeth is the mother of all his children who were all born in England except the youngest Ruth, who was born in Cambridge.

Dr. Comfort STARR and Elizabeth are the parents of:

> **DR. THOMAS STARR (31 Dec 1615--26 November 1658) m. Rachel (1618-1660)**
> Judith Starr, b. 11 Jan 1618
> Mary Starr, b.16 April 1620, m. John Maynard
> Elizabeth Starr b. 1621
>> m1. John Fornisido;
>> m.2 Jno Dix Comfort Starr, b.1624 m. Ann Finch
> John Starr, b. 15 October 1626, m. Martha Bunker Samuel Starr, b. 2 March 1628
> Hannah Starr, b. 22 July 1632, m. John Cutt
> Lydia Starr, b. 22 March 1634, d. 1643; m. Simon Eyrc
> Ruth Starr c. 1637, in Cambridge, Mass., m. Jos Moore

DR. THOMAS STARR (1615-1658) and his wife Rachel Harris (1618-1660), are the parents of the following:

> Samuel Starr (c.1640-) m. Hannah Browster
> Thomas Starr, (c.1642-)
>> m1. Elizabeth Gilbert;
>> m2. Ruth ?
> Comfort (7 June 1644-18 Oct 1693) m. Marah Weld
> Elizabeth Starr, (7 June 1646-) m. John Troadwell
> Benjamin Starr (6 February 1647-) m. Elizabeth Allerton Johosophat (12 November 1650-)
> Constant Starr (1652-Oct 5, 1654, Charlestown)
> William Starr (18 March 1654-) m. Elizabeth Hicks
> **JOSIAH STARR** (1 September 1657-1715) Founder of Danbury Branch, Conn.
> John Starr (c.1658-)

CAPTAIN JOSHUA STARR I, (1 September 1657- 4 January 1715) Married (1) Elizabeth Hicks (1656-1691), in 1692, in Hamstead, LI; **m.2.** Rebekah (1665-1739), in 1685. Captain Josiah Starr served in the French and Indian War. He was born in Charlestown, Massachusetts, lived in Long Island, N.Y., where he married and raised his family, coming to Danbury shortly after it was settled in 1684. He is the founder of the Danbury Branch of the Starr Family, and came to Danbury in 1693. He was the first town clerk, and the second Justice of the peace.

He died in Danbury, at age 57, and his wife Rebekah, died at age 74 and they are both buried beside each other, in the cemetery on what is Wooster Street, today. There are several old headstones at the eastern end of area; there is an upright slab of gray granite, with the inscription nearly obliterated, which marks Joshua and Rebekah's graves.

CAPTAIN JOSHUA STARR (1657-1715) I, and his wife Rebecca (1665-1739) became the parents of:

> Lt. Benjamin STARR (1683-1754)
> Capt. John STARR (1684-1739)

Rachel STARR (1690-1765)
JOSHUA STARR, II (1693-1775)
Daniel STARR (1700-1752)
Capt. Samuel STARR (1704-1778)
Nathaniel STARR 1709-1789)
Abigail STARR (1711-1790)
Elizabeth (1715-1736)
Jehoshaphat STARR, Sr., (1718-1796)

CAPT. JOSHUA STARR II (1693-1778) m. Rebekah Bushnell (1689-1757). They had seven sons and three daughters:

Comfort STARR (1716-1763)
Capt. Joshua STARR (1718-1795)
Captain Thomas STARR (1720-1806)
Major Daniel STARR (1724-1777)
CAPT. JOSEPH STARR (1727-1802) married **Mary "Molly" BENEDICT (1725-1816),** in 1745,
        the daughter of Thomas Benedict (1694-1776) and Abagail Hoyt. (**Revolutionary War**)
Levi STARR (1759-1810)

CAPT JOSEPH STARR (1726-1802) and Mary "Molly" BENEDICT (1725-1816) are the parents of:

Joseph STARR II (1746-1812)
MERCY STARR (1750-1823) married ANDREW COMSTOCK ((1752-1789)
Mary STARR (1753-1839)
Lois STARR (17561823)
Joshua STARR 1757-1838)
Asel STARR (1762-1775)
Jonah STARR (1764-1853)
Rebecca STARR (1767-1847)
Ira STARR (1769-)

ANDREW COMSTOCK and MERCY STARR are the parents of:

Mary COMSTOCK (1774-1775)
Elizabeth COMSTOCK (1775-)
William "Billy" COMSTOCK (1776- 1823)
MARY "POLLY" COMSTOCK (1778-1866) married SAMUEL DIBBLE, JR. (1769-1860)
Rebecca COMSTOCK (1784-1836) Mercy Laura COMSTOCK (1787-1875)

MARY "POLLY" COMSTOCK and SAMUEL DIBBLE, JR. (1769-1860) are the parents of:

Polly or Mary DIBBLE (1798-1876)
ANDREW COMSTOCK DIBBLE (1700-1846)

Rue Mariah DIBBLE (1803-1804)
Horace Benedict DIBBLE (1803-1819)
Philander Virgin DIBBLE (1808-1883)
Samuel Lorenzo DIBBLE (1812-1896)
Cornelius Augustus DIBBLE (1815-1900)

ANDREW COMSTOCK DIBBLE (1800-1846) and **MARTHA SMITH (1800-1849)** are the parents of:

ANDREW HENRY DIBBLE, (1825-1873), Born in Charleston and died in Camden, South Carolina. Married **ELLIE NAOMI NAUDIN (1828-1920)**

Dr. Comfort STARR

ANDREW HENRY DIBBLE, SR.
STARR GENEALOGY

ANDREW HENRY DIBBLE, **SR**. (1825-1873)
(m.) Ellie Naomi NAUDIN (1828-1920), of South Carolina

Son of **ANDREW COMSTOCK DIBBLE** (1800-1846)
Martha Smith (1800-1849), of Connecticut and South Carolina

Grandson of **SAMUEL DIBBLE, JR.** (1769-1860)
(m.) Mary Polly **COMSTOCK (**1778-1866), of Danbury, Connecticut

Great-Grandson of **ANDREW COMSTOCK** (1752-1789)
(m.) Mercy Hickok **STARR** (1750-1841), of Danbury, Conn.

2nd Great-Grandson of **CAPT. JOSEPH STARR, I** (1726-1802)
(m.) Mary "Mollie" **BENEDICT** (1725-1816), of Danbury, Connecticut
(Revolutionary Patriot)

3rd Great-Grandson of **JOSIAH STARR, II** (1693-1778)
(m.) Rebecca BUSHNELL (1701-1757), of Danbury, Connecticut

4th Great-Grandson of **CAPT. JOSIAH STARR, I** (1657-
(m.) Rebecca WHITNEY (1665-1739), of Danbury, Conn.
(French and Indian War)

5th Great-Grandson of **DR. THOMAS STARR II, MD** (1615-1658)
(m.) Rachel HARRIS (1618-1660), of England & Connecticut
(To America, 1635, Three Generations)

6th Great-Grandson of **DR. COMFORT STARR** (1589-1659), England & America
(m.) Elizabeth MITCHELL (1595-1658), England & America
(First Starr to America, 1635)

7th Great-Grandson of **THOMAS STARR, I** (1567-1640), of England & America
(m.) Susanne Hendrickson (1569-1640), of England & America
(First Starr in America, 1635)

Starr

APPENDIX IV

The Fyler Family

England to Massachusetts and Connecticut

WAKEFIELD DIBBLE (1667-1733) married **JANE FYLER (1671-1769)** who descends from the well-known **Lieutenant Walter Fyler (1613-1683),** who came from Devon, England to the Massachusetts Bay Colony in 1630, along with his father George Roman Fyler (1674-1683).

Some of these early settlers who came from England, returned to England, whereas others, like Lt. Walter Fyler, along with about 100 other Puritans left the Massachusetts Bay Colony and walked about two weeks through the wilderness, along an old Indian path to reach Windsor, Connecticut, in 1636. Lt. Fyler became a Freeman in 1634. This means that the Freeman had an advantage in the dividing of lands and were members of the general court, until the representative court system began. We can see he was also literate, where we see his signature that has survived after four hundred years.

LT. WALTER FYLER married Jane IRVING, who was born in 1602, in England and died on September 11, 1690, in Windsor, Connecticut. She arrived in the Massachusetts Bay Colony in 1630. They had two sons: John (1642-1723) and ZERUBABEL FYLER (1644-1714), who was born on December 23, 1644 and died on 21 October 1714, in Connecticut. Walter participated in King Philip War.

Zerubbabel FYLER married Experience STRONG (1650-1714), daughter of Elder John Strong, of Northampton, on 27 May 1669. Zerubbabel Fyler and his wife Experience Strong became the parents of Jane Fyler (1671-1734), who married Wakefield DIBBLE (1667-1733), in 1694.

Jane FYLER married **Wakefield DIBBLE** who was born on September 15, 1667 in Windsor and died on 31 January 1733. Jane was Wakefield's second wife and they had ten children, born between 1695 and 1715, with Lieutenant John Dibble ((1708-1790), being their sixth child.

Jane Fyler and Wakefield Dibble are the parents of ten children:

> Ezra Dibble (1695-1695)
> Ezra Dibble (1697- 1745)
> Mary (1698-1733)
> Sarah Dibble (1701-1791)
> Abigail Dibble (1703- 1791)
> Nehemiah Dibble (1706-1774)
> **JOHN DIBBLE, LT. (1708-1790**)
> Experience Dibble (1720-1774)
> Elizabeth Dibble (1712-1789)
> Ebenezer Dibble (1715-1799

ANDREW HENRY DIBBLE, SR.
FYLER GENEALOGY

ANDREW HENRY DIBBLE, SR., (1825-1873)
(m.) **Ellie Naomi NAUDIN (1828-1920)** of South Carolina

Son of **ANDREW COMSTOCK DIBBLE** (1800-1846)
M**artha Smith (1800-1849)**, of Connecticut and South Carolina

Grandson of SAMUEL **DIBBLE, JR.** (1769-1860)
(m.) **Mary/Polly COMSTOCK (1778-1866),** of Connecticut

Great-Grandson of **SAMUEL DIBBLE, SR.**, (1742-1821)
(m.) **Sarah TROWBRIDGE (1743-1772)** of Connecticut
(Revolutionary War Patriot)

2nd Great-Grandson of **Lieutenant JOHN DIBBLE** (1708-
1790) (m.) **Sarah LEWIS (1708-1787),** of Connecticut
(French and Indian War & Revolutionary War Patriot))

3rd Great-Grandson of **WAKEFIELD DIBBLE (**1667-
1733) (m.) **Jane FYLER (1671-1734),** of Connecticut

4th Great-Grandson of **ZERUBABEL FYLER** (1644-1714)
(m.) **Experience STRONG (1650-1714)***

5th Great-Grandson of **Lieutenant WALTER FYLER (16131683)**
(m.) **Jane IRVING** (1620-1690), of England and Conn.
(First Fyler in America, 1630)
((King Philip's War)

6th Great-Grandson of **GEORGE ROMAN FYLER (1594-1683)**
(m.) **Jane COPE** (1578-1637), of England

FYLER (Filer), Walter (Lieut.), at Dorch(

233

BIBLIOGRAPHY

South Carolina Official Records

Charleston City Directory, 1828, 1829. Printed by James S. Burges, 44 Queen Street, Charleston.
    Charleston, Berkeley County, South Carolina State Free Negro Capitation Tax Books,
    Charleston, Roll 1,

U. S. Census Report, 1800-1950, Camden, South Carolina

U. S. Census Report, 1830, Charleston, Ward 1, South Carolina:
    Shows A. C. Dibble, with One Male "Free Person of Color," living in his household with
    wife (female 20 to 29 yrs.) and one daughter (under 5 yrs.).

U. S. Census Report, 1840, Charleston, South Carolina, shows A.C. Dibble, with his wife,
    1 male, age 5-9; 2 females, ages 5-9; 2 females under than 5 years, and 11 enslaved persons.

U. S. Census Report, 1840, Saint Andrews Parish, Charleston, shows A.C. living with six (6)
    enslaved persons.

U. S. Census Report, 1840, Charleston, South Carolina, Martha Smith

U.S. Census Report for 1850, Charleston, South Carolina

U.S. Census Reports, 1860 thru 1950, miscellaneous counties and states

U.S. Census Report. Topeka, Kansas and St. Louis, Missouri

U.S. Roster of Civil, Military ad Naval Services, 1863-1959. (P.V. Dibble)

Hagy, James H. Charleston South Carolina City Directories for:
    1816, 1819, 1822, 1825.
    1829 Directory, A.C. Dibble & P.V. Dibble Hat Store, 31 Broad Street.
    1830, 1831, 1835-1846, 1837 Directory, A.C. Hat Store., 37 Broad Street.
    1840-41 Directory, A.C. Dibble. Hat Store, 37 Broad Street; Res. 7 Burns Street.
    1829 Directory mentions both Dibble brothers an
    1840-41 Directory, P.V. Dibble in the Firm of Wildman & Dibble, Hat Store.
    1852 Directory, Mrs. A.C. Dibble Boarding House, 219 King Street.
    1855 Directory, Mrs. H. M. Dibble Boarding House, 249 King Street.
    1859 Directory, Mrs. H. M. Dibble Boarding House, 260 King Street
    1860 Directory, Mrs. H. M. Dibble, Boarding House, 160 King Street.

Marriage Notices, Charleston Observer, 15 March 1838, P.V. Dibble.

Sunnyside Cemetery, Orangeburg, S. C.

Kershaw County, Camden, South Carolina

Andrew Henry Dibble, Sr., Last Will, and Testament, 1873
Andrew H. Dibble Estate Papers, 1874
Ellie Naudin Dibble, Last Will, and Testament, 1920
Ellie Naomi Naudin Dibble, Estate Papers
Eugene Heriot Dibble Estate Papers, 1934
John Moreau Dibble, Last Will, and Testament, 1877
Rufus Dennis Dibble Estate papers, 1961
Bonds Conway, Last Will, and Testament, 1843

Camden Archives and Museum

Business Directory for Camden, 1900
Camden City Directory. 1913-1914
Camden City Directory, 1915-1916
Camden City Directory, 1925-1926

South Carolina Wills

Andrew Comstock Dibble, Last Will, and Testament, 1837
Andrew Comstock Inventory and Appraisement of Estate, 9 Oct 1846
Andrew Henry Dibble, Jr. Last Will, and Testament, Chester County, SC
Elizabeth Levy Dibble, Last Will, and Testament, Charlotte, NC

Other Official Records

A Catalogue of Names of he First Puritan Settles of the Colon of Connecticut.
Abstract of Graves of Revolutionary Patriots.
A Genealogical History of the Hoyt, Height and Hight Families.
American Genealogical and Biographical (AGIB).
Ancestry, (www.ancestry.com), Search for numerous Dibble family members.
Confederate Military Service Records.
Congressional Church Cemetery, Bethel, Fairfield County, Connecticut.
Connecticut Town Birth Records, pre-1870 (Barbour Collection).
Connecticut Town Marriage Records, pre 1870 (Barbour Collection).
Connecticut Death Records, 1650-1934).
Connecticut, U.S. Hale Collection of Cemetery Inscriptions and Newspaper Notices, 1629-1934.
Connecticut Wills and Probate Records, 1609-1999.
Connecticut, Church Record Abstracts.
Connecticut French and Indian War Soldiers
Connecticut Revolutionary War Military Lists, 1775-83.
Find a Grave, memorials for numerous Dibble Family members.
Founders of Norwalk, Connecticut, Hoyt
Massachusetts Marriages, 1633-1850.
Massachusetts Town Vital Records, 1620-1988.
Massachusetts, Suffolk County Wills, Starr.
Massachusetts, U. S. Applications for Freemen, 1630-1691.
Hickok Genealogy: Descendants of William Hickok of Farmington, Connecticut.
History of Danbury, Connecticut, 1684-1896.
History and Genealogy of Families of Old Fairfield, Vol. II, Part II.
History of the Old Town of Stratford and the City of Bridgeport, Connecticut.
History of the Starr Family of New England, from the Ancestor, Dr. Comfort Starr. Boston
        Massachusetts in 1635. Hartford, Connecticut, 1879.
National Society of Sons of American Revolution, Application for Membership (Several)
New England Marriages Prior to 1700.
New England, the Great Migration and the Great Migration Begins, 1620-1635.
 North American, Family Histories, 1500-2000.
The Families of Old Fairfield, (Comstock).
Stone Hill Cemetery, Bethel, Connecticut. (A.C. Dibble).
Trowbridge, Francis B. The Trowbridge Genealogy, History of Trowbridge Family in America,
        1908.
(Google Books)
United States International Marriage Records, 1560-1900.
U.S. Newspapers Extractions for Northeast, 1704-1930
U. S. Revolutionary War Rolls, 1775-1783.

U. S. War of 1812 Service Records, 1812-1815.
U.S. Civil War Soldier Records and Profiles, 1861-1865.
U.S. Census Reports for Danbury, Connecticut, for 1790 thru 1900.

Educational Institutions

Atlanta University, Atlanta Georgia.
Bridgewater State College, Bridgewater, Massachusetts.
Claflin University, Orangeburg, SC., SC Normal Program.
Claflin University, College of Arts and Sciences.
Claflin University Normal Program.
Howard University Catalogue of the Officers and Students, 1871-1872.
Howard University, College of Arts and Sciences.
Howard University, Medical College.
Howard University, Dental College.
Johnson C. Smith University (Biddle University), Charlotte, N.C.
Lincoln University, Pennsylvania.
Meharry Medical College, Tennessee.
Columbia College, New York,

Maxwell Documents

Maxwell, Henry J., *Sketches from Columbia News*, c. 1874. Maxwell, Henry J. Bible, 1870.
Maxwell, Henry J., *Diary.*
Maxwell, Henry J., *News article, Philadelphia, Pa., c. 1950.*
Maxwell, Henry J., General Services Administration Letter, January 15, 1975, "Postmaster Appointment."
Maxwell, Henry J., *Enlistment Papers, U. S. Army, 1864.*
Maxwell, Henry J., *U.S.C.T. Muster Roll Papers Maxwell,*
Henry J., *Death Certificate*
Maxwell, Henry J., *Sr., Widow's Pension Application.*
Maxwell, Henry J., *Certificate to Practice Law Before the S.C. Supreme Court, March 6, 1872.*
Maxwell, Henry J., *Marriage Certificate, 1871.*
Maxwell, Henry J., Deeds.
Maxwell, Martha Louisa Dibble, Deeds.
Maxwell, Martha Louisa Dibble, Last Will, and Testament.
Journal of the Senate of South Carolina, 1874-1875. (Maxwell, Henry J.).
Fathers and Lawyers in Reconstruction South Carolina, University of South Carolina Press (2000), Columbia, SC.
Maxwell, Thurston Johnson, *Freedman's Bank Records, 1865-1874*, (12 October 1869).
Maxwell, Henry J., Senator*, Freedman's Bank Records, 22 March 1870.*
Muster Roll Papers, Henry Johnson Maxwell.
Journal of the Senate of South Carolina, 1874-1875.
Fitchett, E. Horace. "A Successful Negro Grocer, "in *The Southern Workman,* December 1933.
Gordon, Asa H. *Sketches of Negro Life and History in South Carolina.* University of South Carolina Press, Columbia. (1971).
Hagy, James H. *Charleston, South Carolina, City Directory, 1840-41.*
Underwood, James L and W. Lewis Burke (ed.). *At Freedom's Door: African American Founding Fathers and Lawyers in Reconstruction Carolina,* University of South Carolina Press (2000), Columbia, *S.C.*
Webber, Paul R., Jr. "The Maxwell Grocery," in *Opportunity: Journal of Negro Life,* March 1940.
Biographical Directory of the Senate of the State of South Carolina, 1776-1985, N. Louise Bailey and Others. University of South Carolina Press, Columbia, South Carolina. (1985).
Posten, Ted. (Staff Correspondent) *The Pittsburgh Courier Newspaper,* Saturday, May 11, 1940, p.5. Miscellaneous Family Records, held by the author.

Walker – Orange Grove Cemetery, Sumter, South Carolina.

Taylor Documents

Ackerman, Hugo, Article in *Times and Democrat Newspaper*, Sunday, June 21, 1987.
Birth and Death Certificates (numerous).
City Directory for Orangeburg, 1935.
Claflin University Catalogue, City Orangeburg, S. C., 1895-1896 and other College records.
Furman University Records on Baptist Ministers.
Cumberland United Methodist Church.
Minutes of the South Carolina Annual Conference of the Methodist Episcopal Church, House at
      Claflin University, Orangeburg, SC.
T. K. Bythewood, "Historical Statement of Trinity Methodist Church, 1866-1966." Original
      document housed in The South Caroliniana Library, University of South Carolina,
      Columbia, S.C.
Orangeburg Cemetery, Orangeburg, S.C.
Orangeburg Deeds and Records.
Times and Democrat Newspapers, Numerous issues 1892 to 1936.
Trinity Methodist Episcopal Church Records, Camden, South Carolina.
Trinity Methodist Episcopal Church Records, Orangeburg, South Carolina
Trinity United Methodist Church Homecoming Souvenir Booklet, 1866-1984.
United States Census Reports, 1900, 1910, 1920, 1930.
 Miscellaneous Family Records held by the author.

Published Sources

Bailey, N. Louise, and Others. *Biographical Directory of the Senate of the State of South Carolina,*
      1776-1985, University of South Carolina Press: Columbia, South Carolina (1985).
Berlin, Ira. *Slaves Without Masters: Free Negro in Antebellum South*. Vintage Books, A Division
      of Random House, New York. (1974).
E. Louise, *Elizabeth Clevland Hardcastle, 1741-1808: A Lady of Color in the South Carolina Low*
      Country. Phoenix Publishers, Columbia, South Carolina. (2001).
E. Louise*, Reflections: A Pictorial History of Certain People of South Carolina*. Phoenix
      Publishers, Columbia, South Carolina. (2009).
Fitchett, E. Horace. "A Successful Negro Grocer, in '*The Southern Workman, December 1933.*
Gordon, Asa H. *Sketches of Negro Life and History in South Carolina.* University of South
      Carolina, Columbia, South Carolina. (1985).
Inabinet, L. Glen and Joan A. eds. *Kershaw County Legacy: A Commutative History.* Kershaw
      County Historical Society, Camden, 1983.
Jacobus, Donald Lines. *"The Trowbridge Ancestry in England," "The American Genealogist,"* 18-
      83, pp. 129-137.
Johnson, Michael. And James L. Roark. *Black Masters: A Free Family of Color in the Old South.*
      W.W. Norton & Company, New York. (1984).
Johnson, Michael and James L. Roark. *No Chariot Let Down: Charleston's Free people of Color on*
      the Eve of the Civil War. University f North Carolina Press. Chapel Hill. (1984).
Koger, Larry. *Black Slaveowners: Free Black Masters in South Carolina, 1790-1860.* McFarland &
      Company, Inc. Publishers. Jefferson, North Carolina, and London. (1983).
McConnell, Catherine Taylor, and Elsie Taylor Goins. *Naudin-Dibble, Selected South Carolina*
      Historic Sites. Photographs by: Will Moreau Goins, Ph.D. (Columbia, (1995).
Outen, Lon D. *Camden's Police Department, 1792-1969.* Sheridan Books, Chelsea, MI. (2015).
      Posten, Ted. (Staff Correspondent) The Pittsburgh Courier Newspaper, Saturday, May 11,
      1940, p. 5.
Stiles, Henry Reed. *The History of Ancient Windsor, Connecticut, Including East Windsor, South*
      Windsor, and Ellington, Prior to 1768, The Date of their Separation From the Old Town.
      2018 Charles B. Norton, 1859, New York. 2918 Reprint.

Underwood, James L. and W. Lewis Burke, (ed.), *At Freedom's Door: African American Founding Fathers and Lawyers in Reconstruction South Carolina.* University of South Carolina Press. (2000).

Van Buren Lamb, Jr., *"Dibble Genealogy," "Your Ancestors."* Van Buren Lamb, Jr., Notes collected.

Webber, Paul R., Jr. "The Maxwell Grocery," *Opportunity: Journal of Negro Life,* March 1940.

Weis, Frederick Lewis. *Ancestral Roots of Certain American Colonists Who came to America before 1700*

Weiss, Ellen. Robert R. *Taylor and Tuskegee: An African American Architect Designs for Booker T Washington.* New South Books, Montgomery, Alabama. (2012).

Genealogical Publishing Co., Inc., Baltimore, MD, Seventh Edition Baltimore 1992, 1993, p. 219.

Newspapers

City Gazette Newspaper (Charleston, South Carolina): A. C. Dibble arriving Charleston, SC on December 10, 1821, as a passenger of the ship *Allen* from New York.

City Gazette Newspaper (Charleston, South Carolina), classified advertisement of his "Deeble" Hat business, June 10, 1822.

National Advocate Newspaper (New York, NY), 19 July 1824. A. C. Dibble arriving in New York by ship, from Charleston, SC.

Charleston Courier Newspaper, 25 July 1822, A.C. Dibble arriving in Charleston from New York.

Charleston Courier Newspaper

Charleston Courier (Charleston, SC), November 2, 1824. A. C. Dibble arriving in the port of Charleston from New York, with a shipment of merchandize.

Charleston Courier (Charleston, SC), November 2, 1824. A. C. Dibble arriving in the port of Charleston from New York, with a shipment of merchandize.

Charleston News and Courier Newspaper, Obituary, September, 1846. (A.C. Dibble).

Charleston News and Courier, August 16, 1918. (Rev. V. C. Dibble).

Times and Democrat Newspaper, Orangeburg, SC., 15 March 1883. (P.V. Dibble).

Times and Democrat Newspaper, Orangeburg, SC, Sunday, June 21, 1987. Article by Hugo Ackerman.

Times and Democrat Newspaper, Orangeburg, SC, Sunday, February 28, 2021.

Times and Democrat Newspaper, Orangeburg, SC, Sunday February 7, 2021, Page A4.

Times and Democrat Newspaper, Orangeburg, SC., Sunday February 6, 2022, Section C.

Times and Democrat Newspaper, Orangeburg, S. C. (Numerous editions, from 1890 thru 1950s).

The Bamberg Hearld Newspaper, November 14, 1901. (Miss Mary H. Dibble).

The Columbia Record Newspaper, Thursday, July 12, 1917. (F.A. Dibble).

Private Collection

Andrew Comstock Dibble Letter to Zalmon Wildman, Postmaster, Danbury, Connecticut, 8 November 1822/24.

Andrew Henry Dibble, *"Certificate of Freedom,"24 August 1860.*

The Conway-Dibble Bible.

The Conway-Boykin Bible.

The Maria T. M. Conway-Vaughan Bible.

John Moreau Maxwell Family Bible.

The Honorable Henry J. Maxwell, Bible, 1870. Held by the author; previously held by The Honorable Stephen Lloyd Maxwell, Jr., District Court Judge, Saint Paul, MN.

The Honorable Henry J. Maxwell, 1866, Diary.

Conversations with Dr. Charles Wendell Maxwell, (c. 1950s) and his nephew: The Honorable Stephen Lloyd Maxwell, Jr., (conversations from 1970s to 2009).

Naudin-Dibble Heritage Foundation Collection.

Miscellaneous Family Photographs and Records held by the author. Obituaries: From numerous newspapers and programs.

ACKNOWLEDGEMENTS

When I hear another express an opinion,
which is not mine, I say to myself,
He has a right to his opinion, as I to mine;
why should I question it.
His error does me no injury. . .

Thomas Jefferson, 1808

I have been involved in family research for more than fifty years, and have enjoyed the excitement of discovering the unexpected things that I happened upon along the way. There has been many ups and downs as new information has come to light while researching. I am most appreciative of all those family members who I came to meet and know, during my youth, young adult years and those whom I have known during the past fifty or more years, while researching my family.

First and foremost, I must acknowledge my sister Catherine Taylor McConnell, who I spent many days and weeks travelling to the court houses and archives of numerous South Carolina towns and cities, during the 1970s and 1980s. We also visited numerous relatives and others, who were helpful in our family research. Those early days of our research, can never be replaced nor forgotten. These memories are important to me, as, I look back on all that we accomplished during that time. After my sister's death in 1996, I have continued my family research, discovering new information.

There were early family members who shared documents, papers, photographs, and family recollections with me. Some of these family members are: Elizabeth (Aunt Bessie) Dibble, who shared the contents of the *"Conway-Dibble Family Bible."* Josephine (Cousin Josie) Dibble Murphy shared the *"Andrew H. Dibble Freedom Papers"* with me and my sister in the late-1960s. Charles Wendell Maxwell, MD, Harold L. Dibble, Wilhelmina Lee Dibble, Catherine Springs Taylor and John B. Taylor, Jr., all shared many recollections of their grandparents, Andrew, and Ellie Naudin Dibble, with me, during those early years.

A sincere thanks goes to my late cousin James Laurence Dibble Palmer, MD, who was kind enough to make a copy of the *"Andrew Dibble Freedom Papers,"* and mail them to my sister and I, during the early 1970s. Jim was also generous in sharing the photograph of Ellie Naomi Naudin, as a young lady with curls, some years later, as well as several other historic photographs, including the one of the original Dibble home and Dibble Stores, made about 1890.

A very special thanks to Wilhelmina Dibble Rettig, my father's first cousin, who brought to my attention at the first family reunion in 1979, that a portrait of Andrew Henry Dibble did exist. Until this time, I was unaware of this large wall portrait, which I have since cherished and held-dear, and honored to have it hanging in my home. Cousin Willie will always have a special place in my heart.

Since our first family reunion in 1979, other family members who have also shared documents, information, and photographs, and much, much more, they are: Leola Kersey Benjamin, Carol Dibble Cook, Justice Stephen Lloyd Maxwell, Dr. James Laurence Dibble and Rose Palmer, Catherine Richardson Hawkins, Emily Means-Willis, Selina Edwards Reed, Carol Reed Sullivan, JD, Lauren Reed, Mabel Murphy Smythe-Haith, Ph.D., Ann Dibble Jordan, Clarice Dibble Walker, Emma Humphrey Pendergrass, JD, Ph.D., Idalean McLain Levy, Zoe Maxwell Tyler and Soleil Maxwell Rofman. Thanks to all, for your support and contribution. Thanks also to other family members, who have contributed in many ways. This has been the journey of a lifetime. Thanks also to my siblings, Joan, Dorothy, and John for their continued support.

A very special thanks to my family, who have endured my adventure during these many years. There were persons who read all or portions of this collection and offered comments, and suggestions. Thanks to my son William, who is no longer with me, for his encouragement, concerns, and thoughts, that are with me every day. Thanks to my son Wendell who has always been encouraging and supportive in all my research, and my daughter Felicia who has always been helpful and encouraging. Both Wendell and Felicia have offered valuable insights and assistance that have helped me navigate through these numerous ancestors, who came to this new land in the 1630s. Without their love and support, I would not have been able to complete this important project. I must also thank my granddaughters who have helped me conquer my many computer challenges.

E. Louise has been doing family research for more than fifty years. She has traveled throughout North and South Carolina collecting information and researching numerous families. E. Louise holds a Bachelor of Science Degree in History and a Master of Science Degree in Education. She is the author of several publications, including: *Elizabeth Cevland Hardcastle, 1741-1808: A Lady of Color in the South Carolina Low Country; Reflections: A Pictorial History of Certain People of South Carolina, 1840s to 1940s;* and *Catherine Smith Springs (1828-1895): Businesswoman, Humanitarian, 'Servant of God'."* She is a member of several historical and genealogical organizations and societies. Among these are the "Descendants of the Founding Fathers of New England," "The National Genealogical Society," "The Society of the Descendants of Charlemagne," "The South Carolina Historical Society," "The South Carolina Genealogy Society," "The Kershaw County Historical Society," "The Society of the First African Families of English America," and "The Descendants of the Founders of Ancient Windsor." E. Louise is the Great-Granddaughter of Andrew Henry Dibble, Sr., of Charleston and Camden, South Carolina.

www.ingramcontent.com/pod-product-compliance
Lightning Source LLC
Chambersburg PA
CBHW080327270326
41927CB00014B/3129